College of William and Mary

**The History of the College of William and Mary**

From it's foundation, 1660 to 1874

College of William and Mary

**The History of the College of William and Mary**
*From it's foundation, 1660 to 1874*

ISBN/EAN: 9783337338619

Printed in Europe, USA, Canada, Australia, Japan

Cover: Foto ©ninafisch / pixelio.de

More available books at **www.hansebooks.com**

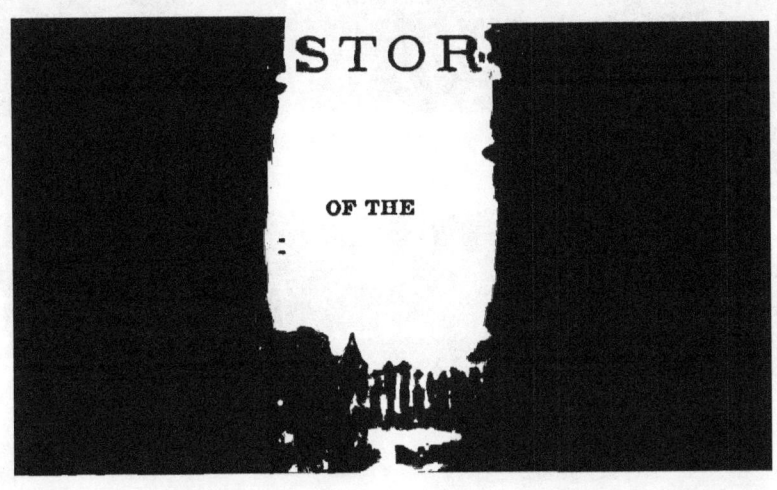

OF THE

J. W. RANDOLPH & ENGLISH,
1318 MAIN STREET, RICHMOND.
1874.

# THE CHARTER

OF THE

# COLLEGE OF WILLIAM AND MARY,

IN VIRGINIA.

WILLIAM AND MARY, by the grace of God, of England, Scotland, France and Ireland, King and Queen, defenders of the faith, &c. To all to whom these our present letters shall come, greeting.

Forasmuch as our well-beloved and faithful subjects, constituting the General Assembly of our Colony of Virginia, have had it in their minds, and have proposed to themselves, to the end that the Church of Virginia may be furnished with a seminary of ministers of the gospel, and that the youth may be piously educated in good letters and manners, and that the Christian faith may be propagated amongst the Western Indians, to the glory of Almighty God; to make, found and establish a certain place of universal study, or perpetual College of Divinity, Philosophy, Languages, and other good Arts and Sciences, consisting of one President, six Masters or Professors, and an hundred scholars, more or less, according to the ability of the said college, and the statutes of the same; to be made, increased, diminished, or changed there, by certain trustees nominated and elected by the General Assembly aforesaid, to wit, our faithful and well-beloved Francis Nicholson, our Lieutenant Governor in our Colonies of Virginia and Maryland; Wm. Cole, Ralph Wormley, William Byrd and John Lear, Esquires; James Blair, John Farnifold, Stephen Fouace and Samuel Gray, clerks; Thomas Milner, Christopher Robinson, Charles Scarborough, John Smith, Benjamin Harrison, Miles Cary, Henry Hartwell, William Randolph and Matthew Page, gentlemen, or the major part of them, or of the longer livers of them, on the south side of a certain river, commonly called York river, or elsewhere, where the General Assembly itself shall think more convenient, within our Colony of Virginia, to be supported and maintained, in all time coming.

I. And forasmuch as our well-beloved and trusty the General Assembly of our Colony of Virginia aforesaid, has humbly supplicated us, by our well-beloved in Christ, James Blair, Clerk, their agent duly constituted, that we would be pleased, not only to grant our royal license to the said Francis Nicholson, William Cole, Ralph Wormley, William Byrd and John Lear, Esquires; James Blair, John Farnifold, Stephen Fouace and Samuel Gray, Clerks; Thomas Milner, Christopher Robinson, Charles Scarborough, John Smith, Benjamin Harrison, Miles Cary, Henry Hartwell, William Randolph, and Matthew Page, Gentlemen, or the major part of them, or of the longer livers of them, to make, found, erect and establish the said college, but also to extend our royal bounty and munificence towards the erection and foundation of the said college, in such way and manner as to us shall seem most expedient: We, taking the premises seriously into our consideration, and earnestly desiring, that as far as in us lies, true philosophy, and other good and liberal arts and sciences may be promoted, and that the orthodox Christian faith may be propagated: And being desirous, that forever hereafter, there should be one such college, or place of universal study, and some certain and undoubted way within the said college, for the rule and government of the same, and of the masters or professors, and scholars, and all others inhabiting and residing therein, and that the said college should subsist and remain in all time coming; of our special grace, certain knowledge, and mere motion, HAVE GRANTED and given leave, and by these presents do grant and give leave, for us, our heirs and successors, as much as in us lies, to the said Francis Nicholson, William Cole, Ralph Wormley, William Byrd and John Lear, Esquires; James Blair, John Farnifold, Stephen Fouace and Samuel Gray, Clerks; Thomas Milner, Christopher Robinson, Charles Scarborough, John Smith, Benjamin Harrison, Miles Cary, Henry Hartwell, William Randolph and Matthew Page, Gentlemen; That they or the major part of them or of the longest livers of them, for promoting the studies of true philosophy, languages, and other good arts and sciences, and for propagating the pure gospel of Christ, our only Mediator, to the praise and honor of Almighty God, may have power to erect, found and establish a certain place of universal study, or perpetual College, for Divinity, Philosophy, Languages and other good Arts and Sciences, consisting of one President, six masters or professors, and an hundred scholars, more or less, graduates and non-graduates, as abovesaid, according to the statutes and orders of the said College, to be made, appointed and established upon the place by the said Francis Nicholson, William Cole, &c., or the major part of them, upon the south side of York river, on the land late of Colonel ——— Townsend, deceased, now in the possession of John Smith, near the port appointed or laid out for York county, by the said General Assembly, within our said colony of Virginia; or if by reason of unwholesomeness, or any other cause, the said place shall not be approved of, wheresoever else the General Assembly of our Colony of Virginia, or the major part of them, shall think fit, within the bounds of the aforesaid colony, to continue for all times coming.

II. And further, of our special grace, certain knowledge, and mere motion, WE HAVE GRANTED, and given leave, and by these presents do grant, and give leave, for us, our heirs and successors, to the said Francis Nicholson, William Cole, &c., that they, or the major part of them, or of the longer livers of them, may be enabled to take, hold and enjoy, and that they may be persons apt and capable in law, for taking, holding and enjoying all Manors, Lands, Tenements, Rents, Services, Rectories, Portions, Annuities, Pensions and Advowsons of Churches, with all other Inheritances, Franchises and Possessions whatsoever, as well spiritual as temporal, to the value of two thousand pounds a year; and all other goods, chattels, monies and personal estate whatsoever, of the gift of any person whatsoever, that is willing to bestow them for this use; or any other gifts, grants, assignments, legacies or appointments, of the same, or any of them, or of any other goods whatsoever: But with this express intention, and upon the special trust we put in them that they the said Francis Nicholson, William Cole, &c., or the major part of them, or of the longer livers of them, shall take and hold the premises, and shall dispose of the same, and of the rents, revenues or profits thereof, or of any of them only for defraying the charges that shall be laid out in erecting and fitting the edifices of the said intended college, and furnishing them with books, and other utensils, and all other charges pertaining to the said college, as they, or the major part of them, shall think most expedient, until the said college shall be actually erected, founded and established, and upon this trust and intention, that so soon as the said college shall, according to our royal intent be erected and founded, the said Francis Nicholson, William Cole, &c., or the longer livers or liver of them, and their or his heirs, executors, administrators or assigns, shall by good and sufficient deeds and assurances in law give, grant and transfer to the said President and masters, or professors, or their successors, the said Lands, Manors, Tenements, Rents, Services, Rectories, Portions, Annuities, Pensions and Advowsons of Churches, with all other inheritances, franchises, possessions, goods, chattels and personal estate aforesaid, or as much thereof as has not been laid out and bestowed upon the building the said college, or to the other uses above mentioned.

III. And seeing the said General Assembly of our Colony of Virginia, has named, elected or appointed, the said James Blair, Clerk, as a fit person to be President of the said college; we of our special grace, certain knowledge, and mere motion, do approve, confirm and ratify the said nomination and election, and do by these presents make, create and establish the said James Blair first President of the said college, during his natural life.

IV. And further, we grant our special license to the said Francis Nicholson, William Cole, &c., and their successors, or the major part of them, that they have power to elect and nominate other apt, fit and able persons, into the places of the masters or professors of the said college; and that, after the death, resignation or deprivation of the said President, or Professors, or any of them, the said Francis Nicholson, William Cole, &c., and their successors, or the major part of them, shall have power to put in, and substitute, a fit person, or persons, from time to time, into his or their place, or places, according to the orders and statutes of the said college, to be made, enacted and established, for the good and wholesome government of the said college, and of all that bear office, or reside therein, by the said Francis Nicholson, William Cole, &c., or their successors, or the major part of them.

V. And further, we will, and for us, our heirs and successors, by these presents, do GRANT, that when the said College shall be so erected, made, founded and established, it shall be called and denominated forever the College of *William* and *Mary*, in Virginia, and that the President and masters, or professors, of the said college, shall be a body politic and incorporate, in deed and name; and that by the name of the President and masters, or professors, of the College of William and Mary, in Virginia, they shall have perpetual succession; and that the said President, and masters, or professors, shall forever be called and denominated the President, and Masters, or Professors, of the College of William and Mary, in Virginia: And that the said President, and masters, or professors, and their successors, by the name of the President, and masters, or professors, of the College of William and Mary, in Virginia, shall be persons able, capable, apt and perpetual in law, to take and hold lordships, manors, lands, tenements, rents, reversions, rectories, portions, pensions, annuities, inheritances, possessions and services, as well spiritual as temporal, whatsoever, and all manner of goods and chattels, both of our gift, and our heirs and successors, and of the gift of the said

Francis Nicholson, William Cole, Ralph Wormley, Wm. Byrd and John Lear, Esquires; James Blair, John Farnifold, Stephen Fouace and Samuel Gray, Clerks; Thomas Milner, Christopher Robinson, Charles Scarborough, John Smith, Benjamin Harrison, Miles Cary, Henry Hartwell, William Randolph and Matthew Page, Gentlemen; or of the gift of any other person whatsoever, to the value of two thousand pounds, of lawful money of England, yearly, and no more, to be had and held by them and their successors for ever.

VI. And also, that the said President, and masters, or professors, by and under the name of the President, and masters, or professors, of the College of William and Mary, in Virginia, shall have power to plead, and be impleaded, to sue, and be sued, to defend, and be defended, to answer, and be answered, in all and every cause, complaint, and action, real, personal and mixed, of what kind and nature soever they be, in whatsoever courts and places of Judicature belonging to us, our heirs and successors, or to any person whatsoever, before all sorts of justices and judges, ecclesiastical and temporal, in whatsoever kingdoms, countries, colonies, dominions or plantations, belonging to us, or our heirs; and to do, act, and receive, these and all other things, in the same manner, as our other liege people, persons able and capable in law, within our said Colony of Virginia, or our kingdom of England, do, or may act, in the said courts and places of Judicature, and before the said justices and judges.

VII. As also, that the said President, and masters or professors, and their successors shall have one common seal, which they may make use of in any whatsoever cause and business belonging to them and their successors; and that the President, and masters or professors of the said College, and their successors, shall have leave to break, change and renew, their said seal, from time to time, at their pleasure, as they shall see most expedient.

VIII. And further of our more especial grace, we have given and granted, and for us, our heirs, and successors, we give and grant our special license, as far as in us lies, to the said Francis Nicholson, William Cole, Ralph Wormley, William Byrd and John Lear, Esquires; James Blair, John Farnifold, Stephen Fouace, Samuel Gray, Clerks; Thomas Milner, Christopher Robinson, Charles Scarborough, John Smith, Benjamin Harrison, Miles Cary, Henry Hartwell, William Randolph and Matthew Page, gentlemen, that they, or any other person or persons, whatsoever, after the said college is so founded, erected, made, created and established, may have power to give, and grant, assign and bequeath, all manors, lands, tenements, rents, services, rectories, portions, annuities, pensions and advowsons of Churches, and all manner of inheritance, franchises and possessions whatsoever, as well spiritual as temporal, to the value of two thousand pounds a year, over and above all burthens and reprisals, to the President, and masters, or professors, of the said College, for the time being, and their successors, to be had, held and enjoyed, by the said President, and masters, or professors, and their successors, forever: And that they, the said President and masters, or professors aforesaid, may take and hold, to themselves, and their successors, forever, as is aforesaid, manors, lands, tenements, rents, reversions, services, rectories, portions, pensions, annuities, and all manner of inheritances, and possessions whatsoever, as well spiritual as temporal, to the aforesaid value of two thousand pounds a year, over and above all burthens, reprisals and reparations: It not being our will, that the said President, and masters or professors of the said College, for the time being, or their successors, shall be troubled, disquieted, molested, or aggrieved by reason, or occasion of the premises, or any of them, by us, our heirs, and successors, or by any of our justices, escheators, sheriffs, or other bailiffs, or ministers, whatsoever, belonging to us, our heirs and successors.

IX. And further, we will, and by these presents, do declare, nominate, ordain and appoint, the said Francis Nicholson, William Cole, Ralph Wormley, William Byrd and John Lear, Esquires; James Blair, John Farnifold, Stephen Fouace and Samuel Gray, Clerks; Thomas Milner, Christopher Robinson, Charles Scarborough, John Smith, Benjamin Harrison, Miles Cary, Henry Hartwell, William Randolph and Matthew Page, gentlemen, and their successors, to be the true, sole and undoubted visitors and governors of the said college for ever: And we give and grant to them, or the major part of them, by these our letters patents, a continual succession, to be continued in the way and manner hereafter specified; as also full and absolute liberty, power and authority, of making, enacting, framing and establishing such and so many rules, laws, statutes, orders and injunctions, for the good and wholesome government of the said college, as to them the said Francis Nicholson, William Cole, &c., and their successors, shall from time to time, according to their various occasions and circmstances, seem most fit and expedient: All which rules, laws, statutes and injunctions so to be made, as aforesaid, we will have to be observed, under the penalty therein contained: Provided nothwithstanding, that the said rules, laws, statutes, orders and injunctions, be no way contrary to our prerogative royal, nor to the laws and statutes of our kingdom of England or our colony of

Virginia, aforesaid, or to the canons and constitutions of the church of England, by law established.

X. And further, we will and by these presents, for us, our heirs and successors, do grant and confirm to the said visitors, and governors of the said college, and their successors, that they and their successors, shall, forever, be eighteen men, or any other number not exceeding the number of twenty, in the whole, to be elected and constituted in the way and manner hereinafter specified; and that they shall have one discreet and fit person, that shall be elected and nominated, out of their number, in the manner hereafter mentioned, that shall be, and shall be called Rector of the said college: And we have appointed and confirmed, and by these presents, do appoint and confirm the said James Blair, to be the present rector of the said college, to be continued in the said office for one year next ensuing the foundation of the said college, and thereafter till some other of the visitors and governors of the said college shall be duly elected, preferred and sworn into the said office; and that from time to time, and in all time coming, after the said year is expired, or after the death of the rector within the year, the visitors and governors of the said college, or the greater part of them, or of their successors, shall have power to elect and nominate another discreet and fit person, from amongst themselves to be rector of the said college; and that he who is elected, preferred and nominated, as abovesaid, into the place of rector of the said college, shall have power to have, exercise and enjoy the said office of rector of the said college, for one whole year, then next ensuing, and thereafter, until some other rector of the said college shall be duly elected, preferred and sworn into the said office: And to perpetuate the succession of the said rector, and of the said visitors and governors of the said college, we will, ordain and appoint, that as often as any one or more of the said visitors and governors of the said college, shall die, or remove himself and family out of our said colony, into any other country for good and all, that then, and so often, the rector for the time being, and the other visitors and governors of the said college, then surviving and remaining within the colony, or the major part of them, shall and may have leave to elect, nominate and choose one or more of the principal and better sort of the inhabitants of our said colony of Virginia, into the place or places of visitor and governor, or visitors and governors, so dead or removed, to fill up the aforesaid number of visitors and governors, for the said college; and that he or they so elected and chosen, shall take his or their corporal oath, before the rector, and the other visitors and governors of the said college, or the major part of them, well and faithfully to execute the said office; which oath the said rector, and two or more of the visitors, shall have power to administer: And that after the taking of the said oath, he or they shall be of the number of the said visitors and governors of the said college.

XI. And further, we will, and by these presents, for us, our heirs and successors, do grant and confirm, to the said President, and masters, or professors of the said college, and their successors, that they and their successors shall have one eminent and discreet person, to be elected and nominated, in the manner hereafter expressed, who shall be, and shall be called chancellor of the said college: And we have appointed and confirmed, and by these presents, for us, our heirs, and successors, do appoint and confirm, our well-beloved and right trusty the reverend father in God, Henry, by divine permission, bishop of London, to be the first chancellor of the said college, to be continued in the said office for seven years next ensuing, and thereafter, until some other chancellor of the said college shall be duly elected and chosen into the said office: And that from time to time, and in all time coming, after these seven years are expired, or after the death of the said bishop, or of the chancellor, for the time being, the rector, and visitors, and governors of the said College for the time being, or the major part of them, shall and may have power to elect, choose and nominate, some other eminent and discreet person, from time to time, to be chancellor of the said college; and that he who is so nominated and elected to be chancellor of the said college, shall and may have, execute, and enjoy, the said office of chancellor of the said college, for the space of seven years then next ensuing, and thereafter until some other chancellor of the said college shall be duly elected and constituted.

XII. Further, we will by these presents and for us, our heirs and successors, do grant and confirm to the said president, and masters, or professors, of the said college, and to their successors, that after the said college is erected, founded, and established, they may retain and appoint some convenient place, or council chamber, within the said college; and that the rector and other visitors, and governors of the said college, or the major part of them, for the time being, as often as they shall think good, and see cause, may convocate and hold a certain court of convocation within the said chamber, consisting of the said rector, and visitors, and governors, of the said college, or the major part of them, in all time coming; and in the said convocation, may treat, confer, consult, advise, and decree, concerning statutes, orders, and injunctions, for the said college.

XIII. And further, we will, and by these presents, for us, our heirs, and successors, do grant and confirm to the said President, and masters, or professors of the said College, and their successors, or the major part of them, that from time to time, and in all time coming, the said rector and visitors, or governors of the said college, and their successors, or the major part of them, shall have power and authority, yearly, and every year, on the first Monday which shall happen next after the feast of the annunciation of the blessed Virgin Mary, to elect and nominate, and that they shall and may elect and nominate one of the said visitors or governors of the said college, to be rector of the said college, for one whole year then next ensuing: And that he, after he is so elected and chosen into the said office of rector of the said college, before he be admitted to execute the said office, shall, on the same day and in the same place, take his corporal oath before the last rector, and visitors, or governors of the said college, or any three of them, well and faithfully to execute the said office; and that after so taking the said oath, he shall and may execute the said office of rector of the said college, for one whole year then next ensuing: And also, that every seventh year, on the same Monday, next after the feast of the annunciation of the blessed Virgin Mary, aforesaid, they shall, in like manner, have power and authority to elect and nominate another chancellor of the said college, to be continued for seven years then next ensuing: And that he who shall be elected, chosen, and nominated, into the office of chancellor of the said college, shall and may, immediately after such election and nomination, execute the office of chancellor of the said college for seven years then next ensuing.

XIV. And that the charge and expense of erecting, building, founding and adorning, the said college at present, and also of supporting and maintaining the said president and masters or professors, for the future, may be sustained and defrayed, of our more ample and bounteous special grace, certain knowledge, and mere motion, we have given, granted, assigned, and made over, and by these presents, for us, our heirs and successors, do give, grant, assign, and make over to the said Francis Nicholson, William Cole, Ralph Wormley, William Byrd and John Lear, Esquires; James Blair, John Farnifold, Stephen Fouace and Samuel Gray, clerks; Thomas Milner, Christopher Robinson, Charles Scarborough, John Smith, Benjamin Harrison, Miles Cary, Henry Hartwell, William Randolph and Matthew Page, gentlemen, and their executors and assigns forever, the whole and entire sum of one thousand nine hundred and eighty-five pounds, fourteen shillings and ten pence, of good and lawful money of England, that has been received and raised out of the quit-rents of the said colony, now remaining in the hands of William Byrd, Esquire, our auditor, or in whosesoever other hands the same now is, for our use, within the said colony: And, therefore, we command and firmly enjoin the said auditor, or any other person with whom the said money is deposited, or who is obliged to pay the same, immediately upon sight of these our letters patents, to pay, or cause to be paid, the said sum of one thousand nine hundred and eighty-five pounds, fourteen shillings and ten pence, to the said Francis Nicholson, William Cole, &c., or the major part of them, or of the longer livers of them, or to their attorney, in that part lawfully constituted, with any other warrant, mandate, or precept to be obtained or expected from us, to be laid out and applied about and towards the building, erecting and adorning, the said college, and to no other use, intent or purpose whatever.

XV. Seeing also, by a certain act of parliament, made the twenty-fifth year of the reign of our royal uncle, Charles the Second, of blessed memory, entitled, An act for the encouragement of the Greenland and Eastland trades, and for better securing the plantation trade, it was enacted, that after the first day of September, in the year of our Lord M.DC.LXXIII., if any ship, which by law, might trade in any of the plantations, should come to any of them to load, and take on board tobacco, or any other of the commodities there enumerated, and if bond were not first given, with one sufficient surety, to carry the said tobacco to England, Wales, or the town of Berwick upon Tweed, and to no other place, and there to unload and put the same on shore, (the dangers of the sea only excepted); in such case there should be paid to our said uncle, and his heirs and successors, one penny for every pound of tobacco so loaded and put on board, to be levied, collected, and paid in such places, and to such officers, and collectors, as should be appointed in the respective plantations, to collect, levy, and receive the same, and under such penalties, both to the officers and upon the goods as for non-payment of his majesty's customs in England: And if it should happen, that any person or persons who are to pay the said duties, shall not have ready money to satisfy the same, that the officers who are appointed to collect the said duties, shall in lieu of the said ready money, take such a proportion of tobacco, that was to be shipped, as may amount to the value thereof, according to the usual rate of the said commodity, in such plantation respectively: All which things are to be ordered, and disposed, and these several duties are to be caused to be levied, by the commissioners of our customs in England, for the time being, under the authority and direction of the lord treasurer of England, or the commissioners of the treasury, for the time being, as by the said act of parliament, amongst other things therein contained, reference being thereto had, doth more fully appear; we, of our more bounteous grace, mere motion, and certain knowledge, have given and granted, and for us, and our successors, do give, and grant, to the said Francis Nicholson, William Cole, &c., and the other trustees above mentioned, and their heirs for ever, the said revenue of one penny for every pound of tobacco in Virginia, or Maryland, in America, or either of them that shall be so loaded, and put on board, as is abovesaid; and the nett produce which shall accrue in England, or elsewhere, by selling there the tobacco that shall be collected in our colonies of Virginia, and Maryland, in lieu of the penny that ought to be paid for every pound of tobacco so loaded and put on board, as is abovesaid: Provided always, that the commissioners of our customs in England, for the time being, shall name and appoint all the collectors and receivers of the said money and tobacco, and their inspectors and comptrollers, from time to time, as they have hitherto done: And that the salaries of the said collectors, receivers, and comptrollers, shall be deducted and paid out of the said revenue; and that the said Francis Nicholson, William Cole, Ralph Wormley, William Byrd, and John Lear, Esquires; James Blair, John Farnifold, Stephen Fouace, and Samuel Gray, clerks; Thomas Milner, Christopher Robinson, Charles Scarborough, John Smith, Benjamin Harrison, Miles Cary, Henry Hartwell, William Randolph, and Matthew Page, gentlemen, and their successors, as also the President, and masters, or professors of the said College, and their successors, for the time being, shall be obliged to receive and observe all such rules, orders, and instructions, as shall be transmitted to them, from time to time, by the said commissioners of our customs in England, for the time being, under the inspection and direction of the lord treasurer, or the commissioners of our treasury in England, for the time being, for the better and more exact collecting of the said duty, as by the said act of parliament, reference being thereto had, is more particularly directed and appointed: but with this express intention, and upon the special trust and confidence we place in the said Francis Nicholson, William Cole, and the rest of the aforesaid trustees, that they, and the longest livers of them, and their heirs, shall take, hold, and possess the said revenue of a penny per pound, for every pound of tobacco aforesaid, with all its profits, advantages, and emoluments, to apply and lay out the same, for building and adorning the edifices and other necessaries for the said college, until the said college shall be actually erected, founded, and established, and with this express intention, and upon the special trust and confidence, that so soon as the said college shall be erected and founded, according to our royal purpose, the said trustees, and the longest livers or liver of them, and his or their heirs, or assigns, shall, by good and sufficient deeds and assurances in law, give, grant, and transfer to the President, and masters, or professors, of the said College, this whole revenue, with all its profits, issues, and emoluments before mentioned, or so much thereof, as shall not have been expended and laid out for the aforesaid uses, to be held, possessed, and enjoyed, by the said President, and masters, or professors, and their successors, for ever.

XVI. And also, of our special grace, mere motion, and certain knowledge, we have given and granted, and by these presents, for us, our heirs, and successors do give and grant to Francis Nicholson, William Cole, and the rest of the said trustees, and to the longest livers or liver of them, and to his or their heirs, the office of surveyor-general of our said colony of Virginia, if the said office be now void, or whensoever and how often soever it shall hereafter fall void, to be had, held and executed, with all its issues, fees, profits, advantages, conveniences, liberties, places, privileges, and pre-eminences whatsoever, belonging to the said office, in as ample form and manner, as any other person, who has heretofore had, executed, or possessed the said office, ever had received or enjoyed, or ought to have, receive, or enjoy, by the said trustees, and their heirs; or by such officers and substitutes, as they or the major part of them, or of the longest livers of them, or of their heirs, shall from time to time nominate and appoint, until the said college shall be actually founded and erected: But with this express intention, and upon this special trust and confidence, which we place in the said Francis Nicholson, William Cole, and the rest of the said trustees, that they and the longest livers of them, and their heirs, shall give back and restore to the President and masters, or professors, of the said college, for the time being, whatsoever money remains in their hands, that has risen from this office, during their administration, not yet laid out upon the building of the said college, and the other above-mentioned uses, so soon as the said college shall be actually erected and founded. And after the said college shall be actually erected and founded, we will, that the said office of surveyor-general, if it be then void, as often as it shall be void, for the time to come, shall be had, held, and executed, with all its profits and appurtenances above-mentioned, by the said President and masters, or professors, and their successors, for ever: Provided always that the said Francis Nicholson, and the rest of the above-mentioned trustees, or the major part of them, or of the longest livers of them, and the President, and masters, or professors, for the time being, shall, from time to time, nominate and substitute such and so many particular surveyors for the particular counties of our colony of Virginia, as our governor in chief, and the council of our said colony of Virginia, for the time being, shall think fit and necessary.

XVII. And also, of our more bounteous special grace, mere motion, and certain knowledge, we have given, granted and confirmed, and by these presents, for us, and our heirs, and succesors, do give, grant, and confirm, to the said Francis Nicholson, William Cole, and the rest of the trustees above-mentioned, ten thousand acres of land, not yet legally occupied or possessed by any of our other subjects, lying, and being, on the South side of the Blackwater Swamp, and also other ten thousand acres of land, not legally occupied or possessed by any of our other subjects, lying and being in that neck of land, commonly called Pamunkey neck, between the forks or branches of York river: which twenty thousand acres of land, we will have to be laid out and measured in the places above-mentioned, at the choice of the said Francis Nicholson, William Cole, and the rest of the fore-mentioned trustees, or the major part of them, or of the longest livers of them, to be had and held by the said Francis Nicholson, William Cole, and the rest of the above-mentioned trustees, and their heirs for ever; but with this intention, and upon special trust and confidence, that the said Francis Nicholson, William Cole, and the rest of the said trustees, or the major part of them, or of the longest livers of them, so soon as the said college shall be actually founded and established, shall give, grant, let, and alienate the said twenty thousand acres of land to the said President and masters, or professors of the said College, to be had and held by them, and their successors, for ever, by fealty, in free and common soccage, paying to us, and our successors, two copies of Latin verses yearly, on every fifth day of November, at the house of our governor, or lieutenant governor of Virginia, for the time being, for ever, in full discharge, acquittance, and satisfaction of all quit-rents, services, customs, dues, and burdens whatsoever, due, or to be due, to us, or our successors, for the said twenty thousand acres of land, by the laws or customs of England or Virginia.

XVIII. And also, of our special grace, certain knowledge, and mere motion, we have given, and granted, and by these presents, for us and our successors, do give, and grant, to the said President, and masters, or professors of the said college, full and absolute power, liberty, and authority, to nominate, elect, and constitute one discreet and able person of their own number, or of the number of the said visitors, or governors, or lastly, of the better sort of inhabitants of our colony of Virginia, to be present in the house of Burgesses, of the General Assembly of our colony of Virginia, and there to act and consent to such things, as by the common advice of our said colony shall (God willing) happen to be enacted.

XIX. And further, it is our pleasure, that such further confirmations and ratifications of the premises shall be granted, from time to time by us, our heirs and successors, to the said Francis Nicholson, and the rest of the trustees above-mentioned, and to their successors, or to the Paesident, and masters, or professors of the said college, or to their successors, for the time being, upon their humble petition under the great seal of England, or otherwise, as the attorney-general of us, our heirs, or successors, for the time being, shall think fit and expedient.

In testimony whereof, we have caused these our letters to be made patent. Witness ourselves, at Westminster, the eighth day of February, in the fourth year of our reign.

*By writ of the Privy Seal,*

PIGOTT.

# THE TRANSFER
### OF THE
# COLLEGE OF WILLIAM AND MARY,
## IN VIRGINIA.

---

TO all to whom these presents shall come, James Blair, of the city of Williamsburg, in the colony of Virginia, and Stephen Fouace, of Chelsea, in the county of Middlesex, clerks, send greeting: Whereas their late Majesties, King William and Queen Mary, of blessed memory, being religiously inclined to promote the Studies of sacred Theology, Philosophy, Languages, and other good Arts and Sciences, to the end the church of Virginia might be supplied with a seminary of ministers of the gospel, and the youth of that country be piously educated in good manners and learning, and the orthodox Christian faith might be propagated among the Western Indians, at the humble suit of the General Assembly of the colony aforesaid, by their letters patents bearing date at Westminster the eighth day of February, in the fourth year of their reign, were pleased of their special grace, certain knowledge, and mere motion to give license to certain trustees, to wit, Francis Nicholson, William Cole, Ralph Wormley, William Byrd, and John Lear, Esqrs.; James Blair, John Farnifold, Stephen Fouace, and Samuel Gray, clerks; Thos. Milner, Christopher Robinson, Charles Scarborough, John Smith, Benjamin Harrison, Miles Cary, Henry Hartwell, William Randolph, and Matthew Page, gentlemen; that they, or the major part of them, or the longest livers of them, might erect, found, and establish a certain general school, or perpetual college, of sacred Theology, Philosophy, Languages, and other good Arts and Sciences, consisting of one President, six masters or professors, and one hundred scholars, more or less, graduates and non-graduates, according to the ordinances and statutes of the said college, by the said trustees, or the major part of them, in that behalf to be made and established, in a certain place upon the south side of York river, near York town, in the county of York, in the colony aforesaid; or if that place, for the unwholesomeness of the air, or any other cause should not be agreeable, in any other place within the said colony which to the General Assembly of the said colony should seem most convenient. And did further grant, that the said trustees, or the major part of them receive, hold, and enjoy manors, lands, tenements, rents, services, rectories, portions, annuities, pensions, and advowsons of churches, with all other hereditaments, franchises and possessions whatsoever, as well spiritual as temporal, to the value of two thousand pounds by the year, and all goods, chattels, money, and personal estate whatsoever, of the gift of any person whatsoever, willing to give the same to this use, or any gifts, grants, assignments, legacies, or appointments whatsoever of them, or any of them, or any other well disposed persons: But to the express intent, and under this special trust, that they, the said trustees, or the major part of them, or the longest livers of them, should take and receive the premises, and dispose the same, or the rents, issues, and profits thereof, only for sustaining and defraying the expenses in erecting and fitting the buildings of and for the said intended college, and in ordaining the same with books and other convenient utensils, and other expenses to the said college pertaining, as to them, or the major part of them, should seem expedient, until the said college should be actually erected, founded and established. And under this trust, and to the intent, that as soon as the said college, according to the royal design aforesaid, should be erected and founded, the said trustees, or the longest livers or the longest liver of them, and his or their heirs, executors, administrators or assigns, by good and sufficient writings and assurances in law, should give, grant, and transfer to the President, and masters, or professors, and their successors, the same manors, lands, tenements, rents, services, rectories, portions, annuities, pensions, and advowsons of churches, with all other hereditaments, franchises, possessions, goods, chattels, and personal estate aforesaid, or so much thereof as should not be before expended and laid out in erecting the said college, or in the other uses aforesaid. And by the said charter did make, create and establish the said James Blair first President of said college, during his natural life. And further, did grant that the said Francis Nicholson, Wm. Cole, Ralph Wormley, Wm. Byrd, John Lear, James Blair, John Farnifold, Stephen Fouace, and Samuel Gray, Thos. Milner, Christopher Robinson, Charles Scarborough, John Smith, Benjamin Harrison, Miles Cary, Henry Hartwell, William Randolph, and Matthew Page, and their successors, or the major part of them, should choose and nominate other able, fit, and capable persons into the places of the masters or professors of the said college; and that after the death, or resignation, or deprivation of the said President, or professors, or any of them, they might from time to time, choose and substitute into his or their places some fit person or persons, according to the ordinances and statutes of the same college, by the said Francis Nicholson, William Cole, Ralph Wormley, William Byrd, John Lear, James Blair, John Farnifold, Stephen Fouace, Samuel Gray, Thos. Milner, Christopher Robinson, Charles Scarborough, John Smith, Benj. Harrison, Miles Cary, Henry Hartwell, William Randolph, and Matthew Page, or their successors, or the major part of them, for the good and wholesome government of the same college, and of all persons enjoying any office or residing therein, to be made, ordained and established. And further, did grant that when the said college should be so erected, made, founded and established, the same should be for ever called and named the College of William and Mary, in Virginia; and that the said President, and masters, or professors, of the said college, should be one body corporate and politic, and by the name of the President and masters, or professors, of the college of William and Mary, in Virginia, should have perpetual succession, and should for ever be called and named the President and masters, or professors of the college of William and Mary, in Virginia; and by the same name should be persons fit, capable, able and perpetual in law to purchase and receive lordships, manors, lands, tenements, reversions, rectories, portions, pensions, annuities, hereditaments, possessions, and services whatsoever, as well spiritual as temporal, and all goods and chattels whatsoever, as well of the gift of their said late majesties, their heirs and successors, as of the gift of the said trustees or any other persons whatsoever, to the value of two thousand pounds of lawful money of England, by the year, and no more, to have and to hold to them and their successors for ever: And did further grant to the said President and masters, or professors, and their successors, divers other liberties, privileges and immunities, in the said letters patents particularly set forth and expressed; and further, did declare, nominate, ordain, and constitute the said Francis Nicholson, William Cole, Ralph Wormley, William Byrd, John Lear, James Blair, John Farnifold, Stephen Fouace, and Samuel Gray, Thomas Milner, Christopher Robinson, Charles Scarborough, John Smith, Benjamin Harrison, Miles Cary, Henry Hartwell, William Randolph, and Matthew Page, and their successors, to be for ever the true and undoubted visitors and governors of the said College; and did give them, or the major part of them, power, from time to time, to make statutes and ordinances for the good government of the said College: And did grant unto them perpetual succession, and that they and their successors should for ever be eighteen persons, or any other number not exceeding twenty; and that one discreet and fit person, out of their number should be rector of the said College, to be elected and appointed as in the said letters patents is expressed; and did appoint the said James Blair first rector of the said College, to continue in that office for one year next after the founding of the said College. And for perpetuating the succession of the said visitors and governors, did grant that as often as any of the said visitors and governors of the said College should die, or remove him or themselves, or their families, out of the said colony, and go into foreign parts with intent not to return, that then it should be lawful for the survivors, or the remaining, or the greater part of them, to choose, nominate, and appoint one other or more of the principal and better inhabitants of the said colony of Virginia, into the place or places of such visitor or governor, or visitors and governors, so dying or removing. And to the end the charges and expenses for erecting, building, founding, and adorning the College aforesaid for the present, and also of keeping and maintaining the President and masters, or professors, in time to come, might be sustained and supported, their said late majesties, of their further special grace, certain knowledge, and mere motion, by the said letters patents, for themselves, their heirs and successors, did give, grant, assign, and transfer unto the said trustees, their executors, and assigns, for ever, that full and entire sum of one thousand nine hundred and eighty-five pounds, fourteen shillings and ten pence, of good and lawful money of England, of the monies received and levied for the quit-rents in the said colony, remaining in the hands of William Byrd, Esq., their said majesties' auditor, or of any other person in the said colony for their use, to be expended and applied in, about, and to the building, erecting, and adorning the College aforesaid, and to no other use, intents, or purposes whatsoever. And for as much as by one act of parliament, made in the twenty-fifth year of the reign of the late king Charles the second, of blessed memory, entitled, an act for the encouragement of the Greenland and Eastland trades, and for the better securing the plantation trade, it was enacted, that after the first day of September, which should be in the year of our Lord one thousand six hundred and seventy-three, if any ship, which by the law of the land might trade in any of the plantations, should go to any of them to trade, or take on board any tobacco or other commodities therein enumerated, and should not first give bond with one sufficient surety, to transport the same tobacco into England, Wales, or the town of Berwick upon Tweed, and to no other place, and there to unload and put the same on shore, the dangers of the sea only excepted; in such case there should be paid to the said king, his heirs and successors, for every pound of tobacco unloaded and put on board, one penny, to be levied, collected, and paid in such place, and to such collectors or other officers in the respective plantations, as should be appointed to collect, levy, and receive the same; and under such penalties, as well on the officers as goods, to be inflicted as for the non-payment or defraying the king's taxes or customs in England ought to be inflicted: And if it should happen that any person or persons who ought to pay the said duties should not have ready money wherewith to satisfy the same, that the officers appointed to collect the same might accept, instead of ready money, such proportion of tobacco, to be laden as aforesaid, as might amount to the value thereof, according to the current rate of that commodity in such plantation respectively: All which matters are to be ordered and managed, and the respective duties to be caused to be levied by the commissioners of the customs in England, for the time being, under the authority and direction of the lord treasurer of England, or the commissioners of the treasury for the time being, as by the same act of parliament, among other things therein contained, relation being thereunto had, more fully appears: Their said late majesties, for themselves, and their successors, did give and grant to the said Francis Nicholson, William Cole, and the rest of the trustees aforesaid and their heirs, for ever, the said revenue of one penny for every pound of tobacco to be shipped as aforesaid, out of Virginia or Maryland, or either of them, and the nett produce which should accrue in England, or elsewhere, by the sale of tobacco to be collected in the colonies of Virginia or Maryland, in lieu of the penny aforesaid to be paid for every pound of tobacco to be shipped. But to the express intent, and under this special trust and confidence, that the said trustees, and the longest livers of them, and their heirs, should hold, take, and possess the said revenue of one penny for every pound of tobacco aforesaid, with all profits, commodities, and emoluments of the same; and the same should apply, and employ, to the erecting and adorning of the buildings and other things necessary for the said College, until the said College should be actually erected, founded, and established; and to the express intent, and under this special trust and confidence, that as soon as the said College, according to the royal design aforesaid, should be erected and founded, the said trustees, and the longest livers or liver of them, and his or their heirs or assigns, by good and sufficient assurances in law, should give, grant, and transfer to the said President and masters, or professors, of the College aforesaid, the entire revenue aforesaid, with all profits, issues and emoluments of the same, or so much thereof as should not be expended and laid out in the uses aforesaid; to be held, possessed, and enjoyed by the said President and masters, or professors, and their successors, for ever. And further, did give and grant to the said Francis Nicholson, William Cole, and the rest of the trustees aforesaid, and the longest livers or liver of them, and to his or their heirs, the office of surveyor-general of the colony of Virginia aforesaid, if the said office should then be vacant: To be had, held, and exercised with all perquisites, fees, allowances, profits, commodities, advantages, liberties, places and pre-eminences to the said office belonging or appertaining, in as ample manner and form as any other person having, exercising, or enjoying the said office ever had, received, or enjoyed, or might have had, received or enjoyed the same, by the said trustees, and their heirs, or by such officers and deputies as they, or the major part of them, or of the longest livers of them, and their heirs, should, from time to time, nominate and appoint, until the said College should be actually founded and erected. But under this express intent, and special trust and confidence, that the said Francis Nicholson, William Cole, and the rest of the trustees aforesaid, and the longest livers of them, and their heirs, as soon as the said college should be actually erected and founded, should render unto the President and masters, or professors, of the said College, for the time being, whatsoever should remain of the monies arising from that office during their administration, which should not be before laid out in erecting the said College, and the other uses aforesaid. And of their further grace did give, grant, and confirm, for themselves, their heirs and successors, to the said Francis Nicholson, William Cole, and the rest of the trustees aforesaid, ten thousand acres of land, not before legally occupied and possessed by any other of their subjects, lying and being on the south side of Black-water swamp: and also other ten thousand acres of land, not before legally occupied or possessed by any other of their subjects, lying and being in that isthmus commonly called Pamunkey neck, between the forks or branches of York river; which twenty thousand acres of land their said late majesties did direct to be bounded and measured in the places aforesaid, wheresoever it should please the said trustees, or the major part of them, or of the longest livers of them: To be held to them the said Francis Nicholson, William Cole, and

## THE TRANSFER. 23

the rest of the trustees aforesaid, and their heirs, for ever. Nevertheless to this intent, and upon this special trust and confidence, that the said trustees, or the major part of them, or of the longest livers of them, when the said College should be founded and established, should give, grant, bargain, and alien the twenty thousand acres aforesaid to the President and masters, or professors of the College aforesaid; to be held to them, and their successors, for ever, by fealty, in free and common soccage, as by the said letters patents, among other things therein contained, relation being thereunto had, more fully and at large doth and may appear. And whereas divers well disposed charitable persons, for encouraging and furthering so good a work, did give unto the said trustees sundry sums of money, amounting to two thousand pounds sterling, and upwards: and the General Assembly of the colony aforesaid, by one act of Assembly made in the fourth year of the reign of the late Queen Anne, entitled, An act for laying an imposition upon skins and furs, for the better support of the College of William and Mary, did lay certain duties upon raw hides and tanned hides, and upon all deer skins and furs that should be exported and carried out of the said colony, either by land or water, to be paid to her said majesty, her heirs and successors, for and towards the better support and maintenance of the said College, as in the said act is more fully expressed. And her said late majesty, Queen Anne, in the          year of her reign, was graciously pleased to give unto the said trustees the sum of one thousand pounds sterling, out of the money arising from the quit-rents of the said colony. And whereas the said trustees since the granting the said letters patents, did purchase one certain parcel of land, containing three hundred and thirty acres, lying and being in the parish of Bruton, in the county of James City, near the City of Williamsburg, for the consideration of one hundred and seventy pounds, which was sold and conveyed to the said trustees by Thomas Ballard by his certain indenture bearing date the twentieth day of December, one thousand six hundred and ninety-three: and have expended divers considerable sums of money in maintaining and supporting a grammar school, for the immediate education of the youth of the said colony, in the Latin and Greek tongues, until the said College should be actually founded as aforesaid, and the number of masters, or professors, in the said letters patents mentioned, made complete: And did also cause to be erected, on part of the said purchased lands, in the parish of Bruton aforesaid, by the appointment of the General Assembly of the said colony, a convenient building of brick for the said College, which some time in the month of October, in the year of our Lord, one thousand seven hundred and five, happened to be destroyed by fire; but by the care of the surviving trustees hath been since rebuilt there, more conveniently than before, and is now fitted with a hall, and convenient apartments for the schools, and for the lodging of the President, masters, and scholars, and hath in it a convenient chamber set apart for a Library, besides all other offices necessary for the said College, and is adorned with a handsome garden; whereby the several sums of money, so as aforesaid contributed, for the carrying on of this work, and the rents, issues and profits, and emoluments, of the said twenty thousand acres of land, and the other revenues aforesaid, have hitherto been in a great measure exhausted, and the founding of the said College delayed and hindered. And whereas the said surviving trustees, pursuant to the trust in them reposed, have established in the said College one school of sacred theology, and one other school of philosophy, besides the grammar school aforesaid, and have appointed certain masters or professors in each of the said schools; that is to say, two masters in the theology school, two other masters in the philosophy school, and one in the grammar school; and have chosen and appointed Bartholomew Yates, late of the parish of Christ Church, in the county of Middlesex, in the colony of Virginia, clerk, and Francis Fontain, late of the parish of York Hampton, in the county of York, in the colony aforesaid, clerk, masters or professors of theology; and Alexander Irwin, of the city of Williamsburg aforesaid, gentleman, and William Dawson, late of Queen College, in Oxford, clerk, masters or professors of philosophy; and Joshua Fry, of Williamsburg aforesaid, gentleman, master of the grammar school in the said College. And whereas the honorable Robert Boyle, Esq., deceased, being in his life-time possessed of a personal estate to the value of ten thousand pounds, and being minded to leave the greatest part thereof to be employed for charitable uses, about the eighteenth of July, in the year of our Lord one thousand six hundred and ninety-one, made his last will and testament in writing, and did thereby, and by one or more codicils, direct that the residue of his personal estate, after debts and legacies paid, should be disposed of by his executors for such charitable and pious uses as they in their discretion should think fit; but recommended unto them the laying out the greatest part thereof for advancement of the Christian religion; and made the right honorable Richard, earl of Burlington, Sir Henry Ashurst, knight and baronet, and John Marr, gentleman, executors of the said will, and soon after died: And the said executors proved his will, and possessed themselves of his personal estate, and had agreed to lay out five thousand four hundred pounds, being looked upon to be the greater half, in the purchase of lands, and to apply the yearly rent thereof towards the propagating the Christian religion amongst infidels; and had agreed with Sir Samuel Gerrard for the purchase of the manor of Brafferton, in the county of York, for the sum of five thousand four hundred pounds, and upon payment thereof, the said Sir Samuel Gerrard was to convey the said estate to them and their heirs; and for the settling the said charity had agreed on the methods following, that out of the said manor the said executors should grant a rent charge in perpetuity of ninety pounds per annum to the company, for propagating the gospel in New England, and the parts adjacent, in America, and their successors, to be paid at Guildhall in London, yearly at Michaelmas and Lady-day, by equal portions, clear of taxes; and that the said company should apply forty-five pounds per annum, one moiety thereof, for the salary of two ministers to instruct the natives, in or near his majesty's colonies in New England, in the christian religion; and the other forty-five pounds per annum, residue of the said rent charge, the said company, and their successors were to transmit unto the President and fellows of Harvard College, in Cambridge, in New England, and their successors, to be by them employed and bestowed for the salary of two other ministers to teach the said natives, in or near the College there, the Christian religion; and that the said manor, subject to the said ninety pounds per annum, should be conveyed to the mayor, commonalty, and citizens of London, and their successors, upon trust, that the rents and profits thereof, over and above the said ninety pounds per annum, receiver's salary, and other incident charges deducted, should be laid out for the advancement of the christian religion in Virginia, in such manner and subject to such methods and rules as the said earl of Burlington, and the Bishop of London, for the time being, should, under their hands and seals, appoint, so as such appointment were made on Lady-day, one thousand six hundred and ninety-seven, and confirmed by the decree of the high court of chancery. But there being delays in the said purchase, some time in Trinity term, in the year of our Lord, one thousand six hundred and ninety-five, sir Thomas Trevor, knight, attorney-general of his then majesty, and dame Elizabeth Gerrard, and Thomas Owen, executors of the last will and testament of the said sir Samuel Gerrard, late deceased, exhibited their bill in the high court of chancery against the right honorable Richard, earl of Burlington, sir Henry Ashurst, knight and Baronet, and John Marr, gentleman, executors of the last will and testament of the honorable Robert Boyle, Esq., deceased: And the said dame Elizabeth Gerrard, and Thomas Owen, being desirous to go on with the said purchase, to that end prayed the said defendants might be decreed to pay the said five thousand four hundred purchase money, on conveyance of a good estate in fee simple. And in as much as it was the proper work of the said court to see charitable uses pursued, the said attorney-general prayed that the defendants might go on with the said purchase, and be decreed to settle the rents thereof on such pious uses as were agreed on, in case the same were according to the testator's mind, or otherwise, as the court should direct: To which bill the said defendants put in their answer, whereupon, and upon the debate of the matters, and hearing what was alleged on either side, the court thought fit, upon the first day of August, one thousand six hundred and ninety-five, to decree that it should be referred to one of the masters of the said court to take an account of the personal estate of the said testator, Robert Boyle, which had come to the hands of the defendants, and to examine and certify whether the five thousand four hundred pounds, agreed to be laid out in the said purchase, were the major part of the said testator's personal estate, and whether the value of the said manor and lands were equivalent to the purchase money agreed to be paid for the same: upon whose report it was, upon the eighth day of August, in the seventh year of the reign of the late king William the third, ordered and decreed, that the defendants should proceed on the said purchase, for the said sum of five thousand four hundred pounds; and that the rules and methods, touching the disposition of the said charity, before mentioned, should be and were thereby ratified and confirmed, with this further addition only, that the yearly account of the said ninety pounds per annum, after the death of the said earl of Burlington and sir Henry Ashurst, should be sent to the President of Trinity College, in Oxford, for the time being, as well as to the several heirs of the earl of Burlington and sir Henry Ashurst, of which College the said Robert Boyle was a member. And it was further decreed, that after the said purchase made, the said defendants should grant the said rent charge of ninety pounds per annum, to the said company, for propagating the gospel in New England, and parts adjacent, in America, and their successors, for the purposes aforesaid; and afterwards should convey the said manor and purchased premises, so charged as aforesaid, unto the mayor, commonalty, and citizens of London, and their successors, subject to the trusts and purposes in the aforesaid rules and agreements made concerning the same. In pursuance of which decree, the said earl of Burlington, and Henry, lord bishop of London, agreed on, and appointed certain rules and methods for the settlement of the said charity in Virginia, under their hands and seals, bearing date the twenty-first day of December, one thousand six hundred and ninety-seven, to the purport and effect herein after mentioned, that is to say: first, that all the yearly rents and profits of the said manor of Brafferton, as well those incurred due since the purchase thereof, as which should thereafter grow due, after the deduction thereout of ninety pounds a year to the College for propagating the gospel in New-England, and other necessary or incident charges, should be by the present or future receivers of the rents thereof paid into the hands of Micajah Perry of London, merchant, agent in London for the President and masters of the College of William and Mary, in Virginia, and to all future agent and agents in England, for the said College, for the time being, for the purposes thereafter mentioned, and such agent or agents receipts and acquittances, should be sufficient discharges to such receiver or receivers for what should be so paid. Secondly, all sum and sums of money already or that should thereafter be received out of the said manor, subject to the deductions aforesaid, should be thereafter remitted to the said President and masters for the time being. Thirdly, that the said President and masters, and his and their successors, should thereout expend so much as should be necessary towards fitting and furnishing lodgings and rooms for such Indian children as should be thereafter brought into the said College. Fourthly, the said President and masters, and his or their successors, should keep at the said College so many Indian children in sickness and health, in meat, drink, washing, lodging, clothes, medicines, books and education, from the first beginning of letters till they should be ready to receive orders, and be thought sufficient to be sent abroad to preach and convert the Indians, at the rate of fourteen pounds per annum for every such child, as the yearly income of the premises, subject to the deduction aforesaid should amount to. Fifthly, that the care, instruction, and education of such children as should be thereafter placed in the said College, should be left to the President and masters thereof, for the time being, but yet subject therein as they were for all their trusts to the visitation and inspection of the rector and governors of the said College, for the time being. Sixthly, that the said President and masters, and his and their successors, should once every year transmit to the earl of Burlington, and lord bishop of London, for the time being, a particular account of what sum and sums of money they should hereafter receive by virtue of the said decree, as also lay out or expend on all or any the matters aforesaid, and the occasion or occasions thereof, as also the number and names of the Indian children that should thereafter be brought into the said College, together with their progress or proficiency in their studies, and of all other matters relating thereto. Seventhly, that the laying out the money from time to time thereafter, to be remitted, as also the manner and method of educating and instructing such children, and all other matters relating to this charity, or the execution of it, should be subject to such other rules and methods, as should from time to time thereafter, be transmitted to the said President and masters, and his and their successors, by the earl of Burlington, and lord bishop of London, for the time being, and in default thereof to such rules and methods as the rectors and governors of the said College, for the time being, should make or appoint: But until such other and further rules were made, the rules and directions thereby given were to take place. Eighthly, and lastly, that the name of the benefactor might not be forgotten, the said earl of Burlington and bishop of London did direct and appoint that the said charity should thereafter be called The Charity of the Honorable Robert Boyle, Esq., of the city of London, deceased. And afterwards at the humble petition of the defendants, preferred to the lord high chancellor of England, praying a day for his lordship's directions for the constitution of the said rules and methods for the settlement of the said charity in Virginia; the right honorable John, lord Somers, baron of Eversham, lord high chancellor of England, the ninth day of June, one thousand six hundred and ninety-eight, ordered, adjudged, and drcreed that the said rules and methods, and all and every of the matters and things therein contained, should be ratified, confirmed and established, with the additions and alterations herein after mentioned, viz: In the sixth rule, that the yearly account therein appointed to be transmitted to the earl of Burlington, and lord bishop of London, for the time being, should be, from time to time, by the said earl and bishop, transmitted into the said court to be filed by the register thereof. And whereas in the seventh rule it is mentioned that the laying out the money, the manner of educating the children, and all other matters relating to the said charity or the execution of it, should be subject to such other rules and methods as should, from time to time thereafter, be transmitted to the said President and masters, and his and their successors, by the said earl of Burlington and bishop of London, for the time being, or in default thereof to such rules and methods as the rector and governors of the said college, for the time being, should make or appoint : it was ordered, that such other rules and methods, touching the charity, at any time so made or appointed, should be first confirmed and approved of by the said honorable court. And it was further ordered, that Micajah Perry, of London, merchant, should be allowed the receiver of the rents and profits of the said trust estate, for the purpose in the said rules and methods mentioned, who was, from time to time, to appoint a receiver under him of the said rents until further order; and also, from time to time, to take and allow such receiver's accounts yearly, and to take the account of the then receiver of the said rents, and of the arrears in his hands, since the time of the said purchase, as by the proceedings and decree of the high court of chancery, in the same court remaining, as of record, relation being thereunto had, more fully, and at large, doth, and may appear. And whereas by reason of the delays in founding the said College, and in completing the full number of masters, by the said letters patents required, the clear rents of the said manor of Brafferton have hitherto been paid to the surviving trustees aforesaid, who have from time to time, applied the same to the education and maintaining such a number of Indian children as could be procured; and out of the said charity have caused to be erected one convenient building of brick, for an Indian school, and for the lodgings of such Indian children as shall hereafter be brought into the said College; and for the educating of them from the first beginning of letters till they should be ready to receive orders, and be thought sufficient to be sent abroad to preach and convert the Indians, have appointed a master who is called the Indian master, and shall hereafter be deemed the sixth master or professor of the said College, and into the place of that master have chosen, nominated and appointed Richard Cocke, gentleman. And whereas by one act of Assembly, made in the fourth year of the reign of his late majesty king George the first, of blessed memory, entitled, An act for granting one thousand pounds out of the public fund for the maintaining and educating of scholars at the College of William and Mary, in Virginia, it is enacted, that the said sum of one thousand pounds current money of Virginia, should be paid to the governors and visitors of said College, to be by them laid out to the best advantage for maintaining and educating such and so many ingenious scholars as to them and their successors should seem fit and expedient, having regard in their elections principally to the learning, virtue and straitened circumstances of such children, and that all natives of the said colony, and no other, should be freely admitted to the said scholarships: Pursuant to which act, the sum of one hundred and fifty pounds, current money of Virginia, hath been laid out in the purchase of one certain tract or parcel of land, containing two thousand one hundred and nineteen acres, lying and being on both sides of Nottoway river, in the counties of Prince George, Surry, and Brunswick; and one other sum of four hundred and seventy-six pounds four shillings, of the like money, hath been laid out in the purchase of seventeen negro slaves, to be employed in tilling and manuring the said lands; and the sum of three hundred and seventy-three pounds sixteen shillings, residue of the said sum of one thousand pounds, for the present, is placed out at interest, the profits of which land and negroes, and the interest of the said money, being judged not sufficient to maintain more than three scholars, after the rate of twelve pounds per annum for each scholar, three scholarships are accordingly settled and appointed pursuant to the said act of Assembly. And whereas, Edward Hill, late of the county of Charles City, Esq., deceased, by his last will and testament, bearing date the     day of     in the year     did give and bequeath unto the said College the sum of one hundred and fifty pounds, to be paid at certain times, in the said will mentioned; which said sum the said trustees have agreed to apply towards the better furnishing the library of the said College with books. And for continuing the succession of the visitors and governors of the said College, the said trustees, as often as any of their number departed this life, or removed him or themselves, and his or their families out of the said colony, with design not to return, have, from time to time, chosen, nominated, and appointed some other person or persons of the principal inhabitants of the said colony into his or their places; and the said Stephen Fouace, many years ago, having removed himself and his family into foreign parts, the present governors and visitors of the said College do consist of the following persons, that is to say, the said James Blair, rector, the honorable William Gooch, Esq., his majesty's lieutenant-governor and commander in chief of the said colony, Alexander Spottswood, Esq., late lieutenant-governor of the said colony, Robert Carter, of the county of Lancaster, William Byrd, of the county of Charles City, Mann Page, of the county of Gloucester, Cole Diggs, of the county of York, Peter Beverly, of the county of Gloucester, John Robinson, of Spotsylvania county, John Carter, of the county of Charles City, John Grymes, of Middlesex county, and William

Randolph, of the county of Henrico, Esqrs., members of his majesty's council in the said colony; Emanuel Jones, of the parish of Petsworth, in the county of Gloucester, Bartholomew Yates, of the parish of Christ-Church, in the county of Middlesex, and John Skaife, of the parish of Stratton-Major, in the county of King and Queen, clerks; John Clayton, John Randolph, and William Robertson, of Williamsburg, Esqrs.; and William Cole, of the county of Warwick, Esq. And whereas, we, the said James Blair and Stephen Fouace, being the longest livers of the said trustees, have made and established certain ordinances and statutes for the better ordering and governing the said College and all persons enjoying any office or residing therein, which are set forth in a certain schedule annexed to these presents. And for as much as the determining the trust aforesaid, and completing the said College, which has been long delayed by the said fire, and the low state of the revenues aforesaid, is adjudged absolutely necessary for promoting the welfare thereof, and the advancement of learning therein; and the General Assembly of the colony aforesaid, hath lately contributed two hundred pounds per annum for one and twenty years for better carrying on the said work. Now know ye, that we the said James Blair and Stephen Fouace, being the only surviving trustees before named, in execution and performance of the trust in us reposed in pursuance of the said recited charter, and for and in consideration of the sum of ten shillings to us in hand paid by the President and masters, or professors of the College of William and Mary, in Virginia, the receipt whereof we do hereby acknowledge, have granted, bargained, sold, aliened, released and transferred, and by these presents, do grant, bargain, sell, alien, release and transfer unto the said President and masters, or professors of the College of William and Mary, in Virginia, all that messuage commonly called the College, situate, lying and being in the parish of Bruton, in the county of James City, aforesaid, near the city of Williamsburg, and all houses, edifices and buildings, courts, gardens and orchards thereunto belonging or appertaining: And all that tract or parcel of land situate, lying and being, in the parish of Bruton, in the County of James City aforesaid, containing by estimation three hundred and thirty acres, purchased of Thomas Ballard as aforesaid: Also all that tract or parcel of land situate, lying and being upon the south side of Black-water swamp, in the county of Surry aforesaid, containing by estimation ten thousand acres: Also all that other tract or parcel of land situate, lying and being in Pamunkey neck aforesaid, containing by estimation ten thousand acres: and also all that other tract or parcel of land situate, lying and being on both sides of Nottoway river, in the counties of Prince George, Surry and Brunswick as aforesaid, containing by estimation two thousand one hundred and nineteen acres. And all houses, edifices, buildings, gardens, orchards, pastures, woods, ways, waters, profits and advantages whatsoever held, used, occupied, or enjoyed with the said lands, or to the same respectively belonging or appertaining, and the reversion and reversions, remainder and remainders of all and singular the premises, and of every part and parcel thereof, and the rents and profits thereunto incident, and belonging; and also all the estate, right, title, interest, trust, claim and demand whatsoever of us the said James Blair and Stephen Fouace in and to the same premises, and every part and parcel thereof; and also the reversion and reversions, remainder and remainders of any other lands and tenements now vested in the said trustees by the gift of any person or persons whatsoever: To have and to hold all and singular the said messuage, lands, tenements, and hereditaments, with the appurtenances, unto the said President and masters, or professors, of the College of William and Mary, in Virginia, and their successors for ever. And we the said James Blair and Stephen Fouace, further, for the considerations aforesaid, have granted, assigned, and transferred, and by these presents do grant, assign, and transfer unto the said President and masters, or professors, of the said College of William and Mary, in Virginia, all the negro slaves by the said trustees, from time to time purchased, now living upon the said lands or any part or parcel thereof, and their increase: Also all that entire revenue of one penny per pound upon all tobacco exported out of Virginia or Maryland to any other of the British plantations in America, with all tobacco profits, issues and emoluments to be had or taken instead thereof, or arising by or from the same: Also the office of surveyor-general of the colony of Virginia aforesaid: Also the said legacy or sum of one hundred and fifty pounds given by the said Edward Hill aforesaid: And also the said sum of three hundred and seventy-three pounds sixteen shillings, residue of the said sum of one thousand pounds given by the said General Assembly as aforesaid, and the interest thereof: And all other debts now due or owing to the said trustees by virtue of the trust aforesaid. And also all the books, household goods, utensils, and furniture to the said College belonging: To have and to hold the said negro slaves, the revenue of one penny per pound upon tobacco exported out of Virginia and Maryland as aforesaid, and the office of surveyor-general aforesaid, and all and singular other the premises last mentioned, with all profits, issues, emoluments, perquisites, fees, advantages, liberties, places and pre-eminences to the same respectively belonging or appertaining to the said President and masters, or professors of the College of William and Mary, in Virginia.

In witness whereof, we have hereunto set our hands and affixed our seals, this twenty-seventh day of February, in the second year of the reign of our sovereign lord king George the second.

JAMES BLAIR, [L. S.]<br>STEPHEN FOUACE, [L. S.]

| Sealed and delivered by the within named JAMES BLAIR, in the presence of<br>WILLIAM GOOCH,<br>MANN PAGE,<br>JOHN GRYMES,<br>JOHN CLAYTON,<br>JOHN RANDOLPH. | Sealed and delivered by the within named STEPHEN FOUACE, in the presence of<br>A. SPOTSWOOD,<br>JOSHUA MONGER,<br>ARTHUR GRYMES,<br>[his mark]<br>SAM'L BLACKSHAW, at Mr. Cuel's, Stationer, Chancery lane, Lond.<br>JOHN RANDOLPH. |
|---|---|

# HISTORICAL SKETCH*

OF THE

# COLLEGE OF WILLIAM AND MARY,

## IN VIRGINIA.

Soon after the settlement at Jamestown (1607) fifteen thousand acres of land were appropriated at the instance of Sir Edwin Sandys, President of the Company in England, to endow a University, to be established at Henrico, for the colonists and Indians. About the same time (1619) fifteen hundred pounds were contributed in England, through the bishops, to endow a College in Virginia for the Indians; and a little later (1621) one hundred and fifty pounds were subscribed to endow the East India School at Charles City, and one thousand acres of land, five servants and an overseer allotted to it. This was designed to be preparatory to the University at Henrico. Mr. George Thorpe, a gentleman of his majesty's privy chamber, came over to be superintendent of the University, but was, on the 22d March, 1622, with three hundred and forty of the colonists, including a number of the College tenants, killed by the Indians.

Thus was defeated the first attempt to establish a College in Virginia. No further steps seem to have been taken in this direction till 1660–61, when the "Grand Assembly," held at James City, March 23d of that year, passed an act entitled "Provision for a Colledge," in these words:

"Whereas the want of able and faithful ministers in this country deprives us of those great blessings and mercies that alwais attend upon the service of God; which want, by reason of our great distance from our native country, cannot in probability be alwais supplyed from thence; Be it enacted, that for the advance of learning, education of youth, supply of the ministry, and promotion of piety, there be land taken upon purchases for a Colledge and free schoole, and that there be, with as much speede as may be convenient,

---

* Much of the matter contained in this sketch is due to the labors and researches of the late Professor Robert J. Morrison, who was an able and zealous member of the College Faculty.

houseing erected thereon for entertainment of students and schollers."

This act was passed in the 13th Charles II.

Again, at the same session of the "Grand Assembly," Act 35th was passed, entitled "A Petition in behalf of the Church." "Be it enacted, that there be a petition drawn up by this Grand Assembly to the King's Most Excellent Majestie for his letters pattents to collect and gather the charity of well disposed people in England for the erecting of colledges and schooles in this countrie, and also for his Majestie's letters to both Universities of Oxford and Cambridge to furnish the church here with ministers for the present, and this petition be recommended to the Right Honorable Governor, Sir William Berkeley."

Again: "Att a Grand Assembly held att James Cittie, in Virginia, 23d March, 1660–61, the following order was made in the government of the Right Honorable Sir William Berkeley, his Majestie's Governor, Mr. Henry Soanes, Speaker:

"Whereas, for the advancement of learning, promoting piety, and provision of an able and successive ministrie in this countrie, it hath been thought fit that a Colledge of students of the liberal arts and sciences be erected and maintayned, in pursuance whereof his Majestie's Governor, Council of State and Burgesses of the present Grand Assembly have severally subscribed several considerable sums of money and quantities of tobacco (out of their charity and devotion), to be paid to the Honorable Grand Assembly, or such treasurer or treasurers as they shall now, or their successors hereafter at any time appoint, upon demand, after a place is provided and built upon for that intent and purpose: it is ordered that the commissioners of the severall county courts do, at the next followinge courts in their severall countys, subscribe such sums of money and tobacco towards the furthering and promoting the said persons and necessary worke, to be paid by them or their heirs, as they shall think fitt, and that they also take the subscriptions of such other persons at their said courts who shall be willing to contribute towards the same. And that after such subscriptions taken, they send orders to the vestrys of the severall parishes in their severall countys for the subscriptions of such inhabitants and others who have not already subscribed, and that the same be returned to Francis Morrison, Esq."

For these acts and order, see 2d volume Henning's "Statutes at Large."

At a Grand Assembly held at James City, March 23, 1661–62, an act to make "Provision for a Colledge,"* the same as that of 1860-61, was passed. Thus was begun and endowed "The Colledge" in Virginia as early as 1660-61.

It was appropriated for by the "Grand Assembly" in lands, subscribed for by members of the goverment, council and House of Burgesses, and contributed to by the Crown, subscribed to by the members of the county courts and parish vestries, and by private individuals largely, and, doubtless, under the regular clergy of the Church of England, was the only College where any regular liberal teaching was had for those of the colonists who could not send their sons to the schools of the mother country. Its charter and regular endowments were obstructed by the revolutionary and disturbing events both in England and the colony; the corporation had no other name than "The Colledge" until the fourth year of William and Mary; it had endowments and was begun as early as 1660-61. That the "Colledge" existed prior to 1693, when it was chartered by the name of William and Mary, is clearly implied by "act III., October, 1693, 5th William and Mary"—the preamble of which recites the charter. That their Majesties had most graciously pleased upon the humble supplication of the Generall Assembly, by their charter, being dated the eighth day of February, in the fourth year of their reign, to grant their royall lycence certaine trustees, to make, found, erect and establish a college named the College of William and Mary, in Virginia, at a certaine place within this government known by the name of Townsend's Land, and *heretofore* appointed by the General Assembly. And for Townsend's Land, previously appointed as the place, was substituted (under authority given in the charter, for the reason, without doubt, of the objections to Townsend's Land—found by experience to exist—to the effect that, "if by reason of unwholesomeness, or any other cause, the said place shall not be approved of, wheresoever else the General Assembly of our colony of Virginia, or the major part of them, shall think fit, within the bounds of the aforesaid colony, to continue for all times coming") the Middle Plantations, now Williamsburg, as the place for erecting the College. Thus it appears that the site of "The Colledge" had at some time previous been selected, and that Townsend's Land was this site. No plausible reason, unless this be so,

---

* This act is taken from Purvis; the act of 1660-61 is taken from a MS. belonging to Thos. Jefferson, late President of the United States, and in his own handwriting, having been transcribed by him from the original in the office of the General Assembly. The true date of the act, doubtless, is therefore March 23, 1660-61. See 2d vol. Henning's Statutes, pp. 17, 25, 37, 56.

can be given for the fact that Townsend's Land, not otherwise known, and being in no other respect noteworthy, was the only place of the colony specified in the charter.

Sir William Berkeley, notwithstanding his prejudices against free schools and printing, favored the order, and promoted the subscriptions for a college. The twenty-third enquiry submitted by the Lords Commissioners of Foreign Plantations to him in 1670, and answered in 1671, was, "What course is taken about instructing the people within your government in the Christian religion? and what provision is there made for the paying of your ministry?"

Answer. "The same course that is taken in England out of towns; every man, according to his ability, instructing his children. We have forty-eight parishes, and our ministry are well paid, and, by my consent, should be better, if they would pray oftener and preach less. But of all other commodities, so of this; the worst are sent us, and we had few that we could boast of since the persecution in Cromwell's tyranny drove divers worthy men hither. But, I thank God, there are no free schools nor printing, and I hope we shall not have these hundred years; for learning has brought disobedience and heresy and sects into the world, and printing has divulged them, and libels against the best government. God keep us from both!" (33, 2d Henning's Statutes at Large.)

This shows how aristocratic was the prejudice of the royal Governor against popular instruction. He was in favor of establishing "a College of liberal arts and sciences"—liberal to the gentlemen, but very illiberal to the people. His ideas of "free schools" and "learning" and "printing" must have been a forecast of Bacon's rebellion, which, five years later, drove him from "James Cittie" across the Chesapeake to Old Plantation on the peninsula of Northampton.

Thus it is claimed that "The Colledge" was in existence from 1660-61, though it had no other name till the fourth year of the reign of William and Mary. The charter constituted trustees of a corporation, but the public and private charity existed in the Grand Assembly, holding by the hands of its treasurer, for the time being, and by Mr. Morrison, its custodian. (This interesting history of the establishment of the "The Colledge" in 1660-61 is condensed from the Appendix to "Seven Decades of the Union," by General Henry A. Wise.)

In 1688-89, an additional sum of twenty-five hundred pounds sterling was subscribed by a few wealthy Virginians and benevolent English merchants to the endowment of "The Colledge," and the

Colonial Assembly, in 1691, sent the Rev. James Blair, afterwards Commissary of Virginia, to solicit a charter from the Crown.

Queen Mary, to whom Mr. Blair first unfolded the object of his visit, was well pleased with the noble design, and zealously espoused it. William concurred with her, and they gave "out of the quit-rents" two thousand pounds towards the building. Mr. Blair was directed to convey to Seymour, the Attorney General, the royal commands to issue the charter. "Seymour remonstrated against this liberality, upon the ground that the nation was engaged in an expensive war; that the money was wanted for better purposes, and that he did not see the slighest occasion for a College in Virginia." The Rev. Mr. Blair represented to him that its intention was to educate and qualify young men to be ministers of the Gospel, and begged Mr. Attorney would consider that the people of Virginia had souls to be saved as well as the people of England. "Souls!" exclaimed the imperious Seymour; "damn your souls, make tobacco!" The charter of the College was prepared, however, and signed on the 8th day of February, in the fourth year of the reign of William and Mary, which date corresponds under the new style with the 19th February, 1693. It was granted "to the end" (nearly identical with that given in the act of 1660–61) "that the church of Virginia may be furnished with a seminary of ministers of the Gospel, and that the youth may be piously educated in good letters and manners, and that the Christian faith may be propagated amongst the Western Indians to the glory of Almighty God." The charter, as has been stated, fixed the location of the College on the land of Colonel Townsend, on the south side of York river, near Yorktown. This is supposed to be Shield's Point. "If, by reason of unwholesomeness or any other cause, the said place shall not be approved of," the College is to be established "wheresoever else the General Assembly of our Colony of Virginia, or the major part of them, shall think fit, within the bounds of the aforesaid Colony, to continue for all times coming."

In the exercise of the power conferred on the General Assembly to move the College from Townsend's land, the 3d act of the Assembly in the fifth year of the reign of William and Mary, before cited, provides: "That Middle Plantation (now Williamsburg) be the place for erecting the said College of William and Mary in Virginia, and that the said College be at that place erected and built as neare the church now standing in Middle Plantation old fields as convenience will permitt."

Trustees named in the charter were constituted the body corporate to establish the College, and to appoint masters or professors, but were required after the establishment to transfer to the President, Masters or Professors, or their successors, the lands, inheritances, chattels, &c.*

The trustees elected by the General Assembly, to whom the royal license was granted, were Francis Nicholson, Lieutenant-Governor of the Colonies of Virginia and Maryland; William Cole, Ralph Wormley, William Byrd and John Lear, Esquires; John Blair, John Farnifold, Stephen Fouace and Samuel Gray, Clerks; Thomas Milner, Christopher Robinson, Charles Scarborough, John Smith, Benjamin Harrison, Miles Carey, Henry Hartwell, William Randolph and Matthew Page, gentlemen.

The charter further provides, that the College "shall be called and denominated forever 'the College of William and Mary, in Virginia;' and 'the President and Masters, or Professors of the said College, shall be a body politic in deed and in name.'"

It was further provided, that after the transfer of the corporate powers, the trustees should be "the true, sole and undoubted visitors and governors of the College."

The charter confirms to the President and Masters, or Professors, that there shall be a chancellor of the College; appoints "the Reverend Father in God, Henry,† by Divine permission, Bishop of London," first chancellor, and requires that the visitors and governors of the College shall elect a discreet person to this office every seven years.

Towards the endowment of the College, William and Mary contributed one thousand nine hundred and eighty-five pounds fourteen shillings and tenpence, raised out of the quit-rents of the colony, and at that time in the hands of William Byrd, Auditor; one penny a pound on all tobacco exported from Virginia and Maryland; the office of Surveyor General, with all its issues, fees, profits, advantages, conveniences, liberties, places, privileges, and pre-eminences whatsoever; ten thousand acres of land lying on the south side of Blackwater swamp, and ten thousand acres lying in that neck of land, commonly called Pamunkey neck, between the forks of York river.

The faculty had the right to elect either one of their own body, one of the visitors of the College, or "one of the better sort of in-

---

* The original record of the charter of the College is in the Chapel of the Rolls, England; and the original record of the transfer, a deed of bargain and sale from the visitors to the faculty, is in one of the courts of record of Westminster Hall, London.—*Robt. J. Morrison.*

† Henry Compton.

habitants of the colony," to represent the College in the House of Burgesses.

The College building was planned by Sir Christopher Wren, and it was designed, says Beverly, "to be an entire square when completed." The first commencement exercises were held in 1700, "at which there was a great concourse of people; several planters came thither in coaches, and others in sloops from New York, Pennsylvania and Maryland, it being a new thing in that part of America to hear graduates perform their exercises. The Indians had the curiosity, some of them, to visit Williamsburg upon that occasion; and the whole country rejoiced, as if they had some relish of learning."*

The General Assembly of Virginia "was held at his Majesty's Royal College of William and Mary," from 1700 until 1705, when, together with library and philosophical apparatus, it was destroyed by fire. "The fire broke out about ten o'clock at night, in a public time. The Governor and all the gentlemen that were in town came up to the lamentable spectacle, many getting out of their beds. But the fire had got such power before it was discovered, and was so fierce, that there was no hope of putting a stop to it, and therefore no attempts were made to that end." The second building was commenced in the time of Governor Spotswood, but owing to the want of available means, and the scarcity of workmen, it was not finished until 1723.

*(Extract from Beverly's History of Virginia, 1722.)*

"The College was burned in the first year of Governor Nott's time, (how, was not known.) It was not rebuilt till Governor Spotswood's time, when it was raised to the same bigness as before."

*(Extract from Present State of Virginia, by Hugh Jones, 1729.)*

"The College front, which looks due east, is double, and is 136 feet long. At the north end runs back a large wing, which is a handsome hall, answerable to which the chapel is to be built. The building is beautiful and commodious, being first modelled by Sir Christopher Wren, adapted to the nature of the country by the gentlemen there; and since it was burnt down, it has been rebuilt, nicely contrived and adorned by the ingenious direction of Governor Spotswood, and is not altogether unlike Chelsea Hospital."

A few years before the fire of 1859, the College building was re-plastered, and when the old plaster was taken down, the traces in the walls of an extensive conflagration† were not to be mistaken. It is beyond doubt that the present site and walls are the original ones.

---

* Campbell's History of Virginia.
†These traces were due to the fire of 1705, or of that of 1781, when the College building was held as a hospital by the French forces.

In 1719 it was occupied by the convention of the colonial clergy. Now that the College was fully established, the transfer of the corporate rights was shortly made to the faculty in 1729, and the trustees became "the visitors and governors of the College of William and Mary, in Virginia."

The first entry in the oldest record book of the faculty is, "In nomine Dei, Patris, Filii et Spiritus Sancti, Amen." Until the Revolution the bishops of London, with a single interregnum, were chancellors of the College. On the 18th of January, 1764, the Earl of Hardwicke had been elected chancellor; but the intelligence of this did not arrive in England until after his death, of which his son and successor in the title wrote to apprise the faculty. Before the war of Independence its presidents were the commissaries or representatives, in the colony, of the bishops of London; and since the Revolution Bishop Madison and other distinguished divines, including the Right Reverend John Johns, now Bishop of Virginia, have presided over it. Indeed, every Bishop of Virginia has been connected with it. As soon as established, the College became the nursery of the church in Virginia, and at later periods proved an efficient support in times of adversity.

Bishop Meade, in "Old Churches, Ministers and Families of Virginia," says: "One thing is set forth in praise of William and Mary which we delight to record, viz: that the hopes and designs of its founders and early benefactors, in relation to its being a nursery of pious ministers, were not entirely disappointed. It is positively affirmed, by those most competent to speak, that the best ministers in Virginia were those educated at the College and sent over to England for ordination. The foreigners were the great scandal of the church."

The condition upon which twenty thousand acres of land were given to the College was, that the President and Professors should pay annually, on the 5th of November, two copies of Latin verses to the governor or lieutenant-governor of the Dominion of Virginia. That this was complied with, we may infer from the following extract from the Virginia Gazette of November 12th, 1736: "On this day sen'night, being the 5th of November, the President, masters and scholars of William and Mary College went, according to their annual custom, in a body to the Governor's to present his honor with two copies of Latin verses, in obedience to their charter, as a grateful acknowledgment for two valuable tracts of land given the said College by their late King William and Queen Mary. Mr. President delivered the verses to his honor, and two of the young gentlemen spoke them. It is further observed that there were upwards of sixty scholars present, a much greater number than has been any year before since the foundation of the College."

The colonial governors, for the most part, took an active interest in the welfare of the College.

(*Extract from Miller's Retrospect*, II. 378.)

"Lord Botetourt attended morning and evening prayers in the College chapel."

WELD, in his travels, 1798, says: "The stature of Lord Botetourt" (now belonging to the College) "was defaced, and the head and arm knocked off during the war (Revolutionary) when party rage was at its highest pitch, and everything pertaining to royalty obnoxious."

Lord Botetourt gave a sum of money, the interest of which was sufficient to purchase annually two gold medals—one to be given to the best classical scholar, the other to the best scholar in philosophy. This medal was annually awarded until the Revolution. The first competitors for the Episcopate of Virginia, the Rev. James Madison and the Rev. Samuel Shield, both received this medal; the former in 1772, the latter in 1773.

This medal was also conferred on Mr. Nathaniel Burwell in 1772; Mr. David Stewart, of King George, 1773; on Mr. Joseph Eggleston, of Amelia, 1774; and the same year, on Mr. Walker Maury, of Williamsburg; and in 1775, on Mr. John White, of King William, and Mr. Thomas Evans, of the Eastern Shore of Virginia.

The Hon. Robert Boyle, who died in 1691, in his will directed his executors, the Right Hon. Richard, Earl of Burlington, Sir Henry Ashurst, Knight and Baronet, and John Marr, gentleman, "to apply his personal estate to such charitable and pious uses as they, in their discretion, should think fit." After some litigation in England, in pursuance of a decree of court, the Earl of Burlington and Henry, Lord Bishop of London, agreed, on the 21st of December, 1697, to bestow the charity in Virginia, arranging that the annual rents, subject to ninety pounds, given to Harvard University at Cambridge, Massachusetts, should be paid to the President and Professors of the College of William and Mary in Virginia, for the purpose of maintaining and educating Indian scholars. The fund was invested in an English estate called the Brafferton, and with the proceeds of it the building on the College green, now known as the Brafferton, was erected; and until the Revolution, Indians were supported and educated by this charity. The Westover manuscripts inform us that "during the sanguinary war with the Indians, in which North Carolina had been engaged, Governor Spotswood demanded of the tribes tributary to Virginia a number of the sons of the chiefs, to be sent to the College of William and Mary, where they served as hostages to keep the peace, and enjoyed the advantage of learning to read and write English, and were instructed in the Christian religion. But on returning to their own people, they relapsed into idolatry and barbarism."

(*Extract from the "Present State of Virginia, by Hugh Jones," published in London in 1724.*)

Speaking of the Indian school of the College, he says: "The young Indians, procured from the tributary or foreign nations with much difficulty, were formerly boarded and lodged in town, where abundance of them used to die, either through sickness, change of provision and way of life, or, as some will have it, often for want of proper necessaries and due care taken with them. Those of them that have escaped well, and have been taught to read and write, have, for the most part, returned to their home, some with and some without baptism, where they follow their own savage customs and heathenish rites. A few of them lived as servants with the English, or loitered and idled away their time in laziness and mischief. But it is a pity more care is not taken of them after they are dismissed from school. They have admirable capacities when their humors and tempers are perfectly understood."

The foundation of the President's house was laid on the 31st of July, 1732—the President (the Rev. James Blair), Mr. Dawson (afterwards Commissary of Virginia), Mr. Fry (afterwards Colonel Fry, under whom Washington served), Mr. Stith (the historian), and Mr. Fox, laying the first five bricks in order one after another. During the American Revolution this building was burnt whilst it was occupied by the French troops, before the siege of Yorktown; but Louis XVI. generously rebuilt it, and about this time presented five or six hundred volumes of great value to the library of the College. The walls, however, had not been much injured by the fire.

The old chapel was first opened on the 28th of June, 1732, and the Rev. James Blair, the President, preached a sermon from the text: "Train up a child in the way he should go, and when he is old he will not depart from it." *Prov.* xxii. 6. In "Old Churches and Families of Virginia," Bishop Meade says: "Williamsburg was once the miniature copy of the Court of St. James, somewhat aping the manners of that royal place, while the old church and its graveyard, and the College chapel were—si licet cum magnis componere parva—the Westminster Abbey and the St. Paul's of London, where the great ones were interred." Sir John Randolph was the first person buried in the College chapel.

(*Extract from Bishop Meade's "Old Churches."*)

"So Williamsburg, while it was the seat of government and of the College of William and Mary, was, to a great extent, Virginia."

The remains of Lord Botetourt rest, it is believed, in the same vault with those of Sir John Randolph.

Peyton Randolph, the President of the first American Congress, and John Randolph, Attorney-General of the Crown for the Colony of Virginia, sons of Sir John Randolph; Bishop Madison, the first Bishop of Virginia, and Chancellor Nelson, were also buried in the College chapel.

(*Extract from Virginia Gazette, Nov. 29th, 1776.*)

"On Thursday last, the remains of our beloved and amiable fellow-citizen, the Hon. Peyton Randolph, were conveyed in a hearse to the College chapel, attended by the Worshipful Brotherhood of Free Masons, Houses of Assembly, a number of other gentlemen, and the inhabitants of the city. The body was received from the hearse by six gentlemen of the House of Delegates, who conveyed it to the family vault in the chapel, after which an excellent oration was pronounced from the pulpit by the Rev. Thomas Davis, in honor of the deceased, and recommending it to the respectable audience to imitate his virtues. The oration being ended, the body was deposited in the vault, when every spectator paid the last tribute of tears to the memory of their departed and much honored friend. The remains were brought from Philadelphia by his nephew, Edmund Randolph, in pursuance of the orders of his widow."

In 1726, a duty was laid on liquors by the House of Burgesses, to be applied to the current expenses of the College and for founding scholarships.

In 1717 Mrs. Philarity Giles, of Isle of Wight, left by will her reversionary interest in lands, on the Blackwater in the same county, to the College.

In 1759, a grant was made by the House of Burgesses to the College of the proceeds of the tax on peddlers.

Before the Revolution, the following donations were made to the College for "foundations of scholarships": General Assembly, one thousand pounds; Col. Edward Hill, of Shirley, Charles City, one hundred and fifty pounds; Robert Carter, of Corotoman, fifty pounds; Mrs. Bray, widow of Capt. Thos. Bray, New Kent, two hundred pounds; Mrs. Elizabeth Harrison, of Surry, three hundred pounds; the Rev. James Blair, five hundred pounds; Philip Lightfoot, Esq., of Sandy Point, five hundred pounds. A gilt cup was presented to the College by Lady Gooch, of England. The Earl of Burlington presented a portrait of his uncle, the Hon. Robert Boyle. It is now,

## HISTORICAL SKETCH.     45

with several other interesting portraits, in possession of the College authorities.

Dr. James Blair, a native of Scotland, and an Episcopal clergyman, was the first President of the College. He was appointed to the office by the charter. At the instance of the Bishop of London, he came as a missionary to Virginia in 1685. He was appointed Commissary or Representative of the Bishop in the Colony in 1689. With justice, he may be considered the god-father of William and Mary College; for his exertions, both in this country and in England, con-tributed greatly to the success of the enterprise. He died in 1743, after having filled the office of President of the College for half a century.

Bishop Meade says of the Rev. James Blair: "He was involved in difficulties with Governors and clergymen, more or less, during almost the whole period of his Commissaryship and Presidency of the College. I have the whole of these controversies spread before me in long and tedious letters from himself and his opponents, to the authorities in England, which never have been published. His first controversy was with Governor Andros, who came to Virginia under no good character, from New York. By royal instructions, Andros was not only Governor of Virginia, but the Ordinary, the Representative of the Bishop of London in church matters, the Commissary being comparatively a negative character." . . . "Dr. Blair being then in England about his College, preferred charges against him as an enemy to religion, to the Church, the Clergy, and the College, bringing proofs of the same. The charges cover thirty-two pages of manuscript and are well written. But Blair had formidable foes to meet in London. Governor Andros sends over in his defence Colonel Byrd, of Westover; Mr. Harrison, of Surry; Mr. Povey, a man high in office in the Colony, and a Mr. Marshall, to arraign Dr. Blair himself before the Bishop of London and Archbishop of Canterbury. Two days were spent in Lambeth Palace in the examination. The charges and the answers are set down, and fill up thirty-seven folio pages of manuscript. Never were four men more completely foiled by one. The accusers seem to feel and acknowledge it, and doubtless wished themselves out of Lambeth Palace long before the trial was over." . . . . "The result of it all was, that Mr. Blair came home with a good sum of money for his College, and Andros was sent back to England to stand his trial, from which he came out badly."

In the dedication by Commissary Blair of his sermons, published in 1722, he says: It is a particular felicity of that country, (Virginia,) not to be infested with the enemies of the Christian faith: so that we have little or no occasion in our sermons to enter the lists with Atheists, Deists, Arians or Socinians, nor are we much troubled with either Popish or Protestant Recusants; or any of those unhappy distinctions by which the Church of England is most unfortunately subdivided in this our mother country.

(*Extract from Preface to Dr. Blair's Sermons, published in* 1740.)

"Therefore, he formed a vast design of erecting and endowing a College in Virginia, at Williamsburg, the Capital of that country, for professors and students in academical learning. In order thereto, he had himself set on foot a voluntary subscription, amounting to a great sum, and not content with that, he came over to England in the year 1693, to solicit the affair at Court. The good Queen (Queen Mary) was so well pleased with the noble design, that she espoused it with a particular zeal; and King William also, as soon as he became acquainted with its use and excellency, very readily concurred with the Queen in it."

### The Presidents before the Revolution were:

The Rev. Dr. Blair, Commissary, from...............................................1693 to 1743
The Rev. William Dawson, Commissary, from............................1743 to 1752
The Rev. William Stith, D. D., the Historian, Commissary, from..1752 to 1755
The Rev. Thomas Dawson, D. D., Commissary, from....................1755 to 1761
The Rev. James Horrocks, D. D.,      "      "      ................1767 to 1771
The Rev. John Camm, D. D.,           "      "      ................1771 to 1777
When Bishop Madison was elected.

Before the Revolution, the College consisted of a school of divinity, one of philosophy, in which natural philosophy and mathematics were taught, a grammar school for instruction in the ancient languages, and an Indian school supported by the donation of the Hon. Robert Boyle, in which, from about the year 1700 to 1776, eight to ten Indains were annually maintained and educated. Some of these Indians came a distance of four hundred miles from the College.

The College long exercised (till 1819) the duties of the office of Surveyor General of the Colony of Virginia; and among the surveyors appointed by it were George Washington, Zachary Taylor, of Orange, the grandfather of the late General Taylor, President of the United States, and Thomas Jefferson.

For about seventy years previous to the Revolution, the average number of students was about sixty; from ten to fifteen of whom were received on the scholarships or foundations. At the beginning of the Revolution the number was seventy.

Prior to the Revolution, the annual income of the College, from duties granted in the charter and by the Colony, from "Boyle's Charity," funded capital and scholarships, was nearly four thousand pounds sterling. In 1776 it was the richest College in North America, and had been the constant recipient of royal, colonial and private benefactions. By the Revolution it lost, in consequence of the depreciation of paper money, all of its endowment, save about two thousand five hundred dollars in money, and the then unproductive land granted by the English Crown.

It furnished to the American Revolution Benjamin Harrison, Carter Braxton, Thomas Nelson and George Wythe, signers of the Declaration; Peyton Randolph, President of the first American Congress; Edmund Randolph, Attorney General and Secretary of State; John Marshall, Chief Justice; Thomas Jefferson* and James Monroe, Presidents of the United States, and a host of others, among them John Tyler, Senior, Governor of Virginia, John Taylor, of Caroline, the Nelsons, the Blands, the Pages, the Harrisons, the Carters, the Nicholases, the Braxtons, the Grymeses, the Burwells, the Lewises, the Lyonses, the Mercers, the Cockes, the Bollings, the Nicholsons, the Carringtons, and many others whose names are national and historic. Thirty students and three professors joined the army at the beginning of the Revolutionary war.

The following extracts from the proceedings of the faculty shed light upon the history of the College before the Revolutionary War:

"June 28th, 1732.—The College chapel was opened. Mr. President (the Rev. Mr. Blair) preached on Proverbs, xxii : 6.

"July 31st, 1732.—The foundation of the President's house at the College was laid. The President, Mr. Dawson, Mr. Fry, Mr. Stith (afterwards the historian), and Mr. Fox, laying the first five bricks in order, one after another.

"At a meeting of y$^e$ President and Masters of William and Mary College, Sep$^r$ y$^e$ 14th, 1752, present,

Y$^e$ Rev. Mr. STITH, President.

Mr. Dawson, Mr. Robinson, Mr. Preston, and Mr. Graham.

Y$^e$ following orders were unanimously agreed to :"

"1. Ordered, Y$^t$ no scholar belonging *to any school in the College*, of what age, rank, or quality soever, do keep any race horse at y$^e$ College in y$^e$ town, or anywhere in the neighborhood. Y$^t$ they be not anyway concerned in making races, or in backing or abetting those made by others, and y$^t$ all race horses kept in y$^e$ neighbourhood of y$^e$ College and belonging to any of y$^e$ scholars, be immediately dispatched and sent off, and never again brought back, and all this under pain of y$^e$ severest animadversion and punishment."

"2. Ordered, Y$^t$ no scholar belonging to y$^e$ College of what age, rank or quality soever, or wheresoever residing within or without y$^e$ College, do presume to appear playing or betting at y$^e$ billiard or other gaming tables, or be any way concerned in keeping or fighting cocks, under pain of y$^e$ like severe animadversions or punishment.

(Signed) WILLIAM STITH."

"Jany. y$^e$ 14, 1754. Resolved, Y$^t$ a person be appointed to hear such boys as shall be recommended by their parents or guardians, a chapter in the Bible

---

*Soon after Mr. Jefferson's entrance into College, Dr. William Small was made *per interim.* Professor of Philosophy, and Mr. Jefferson declared it was Dr. Small's instruction and intercourse that probably fixed his destinies for life.

every school-day, at 12 o'clock, and y$^t$ he have y$^e$ yearly salary of one pistole for each boy so recommended."

"Aug. 29, 1754. Resolved, unanimously, Y$^t$ Mr. Commissary Dawson be allowed y$^e$ use of y$^e$ Hall and great room during y$^e$ meeting of y$^e$ clergy."

Sept. 7th, 1754. The College allows only to the sick, tea to be made and sent by the house-keeper, and wine-whey."

"Jany. 1st, 1756. Richard Collhyon was by them examined, and is thought capable of teaching the Grammar School at Norfolk."

"April 2nd, 1756. Y$^e$ day Benjamin Franklin, Esquire, favored y$^e$ society with his company, and had y$^e$ Degree of A. M. conferred upon him by y$^e$ Rev. G. Dawson, A. M., President, to whom he was in public presented by the Rev. William Preston, A. M."

"March 24th, 1756. Resolved, Y$^t$ y$^e$ young gentlemen, when they leave the Grammar School, shall be obliged to appear in academical dress."

"June 26, 1761. Resolved, That Mrs. Foster be appointed stocking-mender in the College, and that she be paid annually the sum of twelve pounds, provided she furnish herself with lodging, diet, fire, and candles."

"March 2d, 1768. Resolved, that an advertisement be inserted in the Gazette to inform the public that the College is now clear of small-pox.

"June 17th, 1768. Resolved, that the sum of fifty pounds per annum be appropriated out of the College revenue for the purchase of medals and other honorary rewards, to be distributed annually by the president and masters amongst such of the students as shall best deserve them by their public examinations.

"Sept. 4th, 1769. Resolved unanimously, that the college-vote for James City be given to Robt. C. Nicholas and Lewis Burwell, Esqs.

"April 11th, 1771. This day was received from the honorable the president, and the other gentlemen appointed to take care of Lord Botetourt's effects, the following extract of a letter from his grace the Duke of Beaufort: 'I understand that his lordship expressed a desire sometime before he died to be buried in Virginia, so that I do not intend to remove the body to England; but hope the President, &c., of the College will permit me to erect a monument near the place where he was buried, as the only means I have of expressing in some degree the sincere regard and affection I bore towards him. And I flatter myself it may not be disagreeable to the Virginians to have this remembrance of a person whom they held in so high estimation, and whose loss they so greatly lament.' Which being read, the application therein contained received the unanimous assent of the society, who are glad of any opportunity of showing their sincere regard to the memory of Lord Botetourt.

"February 14th, 1772. Upon motion made by Mr. Johnson, it was ordered that the students in the philosophy schools shall speak Latin declamations of their composition, and that by two of them in rotation this exercise shall be performed in the chapel immediately after evening service, every second Thursday during term-time."

"July 29th, 1772. That the medal assigned by his Excellency Lord Botetourt, for the encouragement of students in philosophical learning, be given to Mr. Nathaniel Burwell, as being the best proficient. Resolved, that the medal assigned by his lordship for the encouragement of classical learning be given to Mr. James Madison."

"October 14th, 1773. Agreed, unanimously, that Mr. Thomas Jefferson be appointed surveyor of Albemarle, in the the room of Mr. Nicholas Lewis, who has sent his letter of resignation, and that he be allowed to have a deputy."

"April, 1775. Whereas, we have received from the Bursar the disagreeable news that His Excellency Lord Dunmore entertains thoughts of resigning the office of visitor and governor of the College: Resolved unanimously, that the President and Mr. Gwatkin do wait on his lordship to thank him most cordially for his past favors to the College, and most humbly to request that he will continue to act as a visitor and governor of the College, and to afford his protection to the president and professors as far as they shall appear to him to deserve his countenance."

*(Extract from the Virginia Gazette, September 10th, 1736.)*

"This evening will be performed at the Theatre the Tragedy of Cato; and on Monday, Wednesday and Friday, will be acted the following Comedies. by the gentlemen and ladies of this county, viz: The Busy Body, The Recruiting Officer, and the Beaux Strategem."

*(Extract from the Virginia Gazette, Aug. 15th, 1771.)*

"After prayers and a sermon in the Chapel, two elegant English orations, in praise of the founders and benefactors of the College, were pronounced in the hall by two of the students, Messieurs Edmund Randolph and William Leigh, with such spirit and propriety as to obtain the just applause of a numerous and attentive audience."

*(Extract from the Virginia Gazette, December 8th, 1774.)*

CORRESPONDENCE BETWEEN THE FACULTY AND THE EARL OF DUNMORE, THE GOVERNOR.

"We, his Majesty's dutiful and loyal subjects, the President and Professors of William and Mary College, moved by an impulse of unfeigned joy, cannot help congratulating your Excellency on such a series of agreeable events as the success of your enterprise against the Indians, the addition to your family by the birth of a daughter, and your safe as well as glorious return to the capital of this Dominion. May the great fatigues and dangers, which you so readily and cheerfully undergo in the service of your Government, be ever crowned with victory! May you ever find the public benefits thence arising attended with domestic blessings! And may you always feel the enlivening pleasure of reading in the countenances around you, wherever you turn your eyes, such an expression of affection as can be derived only from applauding and grateful hearts."

*To which his Excellency was pleased to return the following answer:*

GENTLEMEN:—I cannot but receive every instance of the attention of a learned and respectable body, such as yours, with a great degree of satisfaction; but the affectionate and very obliging terms in which you are pleased to express your good wishes towards me on this occasion, demand cordial thanks, and will ever be impressed on my mind."

DUNMORE.

(*Extract from the Virginia Gazette,* 1780.)

. . . "The vacations in the University are from the 1st of April to the 1st of May, and from the 1st of August to the 10th of October."

From the Statutes of the College, published in 1792:

"Be it ordained, That the drinking of spirituous liquors (except in that moderation which becomes the prudent and industrious student) be prohibited."

From a copy of the Old Laws:

"No other person than a student or other member of the College shall be admitted as a boarder at the College table. No liquors shall be furnished or used at table except beer, cider, toddy, or spirits and water.

"The keeper of the College table shall, on no pretext nor for any consideration, furnish or sell to the students wine or any other spirituous liquors, to be drunk at any other time or place, than at their ordinary meals, as aforesaid."

From Weld's Travels: "The Bishop of Virginia is President of the College, and has apartments in the buildings. Half a dozen or more of the students, the eldest about twelve years of age, dined at his table one day while I was there; some were without shoes or stockings, others without coats. During the dinner, they constantly rose to help themselves *at the sideboard.* A couple of dishes of salted meat and some oyster soup formed the above dinner. I only mention this, as it may convey some idea of American colleges and American dignitaries." [The date of the preface to Weld's Travels is December 20th, 1798.]

(*Extract from the proceedings of the Visitors, Sept.* 1*st*, 1769.)

"The Visitation being informed that the Rev'd Mr. John Camm, Professor of Divinity, and the Rev'd Mr. Josiah Johnson, Master of the Grammar School, have lately married and taken up their residence in the city of Williamsburg, by which great inconvenience has arisen to the College and the necessary attention which those Professors ought to pay to the conduct and behaviour of the students and scholars has been almost totally interrupted:

Resolved, That it is the opinion of this Visitation that the Professors and Masters, their engaging in marriage and the concerns of a private family, and shifting their residence to any place without the College, is contrary to the principles on which the College was founded, and their duty as Professors."

(*Extract from same, Dec.* 14*th*, 1769.)

"Resolved, That all Professors and Masters hereafter to be appointed, be constantly resident of y$^e$ College, and upon the marriage of such Professor or Master, that his Professorship be immediately vacated."

The parent society in this country of the Phi Beta Kappa was organized at William and Mary College the 5th December, 1776. The first meeting was held in the Apollo Hall of the old Raleigh tavern of Williamsburg, the room in which the first revolutionary spirit of Virginia was breathed in the burning words of Henry. The original charter of this society is now in the possession of the Historical Society of this State.

When the College broke up in 1781, the records of the Society were sealed up and placed in the hands of the College Steward, and subsequently they came into the possession of the Historical Society of Virginia. On examination in 1850, it was found that one of the old members, William Short, of Philadelphia, still survived. It was also discovered that he was President of the Society when it was interrupted. Measures were immediately taken to revive it in the College with Mr. Short as the connecting link with the original Society. This was done, and it is now in operation.

The names of the original members of this Society are:

| | | |
|---|---|---|
| John Heath, | Thomas Smith, | Richard Booker, |
| Armistead Smith, | John Jones, | Daniel Fitzhugh, |
| John Stuart, | John Starke, | Theodore Fitzhugh, |
| Isaac Hill, | William Short, | John Morrison, |
| Henry Hill, | John Allen, | George Braxton, |
| Thomas Hall, | John Nivison, | Hartwell Cocke, |
| Samuel Hardy, | John Brown, | Archibald Stewart, |
| D. C. Brent, | Thomas Clements, | Thomas W. Ballandine, |
| Spencer Roane, | John Moore, | William Stith, |
| William Stuart, | J. J. Beckley, | Thomas Savage, |
| John Page, | William Cabell, | John Marshall, |
| Landon Cabell, | Thomas Lee, | Bushrod Washington, |
| William Madison, | W. Pierce, | Richard B. Lee, |
| John Swann, | Thomas Cocke, | Paxton Bowdoin, |
| Alexander Mason. | | (*Grigsby's Convention*, 1776.) |

In 1781 the exercises of the College were suspended, and the buildings were alternately occupied the summer before the memorable siege of Yorktown by the British and the French and American troops. Whilst occupied by the latter, the College was injured and the President's house destroyed by fire. This was subsequently rebuilt at the expense of the French government. It does not appear how long the College was closed—probably the exercises were suspended not more than a year. In 1790 there was a respectable number of students.

After the Revolution the General Assembly of Virginia gave to the College the Palace lands and the houses upon them, a tract of land near Williamsburg known as the "Vineyard," and a few acres not far from Jamestown. The organization of the College was now changed. Mr. Jefferson, in his Autobiography. says: " On the 1st of June, 1779, I was appointed Governor of the Commonwealth, and retired from the Legislature. Being elected also one of the Visitors of William and Mary College, a self-electing body, I effected, during my residence in Williamsburg that year, a change in the organization of that institution, by abolishing the Grammar School and the two Professorships of Divinity and Oriental Languages, and substituting a Professorship of Law and Police, one of Anatomy, Medicine and Chemistry, and one of Modern Languages; and the charter confining us to six professors, we added the Law of Nature and Nations, and the Fine Arts, to the duties of the moral professor, and Natural History to those of the professor of Mathematics and Natural Philosophy." The Indian school was abandoned in consequence of the loss of the manor of Brafferton by the Revolution.

In 1788, George Washington was made Chancellor of the College. His letter of acceptance is as follows:

MOUNT VERNON, *April 30th*, 1788.
DEAR SIR:

I am now to acknowledge the receipt of your letter of the 15th instant, in which you did me the favor to enclose an extract from the original statute designating the duties of the office to which I had been appointed.

Influenced by a heartfelt desire to promote the cause of science in general and the College of William and Mary in particular, I accept the office of Chancellor of the same, and request you will be pleased to give official notice thereof to the learned body who have thought proper to honor me with the appointment.

I confide fully in their strenuous endeavors for placing the system of education on such a basis as will render it most beneficial to the State and the republic of letters, as well as to the more extensive interests of humanity and religion. In return, they will do me the justice to believe that I shall not be tardy in giving my cheerful concurrence to such measures as may be best calculated for the attainment of those desirable and important objects.

For the expressions of politeness and friendship blended with your communication, I pray you to receive my best acknowledgments. With sentiments of the highest esteem and regard,

I am, dear sir,
Your obedient and very humble servant,
GEORGE WASHINGTON.

SAMUEL GRIFFIN, ESQ.,
*Rector of the College of William and Mary.*

Notwithstanding the depressed and impoverished condition of the College at the termination of the Revolutionary War, it speedily revived under the guidance and teachings of Bishop Madison and his associates, and sent forth John Tyler, President of the United States, Littleton Waller Tazewell, William B. Giles, John Randolph, Spencer Roane, Bushrod Washington, James Breckinridge, Archibald

## HISTORICAL SKETCH.      53

Stewart, William Brockenborough, James P. Preston, Robert Stanard, William H. Roane, Robert B. Taylor, George M. Bibb, William T. Barry, William H. Fitzhugh, Philip P. Barbour, Benjamin Watkins Leigh, William H. Cabell, Chapman Johnson, Briscoe G. Baldwin, Roger Jones, George Croghan, H. St. George Tucker, John Tayloe Lomax, John Nelson, William S. Archer, John J. Crittenden, John H. Cocke, Powhatan Ellis, Winfield Scott, William C. Rives, and many others of like renown to National and State service.

Since 1835, say twenty-five years of its active existence (within this time its exercises have been for five years suspended), the College matriculation books show an average of seventy-five students who have drunk at the fountains of philosophy, literature and science under the direction of the late Thomas R. Dew, the late Judge N. Beverly Tucker, the Right Rev. John Johns, Bishop of Virginia, and their co-laborers and successors, and who have proved themselves in every way worthy of their predecessors, and, in numerous cases, filled important offices in church and State. During the late civil war, William and Mary followed the fortunes of Virginia. Ninety per cent. of the students at College when the war began, entered the State service. A large number of the alumni held important civil and military positions while the unhappy contest was raging. Some of these, of the highest promise and the fairest prospects, distinguished for learning and genius, sealed their devotion to their State with their blood. With those who have gone before them, they have illustrated Virginia's fame in nearly every important American battle and siege, from the defeat of Braddock to the surrender at Appomattox, by their heroic valor.

Bishop Meade, in his "Old Churches," &c., says, after speaking of Bishop Madison, and of his filling, till he died in 1812, the Presidency of the College, that he was succeeded, after the interval of a year, by Dr. John Augustine Smith, a Virginian, who being "conscious that the aid of heaven, through his church and ministry, ought to be had in order to success, therefore petitioned the now reviving Episcopal Church of Virginia to establish a Professorship of Divinity in the College." The Rev. Dr. Keith was soon after sent for that purpose and made the experiment, which did not succeed. Dr. Smith met with a good degree of success, but did not remain longer than 1826. He was succeeded by the Rev. Dr. Wm. H. Wilmer, who discharged his duties "with zeal and fidelity and with considerable success for one year, at the end of which he died, deeply lamented by all the friends of the church and College." The Rev. Dr. Empie succeeded Dr. Wilmer, and remained eight or nine years, when his place was filled by "Mr. Thomas R. Dew, a Virginia gentleman, a graduate of the College, and a scholar. His amiable disposition, fine talents, tact at management, great zeal and unwearied assiduity were the means of raising the College to as great prosperity as had ever been its lot, notwithstanding many opposing difficulties. To this we must make one exception, viz: as to the classical and mathematical departments, under some of the old and ripe scholars from England, before the Revolution."

"Mr. Dew having been arrested by death in a foreign land in 1846," the College was left for that year and the next in charge of Professor Robert Saunders. The next year, Mr. Saunders having resigned, the College was placed under the direction of Mr. Benjamin S. Ewell, when, by an arrangement with the Episcopal Church, "Bishop Johns was called to the Presidency, which he retained till 1854." His services were most valuable, restoring the College from a seemingly hopeless condition to a state of prosperity.

On the night of the 8th February, 1859, at a time when the alumni of the College were on the eve of celebrating the 166th anniversary of its foundation, the College building, with most of its interesting antiquities, was destroyed by accidental fire.

The following account of the fire of 1859 is extracted from the notes of the late Professor Robert J. Morrison, who lived at the time in part of the President's house:

"About two o'clock in the morning of the eighth of February, 1859, I was aroused from sleep by the cry that the College was on fire. I sprang from my bed and saw the light streaming in through the windows of the President's house. I raised a window, looked towards the College, and saw large volumes of flame issuing from two windows on the north side of the north wing.

"It was evident that the laboratory and the library were in an advanced conflagration. I threw on my clothes in great haste, and rushed towards the scene. Upon opening the front door of the President's house, I was struck with the terrific roar of the flames, which was unusually great for such a fire. This was probably caused by the burning of the books. I had not reached the College when I met President Ewell, who had just returned from the second floor of the building, where he had been to rescue the students who were sleeping in the dormitories. All the students were fortunately saved, though several of them for a short time were in peril. Three or four of them lost their effects. I urged Mr. Ewell, who was not half dressed, to go to his chamber for warmer clothing, as the weather was cold and damp, but he said, "I must first go with him to the basement under the laboratory to discover, if possible, the origin of the fire." (Mr. Morrison came to the conclusion that the fire originated in the laboratory. This was not accepted as the cause. A negro man was cutting wood in the cellar, just under the laboratory, the night before by the light of a candle, and it was his carelessness that produced the conflagration; so it was believed.)

"Soon the citizens of Williamsburg flocked to the sad scene. Ladies and gentlemen were silent, sorrowful spectators of the ravages of the flames. Any attempt to stay their progress would have been vain. The records of the College were saved, as well as the old portraits that hung in the Blue Room. The President saved the College seal. Some of the furniture and the library of the Philomathean Society were also saved. Everything in the chapel was

HISTORICAL SKETCH. 55

burnt. The mural tablets, relics of a past era, crumbled under the influence of the heat.
(Signed) "ROBT. J. MORRISON."
THE COLLEGE OF WILLIAM AND MARY,
February 12th, 1859.

Extract from a letter from Colonel St. George Tucker, who was appointed to recite a poem at the celebration of the 166th anniversary of the foundation of the College, dated

FEBRUARY 9TH, 1859.
MY DEAR MORRISON:

I have just seen the fatal announcement of the loss of old William and Mary. I feel more than I can express at such an awful catastrophe. At any time the destruction of almost the only link which binds Virginia to her golden age, would have awakened emotions of the deepest sorrow; but more particularly now, as I have been fully identifying myself with her destiny, and projecting myself into her early history, does the deepest regret penetrate my soul. . .

Among the coincidences connected with the fire I find, by reference, to the *Dispatch*, that it occurred on the same night and within an hour after I had finished my address.

The library, containing many curious and rare books, with some manuscripts, chiefly presented by kings, archbishops, bishops and governors, and the cabinet of apparatus in which were instruments more than a century old, the gift of the Colonial House of Burgesses, were consumed. The mural tablets in the chapel to the memories of Sir John Randolph and Bishop Madison were also destroyed. Notwithstanding this terrible disaster the celebration took place. The following is part of an eloquent address delivered on that interesting occasion by a most distinguished and honored alumnus—the late ex-President Tyler—at the time of his death Chancellor of the Institution:

Like an aged Nestor, that building has stood until within a few days past, amid civil convulsions which have shaken continents. At the time of its erection, it looked out upon a country in the early infancy of settlement, containing a population in all the English colonies which was not greater than that which at this day is found in the smallest State of the Union. It beheld that population expanding over regions bounded by the two great oceans, to be counted by millions in place of the scattered thousands of that early day. It has seen the colonies shake off the badges of puberty, and put on the *toga virilis*. It saw the Congress before and after it had assembled under the Articles of Confederation, and those articles substituted by the Constitution under which it is now our happiness to live. It re-echoed the words of the forest-born Demosthenes in 1765, asserting the rights of America to be "Natural, Constitutional and Chartered," and in thunder-tones at an after day, its walls resounded to the words "Liberty or Death," uttered by the same eloquent lips. Itself an offspring of the Revolution of 1688, its sons were the warm and enthusiastic advocates of that of 1776.

Under the influence of its teachings, its students threw aside for a season their volumes, and girded on the sword to do battle in the great cause of liberty.

The calm and silver-toned voice of philosophy heard within its walls, has been oftimes hushed by the clangor of drums and trumpets.

At one time it gave reluctant shelter to the British troops as they passed on to Yorktown,* and soon after its gates were opened wide to give willing and exultant reception to the troops with their tattered banners which followed Cornwallis to his last retreat.

Its walls were alternately shaken by the thunder of the cannon at Yorktown, and by the triumphant shouts of the noble bands who had fought and conquered in the name of American independence.

The boy had gone fourth with the surveyor's staff, which it had placed in his hands, into the wilderness of the west, and now returned the hero and the conqueror, and once more stood within its walls, surrounded by the chivalry of France and America, wearing on his brow imperishable laurels, and making the name of Washington foremost on the rolls of fame.

If her catalogue closed with the names of those who belong to the dead generations, might not William and Mary take her place among her sister Universities proudly and rightfully? But it bears the names of men of living generations who add to her renown. In the various pursuits of life they perform well their several parts. The pulpit, from which are uttered those great truths so essential for time and eternity, resounds with their eloquence; while on the bench of justice, at the legal forum, in the State Legislatures, in the National Councils, in the active marts of commerce, in the pursuits of agriculture, in the tented camps, their names are honored, their attainments respected, and their opinions and examples quoted and followed.

The following is extracted from a report made to the Faculty of William and Mary at a meeting on the 8th February, 1860, one year after its destruction by fire, on the general condition of the College:

The new College edifice has been completed and fully furnished. On the 11th October, 1859, the capstone of the building was laid by the Grand Lodge of Virginia, and the College exercises have been conducted in it without interruption from the beginning of the present session. The buildings are in every way suitable, and in an eminent degree convenient and comfortable. The lecture rooms are furnished with all the appliances for illustration in the several departments of instruction. The Philosophical apparatus is very complete. The walls of the lecture rooms of Natural Science are hung with valuable pictoral diagrams. The department of chemistry is well provided with chemicals and instruments for experiment and research. The lecture room of history

---

* During the Revolutionary war the Peninsula was, three times at least, in the possession of British armies, one being led by Arnold. There were one or two engagements in the vicinity of Williamsburg. So far as is known, the College, established and endowed by English beneficence, with its property, including the library, the gift of English "Kings, Lords and Commons," was scrupulously respected.

## HISTORICAL SKETCH.                                57

has been provided with a full set of the most valuable mural maps, geographical and historical, on the largest scale, and of the most accurate construction.

The literary societies of the College have been provided with large and handsome halls, which are furnished in the most comfortable manner. To each of these is attached an apartment for library and reading room.

The chapel has been restored, and the remains of its illustrious dead still lie undisturbed within its walls.

The library has been conveniently and handsomely furnished with cases for books, and already contains about six thousand volumes, obtained partly by purchase and partly by the donations of public spirited individuals.

Thus, within one year, the losses by the fire of February 8th, 1859, have, in every material point of view, been completely restored; and in all the essentials of its building, furniture, apparatus and library, the College is now in a better condition than it was on that day.

In addition, it may be stated that the funds were ample to sustain a full faculty, and the prospects for the future in every way encouraging.

"No *chancellor seems to have been appointed from the death of George Washington until 1859, when Ex-President John Tyler, of Charles City, was appointed; and to the day of his death he felt as honored in succeeding George Washington in that office as he did in the Presidency of the United States. The Visitors named in the charter were *gentlemen* of the highest rank in seventeen counties and of the capital in the colony, and two of them in London. Those of 1723 were such as Alexander Spottswood, Governor of the colony; and Robert Carter, of Corotoman, Secretary of the Council, and their peers. Those of 1758, such as the Hon. John Blair, President of the Council; Hon. William Nelson, and Hon. Thomas Nelson, also Presidents of the Council; the Speaker of the House of Burgesses, Peyton Randolph, Gent., of Williamsburg; Richard Bland, Treasurer and Speaker of the House of Burgesses. From 1761 to 1763, such as Hon. Francis Fauquier, Governor William Robinson, Commissary; Robert Carter Nicholas, Treasurer of the colony, and George Wythe, of Williamsburg. Visitors elected after 1763, such as Right Hon. N. Berkeley, Governor of the colony; Edward Page, Jr., of Rosewell, Governor of Virginia; Right Hon. John, Earl of Dunmore, Governor of the colony; Benj. Berkeley Harrison, of Berkeley, signer of the Declaration of Independence, father of President Wm. H. Harrison; Edmund Randolph General Thomas Nelson, Governor of Virginia; Thomas Jefferson, President of the United States; James Madison, President of the United States; John Marshall, Chief Justice of the United States; Henry Lee, of Westmoreland;

*From "Seven Decades of the Union." By General H. A. Wise.

## HISTORICAL SKETCH.

Littleton Waller Tazewell, Wilson Miles Cary, John Tyler, Sr., William Wirt; John Tyler, Jr., President of the United States; Rt. Rev. J. S. Ravenscroft, Robert Standard, Sr., James M. Garnett, Robert B. Taylor, Edmund Ruffin, Abel P. Upshur, George Loyall, William C. Goode, John S. Millson, James Lyons, Rt. Rev. William Meade, William W. Crump, Tazewell Taylor, Rt. Rev. John Johns, Hugh Blair Grigsby." (Last, but not least, General H. A. Wise.— Editor.)

"In 1859, Ex-President John Tyler was chancellor and rector, and in July, 1871, the Hon. Hugh Blair Grigsby, the gentleman, scholar, and eloquent writer and orator, of the blood of James Blair, the first president of the College, was elected unanimously chancellor, and the Hon. James Lyons, the eminet lawyer and citizen of Richmond, was elected unanimously rector of the College, to succeed another eminent rector, the Hon. William H. Macfarland, who had removed out of the Commonwealth. The very Bursars of the College have ever been gentlemen of the most favorable standing, and the President and Professors such men as James Blair, D. D., William Stith, the Historian, Rt. Rev. James Madison, Dr. John Augustine Smith, Rev. William H. Wilmer, D. D., Rev. Adam P. Empie, D. D., Thomas R. Dew, Esq., Robert Saunders, Rt. Rev. John Johns, Benj. S. Ewell, George Wythe, one of the signers of the Declaration of Independence, St. Geo. Tucker, Judge James Semple, Judge N. Bev. Tucker, Judge George P. Scarburgh, Rev. Charles Minnegerode, William B. Rogers, and Dr. John Millington.

A College thus organized and instructed by such men could not but yield the rarest and richest Alumni. Before the Revolution there was a long succession of the most eminent Colonial men, who were proud to be called her sons; and since, her brood has been multiplied fourfold without loss of grade. About four hundred different names on her rolls have been put upon the rolls of distinction, and many on the heights of eminence, by her teaching and training. Not only was her teaching after the Oxford order of the Humanities, but her training was that of the most refined and urbane manner. Williamsburg was the site of the Vice Royal Palace, and her court was far more moral than that of Charles II., and quite as ornate in manners. The breeding and cultivation were of the old regime of Knights, under the guidance of the Episcopal clergy; and to this day there is a marked superiority of address among the old families, and old servants even, of Williamsburg over any other people of town or country, in Virginia. She is so retired and ancient that "Young America" and modern manners have not yet fully abashed her gentle, soft and polished politeness as elsewhere—almost everywhere in the land. It is, and ever was, one of the chief attractions of the sons of gentlemen to her halls of learning and houses of hospitality. No man of his day more kept up that *"ancien regime"* than John Tyler—plain, genial, polished, kind, gentle, affable—young men were his proteges and pets—and he was one of their best models.

" A part of the great good he did for his Alma Mater was to protect her corporate franchise. When many erroneously urged that William and Mary was part of the 'establishment'—yea, was the very 'red shawl of the Babylonish woman'—and were for depriving her of her charter, claiming that she was a State or public political institution, and might be abolished, Mr. Tyler nobly stood among others by her side, and maintained that though she had a Burgess in the Grand Assembly, and was represented as a municipal corporation in the Convention even which formed the State Constitution which excluded her for the first time from representation in the Legislature, yet she was founded on private subscription mainly, and stood safely on the ground taken by Mr. Webster in the case of Dartmouth College. There she has stood, and still stands, unassailable; and it would be sacrilege to question her corporate rights now, after giving twenty-seven of her students to the achievement of American independence, among whom were a Bolling, a Burwell, a Byrd, two Carters, a Claiborne, a Cooke, a Cocke, a Dade, a Digges, an Eggleston, an Evans, a Harrison, a Mercer, a Monroe, a Nelson, a Nicholson, two Pages, four Randolphs, a Roberts, a Saunders, G. Smith, and Dr. James Lyons (father of James Lyons)—names forever to be cherished. Besides her long roll of most eminent divines, lawyers and physicians in private life, she has given to the country two eminent Attorney Generals of the United States; to the House of Representatives of the Congress of the United States nearly twenty members, and to the Senate of the United States fifteen Senators; to Virginia and other States seventeen Governors; to the country one historian and numberless eminent writers; to the State and the United States thirty-seven judges; to the Revolution twenty-seven of her sons; to the army of the United States a lieutenant-general and a score of principal and subordinate officers; to the United States navy a list of Paladins of the sea, headed by Warrington and Thomas Ap. Catesby Jones; to the Colleges and University twelve professors; to the nation three Presidents—Jefferson, Monroe, and John Tyler; to Independence four signers of its Declaration; to the first American Congress its President; to the Federal judiciary the most eminent Chief Justice, John Marshall; to the Federal Executive seven Cabinet officers, and to the convention which framed the Constitution of the United States, Edmund Randolph, its chief author and draftsman. In all she has given to her country more than two hundred heroes and sages who have been pre-eminently distinguished in public service and place. These are wonderful facts, and their number and value, compared with the number of alumni, show her to be first in fruits, if not first in time, compared with any other College in America. Counting her time from 1693 to the present day (1871)," the period of her existence is one hundred and seventy-eight years; from 1661, two hundred and ten years; in a word, for about two hundred years she has for and during the period of her existence yielded to her State and country, to mankind and the world, more than one jewel of the first water per annum of inestimable value. Who would see that fountain of truth, of light, of honor, of law and liberty fail?

"John Tyler, ex-President of the United States, was devoted to the task of keeping her full up to the mark of her memories of the past, and of her high calling for the future; and the Congress of the United States will, doubtless, at its next session repair liberally all the damages done by civil war to her venerable walls and to her precious paraphernalia and archives."

Early in May, 1861, the actual existence of war at its very threshold rendered it necessary to suspend the College exercises and to

---

NOTE.—The following is from a speech of the Hon. George F. Hoar, M. C., from Massachusetts, in support of a bill before the Congress of the United States for the relief of the College because of its losses during the civil war:

"To spare, and if possible to protect, institutions of learning, is an obligation which the most civilized nations impose on themselves. Whenever, by accident or design, these institutions have been injured in war, such governments desire, if possible, to make reparation. History contains many conspicuous and interesting examples of this generous recognition. . . . . In her bloodiest and angriest civil strifes, all factions in England have revered her institutions of learning. Her schools and colleges, whatever side they may have taken in civil war, have enjoyed immunity from its injuries, when even her stately and venerable cathedrals have not been spared. Think what permanence these schools enjoy, shielded from the storms of war by the beneficent principle we invoke. Wherever civilization exists, wherever men are humane and Christian, the College or the school, wisely founded, shall endure. I purchased at Eaton, a few years since, a little book containing the history of the ten great schools of England. I was struck, in looking over it, to see dates of their endowment: Eaton, in 1440; Winchester, 1380; Westminster, 1560; St. Paul's, 1509; Merchant Taylors', 1560; Charter House, 1611; Harrow, 1571; Rugby, 1567; Shrewsbury, 1549; Christ's, 1552; while the origin of Oxford and Cambridge is lost in the darkness of antiquity.

These schools have survived all the changes of dynasty, all the changes of institutions and manners; Puritan and Cavalier, York and Lancaster have fought out their battles, and yet, in the wildest tempests of popular excitement, they

"Lift not their spears against the Muses' bower."

At Winchester William of Wykeham founded, in 1380, a school which still stands and has remained through four dynasties. Guelph, Hanover, Tudor, York, Lancaster and Plantagenet close its doors. The building was soon after seized by the military, and used first as a barrack and next as a hospital, until the evacuation of Williamsburg in May, 1862. Williamsbusg is, to a force holding James and York rivers, the strategic point of the Peninsula. The tides in deep creeks, emptying into the James and the York, and flanked by impassable morasses, ebb and flow within a mile of the city. The position is a narrow gorge, where the roads from above and below converge into a single one, passing directly through the place. It was, therefore, held by the United States army in the Peninsula from the time of General McClellan's advance on Richmond till the close of the war, almost without intermission, as an important post. At times, however, it was debatable ground, and was alternately in the possession of the contending forces. A conflict occurred on the 9th September, 1862, between a detachment of Confederate cavalry and the United States garrison, then consisting of the 5th regiment Pennsylvania cavalry, in which the latter was worsted. The Confederates took possession of the town early in the day, but withdrew in a few hours. After they had retired (by 11 A. M. of the same day all had gone), returning stragglers of the garrison, provoked by their defeat, under the influence of drink and before organization, or subordination was restored, fired and destroyed the principal building, with furniture and apparatus. For this, it is believed, no authority was given by the officers in command.

---

have successively struggled for and occupied the English throne, while in the building, which Wykeham in his lifetime planned and built, the scholars of Winchester are still governed by the statutes which he framed.

You will scarcely find an instance, in England or America, where a school or college, wisely founded, has died. "Whatever perishes, that shall endure." . . . . . .

But William and Mary has also her own peculiar claim on our regard. The great principles on which the rights of man depend, which inspired the statesmen of Virginia of the period of the Revolution, are the fruits of her teaching. The name of Washington, to whose genius in war, and to whose influence in peace we owe the vindication of our liberties and the successful inauguration of our constitution, is inseparably connected with William and Mary. She gave him his first commission in his youth; he gave to her his last public service in his age. Jefferson, author of the declaration of independence, who announced the great law of equality and human rights, in whose light our Constitution is at last and forever to be interpreted, drank his inspiration at her fountain. Marshall, without whose luminous and farsighted exposition our Constitution could hardly have been put into successful and harmonious operation, who imbedded forever in our constitutional law the great doctrines on which the measures that saved the Union are based, was a son of William and Mary. By the cession of the great Northwestern territory, largely due to the efforts of one of her illustrious sons, she lost a great part of her revenues.

Next to Harvard she is the oldest of American Colleges. The gift of the famous Robert Boyle was held by her for many years, on condition of an annual payment of £90 to Harvard. Boyle was the friend of many of the early friends and benefactors of Harvard, and a correspondent of one of its first Presidents. Each of these two seminaries, in its own part of the country, kindled and kept alive the sacred fire of liberty. In 1743, the year Jefferson was

## HISTORICAL SKETCH.

Extracts from the depositions of Mrs. Maria T. Peyton and Miss Mary T. Southall, both of Williamsburg, in relation to the destruction of the College in September, 1862, taken before Dr. R. M. Garrett, magistrate of the town:

Miss Southall deposes: "That she resided at the time on the College grounds in the President's house, and that she was alarmed, on the evening of the 8th of September, by the cry of fire. She went out and found that the College Building was on fire; that soon a crowd gathered and extinguished the flames; and that while carrying a bucket of water, she met three United States soldiers; one of them told her if the College was not burned that day, it would be the next, or words to that effect; that early the next day, a detachment of the Southern cavalry entered and, after a short contest, retired, the last one of them leaving by ten minutes after ten o'clock A. M.; that shortly afterwards, the College yard was crowded with United States soldiers, many of them drunk and boisterous; that she and her sisters were advised, so unruly were they, to leave the premises, which they did; that about five o'clock, P. M., she was told of the College being on fire, and advised to return, as the house in which she lived was in great danger. This she did, and soon after the College was a smoking ruin; and that there is no doubt of the destruction having been designedly effected by drunken United States soldiers."

Mrs. Maria T. Peyton deposes essentially to the same facts respecting the fire on the 9th of September, resulting in the burning down of the Building; and further deposes that she went to Lieut. Col. Smith, who, by the capture of Col. Campbell, became the Commandant of the Post and the Regiment which was its garrison, the Fifth Pennsylvania Cavalry, and told him there was a rumor the town was to be fired. He replied: "No such orders had been or would be given." A short time after, the affiant saw the College on fire, and immediately said to Col. Smith: "See, sir, the destruction has begun." He replied, that it had, but that it would be now impossible to save the building for want of buckets. He said further, he had a set of

---

born, Samuel Adams maintained, on taking his degree of Master of Arts at Harvard, the affirmative of the thesis, whether it be lawful to resist the Supreme Magistrate, if the Commonwealth cannot otherwise be preserved ? In this hour of the calamity of her sister College I am glad to believe that Harvard does not forget the ancient tie. The mother of the Otises and Adamses would gladly extend her right hand to the mother of Jefferson and Marshall.

If civil strife or foreign war shall ever again disturb our peace, every College in the land will be safer if Congress shall to-day make this solemn recognition of the rule we invoke. To deny it is to deny to the College of Washington the justice he did to Princeton. To deny it is to deny to Virginia the generous treatment which Connecticut received from Tryon, Philadelphia from Cooke, and William and Mary herself from Louis XVI. of France. The hallowed associations which surround this College prevent this case from being a precedent for any other. If you had injured it, you surely would have restored Mount Vernon; you had better honor Washington, by restoring the living fountain of learning, whose service was the pleasure of his last years, than by any useless and empty act of worship or respect towards his sepulchre.

No other College in the country can occupy the same position. By the fortune of war that sacred institution, which has conferred on the country a hundredfold more benefit than any other institution or College in the South, has become a sufferer. I desire to hold out the olive branch to the people of Virginia, to the people of the South, to show them that we will join them in rebuilding the sacred place laid waste by the fortunes of war."

drunken soldiers, and that it would take two sober men to control one drunken one. The affiant turned again to Col. Smith and said: "Do, sir, try and save William and Mary College, for it will be a stigma on the page of history if you suffer it to be lost." He replied: "I have no means of putting out the fire; it cannot now be saved." The affiant distinctly understood from Col. Smith, that no order had been given to burn the College, but that it was done by drunken soldiers whom he could not control.*

At later periods of the war all the remaining houses on the College premises and the enclosures were burned, or pulled entirely to pieces, or greatly injured.

The vaults in the College chapel were broken open and robbed of the silver plates attached to the coffins, and of whatever else of value they were found to contain. This desecration was checked, as is stated, when it became known to the military commander.

These facts are fully substantiated by the affidavits of eye-witnesses.

It will require at least eighty thousand dollars to repair these losses and restore the College to what it was in 1860.

The College grounds and buildings not destroyed were held by the United States Army from May, 1862, to September, 1865, for depots and for other purposes.†

---

* It was further declared by eye-witnesses, that while the College was burning, some of the Fifth Pennsylvania Cavalry, a regiment said to have been raised in Philadelphia, surrounded the building, with drawn swords, to prevent any attempt at extinguishing the flames.

† The difficulties in the way of restoring the College at Williamsburg, appeared so formidable, at the close of the late civil war, as to cause some of its best friends to think seriously of its removal. Fortunately, the attempt was not made. The following extracts from a letter, written by the President of the College, to Sydney Smith, Esq., of the House of Delegates, relate to the subject:

SHALL WILLIAM AND MARY COLLEGE BE REMOVED?

WILLIAMSBURG, *January* 3, 1867.

*Dear Sir*—Thinking with you that a statement of the difficulties attending an attempt to carry the College of William and Mary from its present classical, time-honored site, may have a tendency to stop the discussion of the subject, I will comply with your request, and mention some of them.

And first, let me ask, in whom does the power to move vest? In the first section of the charter—granted in 1692—the Trustees therein named, Francis Nicholson, William Randolph, Benj. Harrison, Mathew Page, and others, are directed to establish the College "upon the South side of York river, on the lands of Colonel Townsend, deceased," "or, if by reason of unwholesomeness or any other cause, the said place shall not be approved of, wheresoever else the General Assembly of our Colony of Virginia, or the major part of them, shall think fit, within the bounds of the aforesaid Colony—to continue for all times coming." The site of the College was changed about a year after it was fixed by the Charter to the Middle Plantations, now Williamsburg, by statute.

It would seem that in making this statute, the General Assembly exhausted the power conferred by the Charter as to the location of the College. In section IX of the Charter, the gentlemen named as trustees, and their successors, are appointed "the true, sole, and undoubted visitors and governors of the said College forever," with full and absolute authority to make "rules, laws, statutes, orders, and injunctions, for the good and wholesome govern-

## HISTORICAL SKETCH.

At a convocation of the Board of Visitors and Governors held during the month of August, 1865, in Richmond, it was determined to re-open the College at the usual time, to repair some of the College buildings for recitation rooms, and to provide other accommodations necessary for the students. This was done, and sufficient temporary arrangements made.

At the same time, a grammar school was established, to be under the care and supervision of the Faculty.

The wisdom of this action is abundantly confirmed by the result. At this time, January 15th, 1866, there is a grammar school in successful operation. The numbers composing the College classes exceed the anticipations of the most sanguine; nearly sixty attend the academic exercises.

In 1867, to continue this historical sketch to the present time, the

---

ment of the said College," to elect a chancellor, a rector, to fill vacancies in their own body, and to elect a president, and masters or professors when necessary. No other powers seem to be conferred by the Charter on the visitors and governors. As trustees, they were ordered to receive and dispose of the College property until the College should be actually established, when their functions as trustees, with the property, were to be transferred to the president, and masters or professors, or their successors, who "shall be a body politic in deed and name," who "shall have perpetual succession," with the right to hold property, to sue and be sued, &c., and who shall "have a common seal," &c. In short, the Charter does not provide for a removal, but intended that wherever established, the College was "to continue," and "to be supported and maintained for all time coming." (See Charter.)

An exercise of such authority by the Legislature would be a usurpation; by the Visitors and Governors, or Faculty, a *felo-de-se*. If removed, the old College of William and Mary, the alma mater of Virginia's greatest and best sons, the Institution identified with Washington, and Jefferson, and Monroe, and Marshall, and Tyler, and others as worthy, whom time and space do not allow me to name, would cease to exist. A new Institution, bearing the same name, of greater wealth, and perhaps, of equal usefulness, might be established; but old William and Mary would be among the things of the past.

But assume that this power exists, ought it to be exercised? If established in Richmond, or Alexandria, or Petersburg, or Norfolk, the number of students would be larger, and the Professors' fees remunerative, but I doubt if the number of young men in attendance from a distance would equal the average here. In a town like this, College students have all the advantages of society, and may be supervised and controlled. In a city, they would be lost sight of. Experience, in all parts of this country, has demonstrated that Universities and Colleges do not prosper in cities. The classes are all filled up for the most part with boys, studying what they could much better learn in academies and private schools, with but few advanced scholars. What constitutes the prosperity of a College? The following answer was given to this question by the Rev. Dr. Horrocks, President of William and Mary, a century ago:

"The flourishing state of a college is not to be estimated by the number of wild and uncultivated minds which may be brought together," "but purely by the number of competent scholars and well-behaved gentlemen which are sent by any seminary of learning into the larger society, where they vie to display improved talents for their own benefit and the public emolument."

If the question of locality was an open one, a city ought not to be selected. What is the matter with Williamsburg? Its position is central in the tide-water country. In this respect it is a suitable site for the only College in lower Virginia. To be sure, the College is doing but little at present beyond local instruction; but recollect that its endowment funds are entirely unproductive, excepting that part invested in State Stocks, and that its buildings, burned or otherwise destroyed during the war, have been but partially restored.

## HISTORICAL SKETCH.

visitors and governors encouraged by the interest manifested in the restoration of the College by distinguished persons in every part of the country, and the substantial aid furnished by W. W. Corcoran,* of Washington city, A. T. Stewart, James T. Soutter, Hon. A. E. Borie, and other prominent gentlemen of New York, Philadelphia and Baltimore, and the decree of the English courts giving the "Matty Fund" "in trust" to the College, took the necessary steps to rebuild and reorganize the Institution.

The wise policy of the Visitors has been to permit no expenditures by which the endowment might be diminished, and to preserve the Institution free from debt, knowing it to be better to let the College linger, or even to suspend it for a time—for what are a few years in comparison to the life-time of a College?—than to weaken its vitality by investing its capital stock in bricks and mortar. Are Oxford and Cambridge less valuable or less dear to Englishmen now because of their mutations of fortune during the thousand years of their existence? As to health, I assert that Williamsburg is, during the entire College session, one of the very healthiest places in Virginia. Living is cheap here, and will be cheaper.

Is this old Colonial Capital, with all its cherished traditions, and associations, and existing attractions, to go for nothing, because it has been desolated by war? Other places may be ahead of it in promise and progress, but they are farther behind it in tone, in refinement, in civilization. There is no College in the United States where the intercourse between citizen, professor and student is more cordial and mutually beneficial in all respects.

As to the fitness of the place and its surroundings for study and improvement, judge of the tree by its fruits. Among the students of the last thirty years, some of the brightest and best of whom have sealed their devotion to Virginia with their blood, are to be found scholars and patriots, fit successors of the illustrious men educated here in the last century.

As yet I have not adverted to the losses of property the College would sustain by a removal. Directly and indirectly, the losses would be $40,000 at least. What, too, if the heirs of private donors to the College of William and Mary, at *Williamsburg*, were to assert their claims to the gifts of their ancestors? Nearly the whole endowment would be swept away. The condition of the College is by no means desperate. It is better off to-day than it was in 1783. In 1776 its revenue was about $12,000; in 1783, it had $2,500 in money, and the land given in 1692 by William and Mary. Now its endowment is over $100,000. Though dismantled, the College has yet much capacity for future good. In its present state, it is an apt type of Tide-Water Virginia, scourged and desolated by war. Through patient industry, this region will "smile and blossom" as it never has before, and with it the College will rise from its ashes, develop itself anew to meet the wants of the people, and in good time reach the full measure of its former prosperity. You agree with me, I feel fully assured, that Virginians are bound by considerations of the past and present to continue the College where it is, and that by them it ought to be supported and maintained for all time coming.

Very respectfully,

BENJ. S. EWELL.

*Mr. Corcoran founded a Scholarship, as did Mr. Soutter.

*The Scholarships Founded in the College before 1776, are:*
The House of Burgesses Scholarships, 3. Founded by the House of Burgesses.
The Hill Scholarship, 1. Founded by Col. Edward Hill, of Shirley.
The Carter Scholarship, 1. Founded by Robert Carter, (King), of Corotoman.
The Bray Scholarship, 1. Founded by Mrs. Thomas Bray, of New Kent.
The Harrison Scholarship, 1. Founded by Mrs. Elizabeth Harrison, of Surry.
The Lightfoot Scholarships, 2. Founded by Philip Lightfoot, of Sandy Point.
The Blair Scholarships, 2. Founded by Rev. Dr. James Blair, of Williamsburg,

*Those Founded since are:*
The Corcoran Scholarship, 1. Founded by W. W. Corcoran, of Washington City, 1867.
The Soutter Scholarship, 1. Founded by James T. Soutter, of New York, 1869.
The Grigsby Scholarship, 1. Founded by Hugh Blair Grigsby, LL. D., of Norfolk, 1871.
The Graves Scholarship, 1. Founded by Rev. Robt. J. Graves, D. D., of Pennsylvania, 1872.

In July, 1869, the main building being substantially restored, the Faculty was reorganized with a sufficient corps of academic professors; the course of studies revised and modified; and the College ordered to be regularly opened for students, for the first time with a full Faculty since 1861.

The session commenced encouragingly, notwithstanding the short notice, and there is now every prospect of reasonable success. The building is well constructed and suitable. The library numbers about five thousand volumes, having been increased by some twelve hundred volumes within the last twelve months; the gift for the greater part of Little, Brown & Co., of Boston; D. Appleton & Co., A. J. Barnes & Co., D. Van Nostrand, and Harper and Brothers, of New York; J. B. Lippincott & Co., of Philadelphia; and J. Murphy & Co., of Baltimore, publishers; and of a few gentlemen of England, among them Mr. R. Potts, A. M., of Trinity College, Cambridge, and the Earl of Derby. The philosophical and chemical apparatus is in good order, and ample for purposes of experiment, illustration and research. With the "Matty Fund," the recovery of which has been mentioned, the preparatory department has been endowed and is in successful operation. Mrs. Mary Whaley, of Bruton parish, by her will, dated February 16th, 1741, devised to Rev. Thomas Dawson, rector; John Blair and Thomas Jones, church-wardens; and to Peyton Randolph, Thomas Cobbes, Henry Tyler, Matthew Pierce, Lewis Burwell, Benj. Waller and William Parks, and their successors, a piece of land, just north of Dr. R. P. Waller's residence, on the road to the capital landing, containing about ten acres, on which were erected a school-house, called "Matty's School," and a dwelling house for the master, "upon trust to continue the same for the use of the said school, viz: and to teach the neediest children of the said parish in the art of reading, writing and arithmetic, to eternalize Matty's school forever." The testatrix also gave fifty pounds sterling, and the residue of her estate, after paying certain legacies. Mrs. Whaley died in 1742. The executor failed to comply with the terms of the will, and a suit was, in consequence, instituted in the Colonial court, and a decree obtained requiring the heir-at-law to convey the land, and the executor, Mr. James Fraunces, to pay the fifty pounds and account for the residue. The conveyance was soon after made, but the money was not paid, and a suit was brought against the executor in the English court of chancery, where it was decreed in 1752, that the charity ought to be established, and that the executor should pay into the court five hundred pounds sterling. This sum was paid and ordered to be invested in English securities.

Nothing further was done till 1866, when an English attorney, Mr. C. M. Fisher, after corresponding with the Faculty, and learning that the College would consent to execute the trust to the extent of receiving into the preparatory department of the College, without charge for tuition, fifteen of the neediest boys of the Parish, applied to the chancery court for, and obtained a decree, directing the whole sum to be paid to the College on the condition mentioned. The net amount received was about eight thousand two hundred dollars.

The correspondence was commenced by Mr. Fisher in 1859, and was first directed to the rector of the parish, and by the rector referred to the College.

This whole transaction reflects great credit on the English people and government. That a sum of money, and its accumulation of dividends, belonging to parties in a foreign land, should be paid, without dispute or cavil, after the lapse of more than a century, notwithstanding the bitterness of feeling resulting from two severe wars, is an evidence of national integrity and honor that ought to make every American, who has English blood in his veins, feel proud of his ancestry.

The preparatory department, its name being in virtue of a second condition, changed to the "Grammar and Matty School," thus endowed, bids fair to become useful and prosperous.

It may be observed, that the city of Williamsburg, in which the College is located, has a population of nearly two thousand, and has long been celebrated for the hospitality of its inhabitants, making it a most agreeable residence for the student. Of late, the town and the adjacent country have been much improved. Timber has been cleared away, and a better system of cultivation introduced; and the result has been a decided improvement in the healthiness of the locality. Few places in the State can boast a more sulubrious climate than this during the College session. Diseases peculiar to the low country prevail only in the months of August and September, and of late years, these have been very mild in their character and easily controlled by medicines. From October to July, while the College is in session, these diseases are never contracted. The winter climate is delightful, the cold being moderated by the large bodies of salt water in the vicinity, while it is too far distant from the ocean to be much affected by storms. The heat of summer is neutralized by the same means, so that in the hottest weather the thermometer ranges from three to five degrees lower than in Richmond.

Students from the upper country need be under no apprehension from the effect of the climate; while to those predisposed to pulmonary complaints it would be decidedly beneficial. During the present century, only seven deaths have occurred among the students of the College, and two of these were from drowning.

The College of William and Mary, as well by its past history as its capacity for future usefulness, has a just claim to the sympathy and aid of the friends of learning, wherever they are to be found.

More especially does this claim apply to Episcopalians in behalf of what was the oldest church institution in America.

The following is from the address before quoted:

The associations which cluster around this locality, render it peculiarly appropriate for a seat of learning. Can the young heart maintain a quiet pulse in wandering amid the ruins which tell of a glorious past, and everywhere meet his eye? Will he not gather from the very fragments which lie scattered over the earth at Jamestown, almost in sight of this spot, a lesson never to be forgotten, inspiring him with courage and perseverance in the great battle of life?

Will not these fragments tell him a tale of hardship and suffering on the part of the early settlers, unequalled in the history of his race, and of an ultimate triumphant conclusion more grand in its results than fancy ever sketched or poet in rapt imagination ever sang?

Will not that broken steeple, reared centuries ago in honor of the living God, preach to him like an aged minister, and impress upon his heart the all-governing truth that without Divine assistance nothing great and nothing good can ever be accomplished?

Does he seek incentives to an ardent and burning patriotism? Let him visit the ruins of the old capitol, and ponder there until his heart expands and his lips give utterance to that exclamation which aroused a continent from slumber.

Let him, then, find his way to the Apollo Hall of the old Raleigh Tavern, and mix with the noble spirits in their deep deliberations on the great crises that had arisen. Those who assembled there were for the most part his elder brothers, sons of the same Alma Mater.

In a few hours thereafter he may find himself wandering over the entrenchments at Yorktown, behind which British power made its last defence.

These memorials of the mighty past are not dead and voiceless. They speak more eloquently than the Roman or Athenian of old before the Senate or Assembly of the people. They tell of past glory and are the oracles that unveil the future. Sinking deep into the heart of youth, they inspire it with the lofty desires which make ambition virtue.

The oldest, save one, of all the literary institutions of the United States, William and Mary has contributed its full share to the public enlightenment, and made a mark in history which neither fire can consume nor dust nor ashes obscure. Thrice now has its genius been driven by cruel flames from the edifices erected for her abode. To-day she is banished from her ancient temple—that temple is now in ruins.

## HISTORICAL SKETCH. 69

These hallowed walls, in which the calm voice of philosophy has for so many generations been heard, have not been allowed to stand a blackened monument of the desolations of war and a reproach to our age and people. On the contrary, new and more beautiful temples have arisen to receive and welcome the genius of education, and to foster that philosophy and those arts and sciences, the achievements of which it is the glory of a nation to honor as the noblest victories of peace.*

---

*The appeal made after the fire of 1859, to Virginians and others, for aid to the College, was liberally responded to in this State and New York. Among those who made donations in sums of five hundred dollars and upwards, were:

| | |
|---|---|
| Hugh Blair Grigsby, LL. D., Norfolk, for a vested library fund | $1,000 00 |
| Richard Baylor, Rosegill, Essex county | 1,000 00 |
| William Beverly, Blandfield, Essex county | 1,000 00 |
| Philip St. George Cocke, Powhatan | 1,000 00 |
| William B. Harrison, Upper Brandon, Prince George | 1,000 00 |
| George Harrison, Lower Brandon, " " | 500 00 |
| Miss Belle Harrison, Lower Brandon, " " | 500 00 |
| Williams Carter, Hanover | 500 00 |
| Dr. Robert P. Waller, Williamsburg | 500 00 |
| Dr. Nath. M. Osborne, Prince George | 500 00 |
| Alexander T. Stewart, New York city | 500 00 |
| James T. Soutter, " " " | 500 00 |
| John Tyler, late President of the United States | 500 00 |

The subscribers of less sums were numerous. There is no authentic list of these names within reach. All the members of the Board of Visitors made liberal subscriptions, including Governor Henry A. Wise, Tazewell Taylor, Esq., William S. Peachy, Colonel E. T. Tayloe, Judge W. W. Crump, Dr. Nathaniel M. Osborne, James Lyons, &c.

*Among the Subscribers during and since 1867, are to be found the names of:*

| | |
|---|---|
| His Grace, the Archbishop of Canterbury | England. |
| The Secretary of the Archbishop | " |
| Robert Potts, A. M., Cambridge University | " |
| The Earl of Derby | " |
| J. S. Pendergrast, Esq | " |
| Miss Goddard | " |
| Miss Sarah B. Nevins | " |
| Williams & Norgate | " |
| Maxon & Co | " |
| John Murray, Esq | " |
| A. T. Stewart | New York City. |
| James T. Soutter | " " |
| Wm. E. Dodge | " " |
| August Belmont | " " |
| Robert Bonner | " " |
| S. Cooke | " " |
| Charles Scribner & Co | " " |
| A. J. Barnes & Co | " " |
| Harper & Brothers | " " |
| D. Appleton & Co | " " |
| D. Van Nostrand | " " |
| Van Evrie & Horton | " " |
| Dr. Thomas Dunn English | " " |
| Udolpho Wolfe | " " |
| George B. Field | " " |

INSCRIPTION FROM THE MURAL TABLET, IN MEMORY OF SIR JOHN RANDOLPH, WHICH WAS DESTROYED BY FIRE IN THE COLLEGE CHAPEL OF WILLIAM AND MARY IN 1859.

Hoc juxta marmor S. E.
Johannes Randolph, Eques.;
Hujus Collegii dulce ornamentum, alumnus;
Insigne præsidium gubernator,
Grande columen Senator,
Gulielmum patrem generosum,
Mariam ex Ishamorum stirpe.
In agro Northamptoniensi matrem
Præclaris dotibus honestavit,
Filius natu Sextus
Literis humanioribus
Artibusque ingenuis fideliter instructus;
(Illi quippe fuerat tum eruditionis,
Tum doctrinæ sitis nunquam explenda.)
Hospitium Graiense concessit,
Quo in domicilio
Studiis unice deditus,
Statim inter legum peritos excelluit,

| | |
|---|---|
| J. D. Alsop | New York City. |
| John J. Williams | " " |
| James S. Thayer | " " |
| Currier, Sherwood & Co | " " |
| Treadwell & Jarman | " " |
| A. A. Lowe | " " |
| Rev. Francis Vinton, D. C. L. | " " |
| Hon. A. E. Borie | Philadelphia. |
| A. J. Drexel | " |
| J. G. Fell | " |
| G. W. Childs | " |
| Edward Coles | " |
| Z. W. Clark & Co | " |
| J. B. Lippincott & Co | " |
| Miss Laura Robinett | " |
| Henry C. Lea | " |
| Moncure Robinson | " |
| Rev. Christopher B. Wyatt, D. D. | San Francisco. |
| Francis E. Parker | Boston. |
| L. Saltonstall | " |
| Alex. H. Rice | " |
| Little, Brown & Co | " |
| Mrs. Isabella Brown | Baltimore. |
| Rev. E. A. Dalrymple, D. D. | " |
| William Reynolds, Jr | " |
| G. S. Brown | " |
| John Murphy | " |
| Bartlett & Robins | " |
| Collins & Heath | " |
| J. M. Orem | " |
| R. M. Proud | " |
| Rev. M. Mahan, D. D. | " |

## HISTORICAL SKETCH.

>Togamque induit;
>Causis validissimus agendis.
>In Patriam
>Quam semper habuit charissimam reversus,
>Causidici
>Senatus primum clerici deinde prolocutoris
>Thesaurarii
>Legati ad Anglos semel atque iterum missi,
>Glocestriæ demum curiæ judicis primarii,
>Vices arduas honestasque sustinuit
>Perite, graviter, integre ;
>Quibus in muniis,
>Vix parem habuit
>Superiorem certe neminem.
>Hos omnes quos optime meruit honores,
>Cum ingenua totius corporis pulchritudo,
>Et quidam senatorius decor,
>Tum eximium ingenii acumen
>Egregie illustrarunt.
>At Æquitas summi juris expers,
>Clientum fidele omnium
>Pauperiorum sine mercede patrocinium,

---

| | |
|---|---|
| Samuel G. Wyman | Baltimore. |
| Rev. Peyton Harrison | " |
| Mrs. Peyton Harrison | " |
| J. P. Pleasants | " |
| John W. Garrett | " |
| Union Club, through Mr. J. R. Patridge | " |
| C. Morton Stewart and others | " |
| J. Glenn | " |
| S. Teackle Wallace | " |
| Otho Williams | " |
| W. W. Corcoran | Washington City. |
| Mrs. M. Berry | Georgetown, D. C |
| Miss E. S. Ewell | "      " |
| John Lindesay | Virginia. |
| Peter T. Powell | " |
| W. W. Vest | " |
| Talbot Sweeny | " |
| Robert F. Cole | " |
| Alex. Dunlap | " |
| M. R. Harrell | " |
| W. H. E. Morecock | " |
| John Motley | " |
| Dr. Leonard Henley | " |
| Wm. S. Peachy | " |
| H. M. Waller | " |
| Santos & Brother | " |
| Archer Brooks | " |
| P. M. Thompson | " |
| Dr. Charles Coleman | " |
| Colonel A. Ordway | " |
| General J. Mulford | " |
| John R. Thompson | " |

Hospitium sine luxu splendidum,
Veritas sine fuco,
Sine fastu Charitas.
Ceteris animi virtutibus
Facile præluxerunt.
Tandem
Laboribus vigiliisque fractus,
Morboque lentissimo confectus
Cum sibi satis, sed amicis, sed Reip: parum vixisset,
Susannam
Petri Beverley Armigeri
Filiam natu minimam,
Conjugem delectissimam,
(Ex qua tres filios filiamque unicam susceperat,)
Sui magno languentem desiderio
Reliquit
Sexto Non: Mar: Anno Dom: 1736-7
Ætat: 44.

(*From the Virginia Gazette, November* 11, 1775.)

Sacred
To the memery of
The Hon. Peyton Randolph, Esq'r,
Whose distinguished virtues in every station of life
Gained him
The affection and confidence of his Country.
Descended from an ancient and respectable family,
He received a liberal and polite education
In William and Mary College.
Removing (from) thence to the Inner Temple,
He was advanced to the Degree of Barrister at Law,
And appointed Attorney General of Virginia.
In this Office
His regard to the peace and security of Society,

| | |
|---|---|
| Charles Hansford | Virginia. |
| Rev. Samuel Cheevers | " |
| Charles Gallagher | " |
| Miss R. L. Ewell | " |
| H. S. McCandlish | " |
| T. T. L. Snead | " |
| T. P. McCandlish | " |
| Robert A. Bright | " |
| T. J. Barlow | " |
| Benjamin S. Ewell | " |
| Junius Lamb | " |
| Richardson Henley | " |
| General R. S. Ewell | " |
| T. S. B. Tucker | " |
| Dr. B. St. G. Tucker | " |
| Mrs. Cynthia B. T. Coleman | " |

His humanity and benevolence
To the criminal his duty obliged him to prosecute,
Were not more conspicuous
Than his Learning and Integrity in his Profession.
After an extensive practice in the General Court,
He resigned his Law employments;
And being elected Speaker of the House of Burgesses,
Discharged the duties of that high office
With such Ease, Dignity and Impartiality,
That he was frequently called to the Chair, by the
Unanimous voice
Of the Representatives of the People.
When the measures of the British Ministry
Compelled the American Congress to unite their Councils
In General Congress,
He was chosen first Delegate for this Colony
To that illustrious Assembly;
And was by them unanimously elected their PRESIDENT.
While he was a third time attending to that great Great Council,
A sudden stroke of the Palsy deprived
America of a firm Patriot,
His Country of a wise and faithful Senator,
His acquaintance of an invaluable Friend,
His family of the most affectionate Husband
And kindest Master.
Upon the 22d Day of October, 1775,
In the 54th Year of his Age.

# CATALOGUE

OF THE

# COLLEGE OF WILLIAM AND MARY,

IN VIRGINIA,

FROM ITS FOUNDATION TO 1874.

---

The names of the Visitors, Bursars, Faculty and Students at College after 1788, in the following Catalogue, are taken from papers and records in possession of the Faculty. The names of Students of an earlier date were obtained from different sources.

The College records containing the names of Students before 1827, being exceedingly imperfect and in a mutilated condition, it is certain a great number are omitted. Any person who may detect an error in this Catalogue will confer a favor on the Faculty, by communicating it without delay to the Faculty of the College.

---

## CHANCELLORS.

| NAMES. | RESIDENCES. | REMARKS. |
|---|---|---|
| The Bishops of London | *England* | Until 1764. |
| The Earl of Hardwicke | " | 1764. |
| The Bishops of London | " | From 1764 to 1776. |
| Gen. George Washington | *Mount Vernon* | From 1788 to 1799. |
| John Tyler, Ex-Pres. of U. S., | *Charles City* | From 1859 to 1862. |
| Hugh Blair Grigsby, LL. D. | *Charlotte* | From 1871. |

## VISITORS

NAMED IN THE CHARTER.

| NAMES. | RESIDENCES. | REMARKS. |
|---|---|---|
| Francis Nicholson, Esq | *Williamsburg.* | |
| William Cole, Esq | *Warwick.* | |
| Ralph Wormley, Esq | *Middlesex.* | |
| William Byrd, Esq | *Westover, Charles City.* | |
| John Lear, Esq | *Nansemond.* | |
| James Blair, Clerk | *Williamsburg.* | |
| John Farnifold, Clerk | *London.* | |
| Stephen Fouace, Clerk | " | |
| Samuel Gray, Clerk | *Southampton.* | |

CATALOGUE OF ALUMNI.  75

| NAMES. | RESIDENCES. | REMARKS. |

Thomas Milner, Gent............*Nansemond.*
Christopher Robinson, Gent....*Middlesex.*
Charles Scarborough, Gent......*Accomac.*
John Smith, Gent.
Benjamin Harrison, Gent........*Surry.*
Miles Cary, Gent..................*Warwick.*
Henry Hartwell, Gent............*James City.*
William Randolph, Gent.........*Henrico.*
Matthew Page, Gent...............*Gloucester.*

## Visitors in 1723.

| NAMES. | RESIDENCES. | REMARKS. |

Alexander Spotswood, Esq..... *Williamsburg* .........Governor of the Colony.
Robert Carter, Esq................*Corotoman, Lan. co.*..Secretary of the Council.
William Byrd, Esq.................*Westover, Charles City.*
Nathaniel Harrison, Esq.........*Wakefield, Surry co.*
Cole Digges, Esq...................*Williamsburg.*
Peter Beverly, Esq.................*Gloucester.*
John Clayton, Esq..................     "         .............The eminet botanist.
John Robinson, Esq...............*King and Queen.*
William Bland, Clerk.............*Williamsburg.*
Emmanuel Jones, Clerk.........     "
Bartholomew Yates, Clerk......     "
John Skaife, Clerk.................*Gloucester.*
William Randolph, Gent.........*Chatsworth, Henrico.*
John Randolph, Gent.............*Tazewell Hall, Williamsburg.*
William Robertson, Gent........*Williamsburg.*
John Grymes, Gent................*Middlesex.*
William Cole, Gent.................*Warwick.*

## Visitors in 1758.

| NAMES. | RESIDENCES. | REMARKS. |

Hon. John Blair, Esq..............*Williamsburg* .........President of the Council.
Hon. William Nelson, Esq......*York* .....................     "           "
Hon. Thomas Nelson, Esq......     "         .....................     "           "
Philip Grymes, Esq................*Middlesex.*
Richard Corbin, Esq...............     "
Philip Ludwell, Esq................*James city.*
William Lightfoot, Esq...........*Sandy Point, Chas. City.*
Thomas Dawson, Clerk..........:...................Commissary.
Mann Page, Gent...................*Rosewell, Gloucester co.*
Peyton Randolph, Gent..........*Williamsburg* .........Speaker House of Burgesses
Charles Carter, Gent..............*Shirley, Chas. City co.*
Richard Bland, Gent..............*Prince George*.........Treasurer and Speaker House of Burgesses.

## CATALOGUE OF ALUMNI.

### VISITORS FROM 1761 TO 1763.

| NAMES. | RESIDENCES. | REMARKS. |
|---|---|---|

Hon. Francis Fauquier............ *Williamsburg* .........Governor.
C. Thacker, Clerk................. *Gloucester.*
John Fox, Clerk..................... "
William Robinson, Clerk........*King and Queen*......Commissary.
Francis Willis, Gent............ *Gloucester.*
Charles Robinson, Gent.
Robt. Carter Nicholas, Gent... *Williamsburg* .....Treasurer of the Colony.
Lewis Burwell, Gent............*James City.*
Peter Randolph, Gent........... *Chatsworth, Henrico.*
George Wythe, Gent............. *Williamsburg.*

### VISITORS ELECTED AFTER 1763.

| NAMES. | DATE OF ELECTION. | RESIDENCES. | REMARKS. |
|---|---|---|---|

John Page........................1764... *Gloucester.*
Hon. Dudley Digges.........1764...*James City.*
Charles Carter..................1764... *Corotoman.*
Rev. Bartholomew Yates..1766... *Williamsburg.*
Rev. James M. Fontaine...1767... *Gloucester.*
Dr. Arthur Lee................1767... *Williamsburg.*
Rt. Hon. N. Berkeley,
  Baron De Botetourt......1768...     "      ......Governor of the Colony.
John Page, Jun............ .....1768...*Rosewell*..............Governor of Virginia.
Hon. William Byrd..........1769... *Westover.*
Carter Braxton...............1769...*King William county.*
Edward Ambler..............1769...*James Town.*
Thomas Nelson, Jun........1770... *York.*
Richard Randolph............1770... *Curls, Henrico.*
Right Hon. John, Earl of
  Dunmore....................1772... *Williamsburg*........Governor of the Colony.
Rev. Thomas Field...........1773
Col. Benjamin Harrison...1773...*Berkeley, Ch. City.*
Robert Beverly...............1775...*Blandfield.*
Nathaniel Burwell...........1775... *Gloucester.*
Hon. Ralph Wormley.......1775...*Middlesex.*
John Bannister........... ......1777...*Dinwiddie.*
Warner Lewis..................1777... *Gloucester.*
Edmund Randolph...........1777... *Williamsburg.*
Benjamin Harrison...........1777...*Brandon, P. Geo.*
Gen. Thomas Nelson........1777... *York*...............Governor of Virginia.
Thomas Jefferson............1779...*Albemarle*............Pres't of United States.
James Madison...............1779...*Orange*................  "    "    "
James Innes....................1782... *York.*
Richard Henry Lee...........1784... *Westmoreland.*
Beverly Randolph.. ...........1784... *Cumberland.*

## CATALOGUE OF ALUMNI. 77

| NAMES. | DATE OF ELECTION. | RESIDENCES. | REMARKS. |
|---|---|---|---|
| Robert Beverly | 1784 | Blandfield, Essex. | |
| Henry Tazewell | 1786 | James City. | |
| Samuel Griffin | 1786 | Williamsburg. | |
| Francis Corbin | 1788 | Caroline. | |
| Philip Ludwell Grymes | 1788 | Middlesex. | |
| Mann Page | 1788 | Spottsylvania. | |
| St. George Tucker | 1788 | Williamsburg. | |
| David Stuart | 1790 | Fairfax. | |
| John Marshall | 1790 | Fauquier county | Chief Justice. |
| Philip Barraud | 1791 | Williamsburg. | |
| Hugh Nelson | 1791 | York. | |
| John Carter Byrd | 1791 | Williamsburg. | |
| Joseph Prentis | 1791 | " | |
| William Nelson | 1791 | York. | |
| Cyrus Griffin | 1791 | Williamsburg. | |
| Otway Byrd | 1791 | Norfolk. | |
| Henry Lee | 1792 | Westmoreland. | |
| Arthur Lee | 1792 | " | |
| Rev. John Dunbar | 1792 | Williamsburg. | |
| Burwell Basset | 1792 | " | |
| William Nelson | 1792 | Charles City. | |
| John Ambler | 1794 | James City. | |
| William Lee | 1800 | " | |
| John Blair | 1800 | Williamsburg. | |
| Littleton W. Tazewell | 1800 | Norfolk. | |
| Robert Saunders | 1800 | Williamsburg. | |
| Thomas Nelson | 1800 | York. | |
| William Coleman | 1800 | Williamsburg. | |
| Robert Greenhow | 1800 | " | |
| Wilson Miles Cary | 1800 | Elizabeth City. | |
| Champion Travis | 1800 | Jamestown. | |
| Mann Page, Jun. | 1800 | Gloucester. | |
| John Minson Galt | 1800 | Williamsburg. | |
| William Tazewell | 1800 | " | |
| Robert P. Waller | 1800 | " | |
| James Semple | 1803 | " | |
| Samuel Tyler | 1804 | Charles City | Chancellor. |
| John Tyler | 1804 | " | First Governor of Virginia of that name. |
| William Wirt | 1804 | " | U. S. Attorney General. |
| Nicholas Faulcon | 1804 | Surry. | |
| John B. Seawall | 1808 | Gloucester. | |
| Alexander D. Galt | 1808 | Williamsburg. | |
| Robert Nelson | 1808 | " | |
| Gawin L. Corbin | 1810 | York. | |
| John H. Smith | 1812 | King & Queen. | |
| William Armistead | 1812 | | |
| William Browne | 1812 | Williamsburg. | |

## CATALOGUE OF ALUMNI.

| NAMES. | DATE OF ELECTION. | RESIDENCES. | REMARKS. |
|---|---|---|---|
| Robert G. Scott | 1814 | Richmond. | |
| Thomas Griffin | 1814 | York. | |
| John Tyler | 1814 | Charles City | Second Gov. of that name in Va., Pres. U. S., Rector, and Chancellor in 1859–62. |
| Henry Skipwith | 1814 | Williamsburg. | |
| William H. Macon | 1814 | New Kent. | |
| Thomas G. Smith | 1814 | Middlesex. | |
| John C. Pryor | 1816 | Hampton. | |
| Charles Everett | 1817 | Albemarle. | |
| Rt. Rev. Rich. C. Moore | 1817 | Richmond. | |
| Hugh Nelson | 1818 | Albemarle. | |
| Rt. Rev. J. S. Ravenscroft | 1821 | Brunswick. | |
| John D. Watkins | 1824 | New Kent. | |
| Robert Stanard | 18.. | Richmond. | |
| James M. Garnett | 1824 | Essex. | |
| Robert B. Taylor | 1824 | Norfolk. | |
| Joseph Prentis | 1824 | Williamsburg. | |
| Robert McCandlish | 1826 | " | |
| John Page | 1827 | " | |
| William Robins | 1828 | Gloucester. | |
| Edmund Ruffin | 1833 | Prince George. | |
| Thomas G. Peachy | 1833 | Williamsburg. | |
| Thomas Martin | 1833 | James City. | |
| Abel P. Upshur | 1830'40 | Northampton | Secretary of State. |
| George Blow | 1833 | York. | |
| Charles F. Osborne | 1833 | Petersburg. | |
| Edward H: Carmichael | 1842 | Richmond. | |
| George Loyall | 1842 | Norfolk. | |
| William O. Goode | 1842 | Mecklenburg. | |
| John C. Mercer | 1844 | Williamsburg. | |
| John B. Christian | 1844 | " | |
| Thomas L. Gholson | 1844 | Petersburg. | |
| John S. Millson | 1844 | Norfolk. | |
| James Lyons | 1844 | Richmond. | |
| Colin Clarke | 1845 | Gloucester. | |
| John E. Shell | 1845 | Brunswick. | |
| Corbin Braxton | 1847 | King William. | |
| Richard K. Meade | 1847 | Petersburg. | |
| William Boulware | 1847 | King and Queen. | |
| Henry A. Wise | 1848 | Accomac | Governor of Virginia. |
| Rt. Rev. William Meade | 1848 | Clark. | |
| William H. Macfarland | 1848 | Richmond | Rector 1869–71. |
| Edward P. Scott | 1848 | Greensville. | |
| Willoughby Newton | 1848 | Westmoreland. | |
| Tazewell Taylor | 1849 | Norfolk. | |
| Eustace Conway | 1849 | Fredericksburg. | |

## CATALOGUE OF ALUMNI.

NAMES.    DATE OF ELECTION.    RESIDENCES.        REMARKS.

William B. Harrison........1849...*Brandon.*
Nathaniel M. Osborne......1851...*Prince George.*
Robert B. Bolling............1851...*Petersburg.*
Rev. George Woodbridge..1851...*Richmond.*
Edward T. Tayloe...........1851...*King George.*
Otway B. Barraud...........1852...*Norfolk.*
William W. Crump..........1853...*Richmond.*
David May......................1853...*Petersburg.*
Rt. Rev. John Johns........1854...*Fairfax.*
Hugh Blair Grigsby.........1855...*Norfolk.*
James Lyons...................1855...*Richmond.*............Rector 1871.
George W. Lewis.............1858...*Westmoreland.*
Wm. S. Peachy................1866...*Williamsburg.*
Rev. E. C. Murdaugh......1866...*Prince George.*
William Lamb.................1867...*Norfolk.*
P. Montagu Thompson.....1869...*Williamsburg.*
Charles S. Stringfellow.....1869...*Petersburg.*
Robert L. Montague........1870...*Middlesex,*............Ex-Lieut. Gov. of Virginia.
Wm. B. Taliaferro...........1870...*Gloucester.*
Dr. A. N. Wellford..........1870...*Richmond county.*
Rev. J. H. D. Wingfield...1871...*Petersburg.*
Rev. Chas. Minnegerode...1871...*Richmond city.*
Warner T. Jones.............1873...*Gloucester.*
John Goode, Jr...............1873...*Norfolk.*

### VISITORS IN 1859.

JOHN TYLER, *Rector.*

Colin Clarke,
William Boulware,
William H. Macfarland,
Dr. Edward P. Scott,
William B. Harrison.
Tazewell Taylor,
Hon. Henry A. Wise,
Rev. George Woodbridge,

Edward T. Tayloe,
Dr. Nathaniel M. Osborne,
Judge William W. Crump,
David May,
Right Rev. John Johns,
George W. Lewis,
Hugh B. Grigsby,
James Lyons.

### BURSARS SINCE 1735.

NAMES.      DATE OF APPOINTMENT.      RESIDENCES.

Rev. Richard Graham...................1735.................. *Williamsburg.*
John Blair ...................................1754................. "
Robert Miller................................1772
John Carter..................................1776................. *Williamsburg.*
William Pierce..............................1777................. "
Rev. Robert Andrews...................1790................. "
William Coleman.........................1807................. "
Edmund Christian........................1824................. "
Tazewell Taylor............................1850.................Norfolk.

# FACULTY,

*Including Presidents, Masters or Professors, and Teachers in the Grammar Schools.*

## PRESIDENTS.

| NAMES. | DATE OF APPOINTMENT. | REMARKS. |
|---|---|---|
| James Blair, D. D | 1692......Commissary. | Died 1743. |
| Rev. William Dawson | 1743......Died 1752. | |
| Rev. William Stith | 1752......Died 1755. | |
| Rev. Thomas Dawson | 1755......Commissary. | Died 1761. |
| Rev. William Yates | 1761......Died 1764. | |
| Rev. James Horrocks | 1764......Died 1791. | |
| Rev. John Camm | 1771......Commissary. | |
| Rt. Rev. James Madison | 1777......Died 1812. | |
| Rev. John Bracken | 1812 | |
| Dr. John Augustine Smith | 1814 | |
| Rev. Wm. H. Wilmer, D. D | 1826......Died 1827. | |
| Rev. Adam P. Empie, D. D | 1827 | |
| Thomas R. Dew | 1836......Died in 1846. | |
| Robert Saunders | 1847......Died in 1868. | |
| Benjamin S. Ewell | 1848 | |
| Rt. Rev. John Johns | 1849 | |
| Benj. S. Ewell | 1854 | |

## PROFESSORS.

| NAMES. | DATE OF APPOINTMENT. | REMARKS. |
|---|---|---|
| Rev. Francis Fontaine | 1729......Professor of Oriental Languages. | |
| Rev. Bartholomew Yates | 1729......Professor of Divinity. | |
| Rev. John Dixon | 1770...... | " " |
| Rev. R. Keith, D. D | 1822 | " " |
| Hon. George Wythe | 1779......Professor of Law. | |
| Judge St. George Tucker | 1800...... | " " |
| Judge William Nelson | 1804...... | " " |
| Robert Nelson | | " " |
| Judge James Semple | 1820...... | " " |
| Judge N. Beverly Tucker | 1833...... | " " |
| Judge George P. Scarburgh | 1852...... | " " |
| Lucian Minor | 1855...... | " " |
| Charles Morris | 1859...... | " " |
| James McClung | 1779......Prof. of Anatomy and Medicine. | |
| Rev. John Bracken | 1792......Professor of Humanity. | |
| Rev. R. Keith | 1822...... | " " |
| Dabney Browne | 1826...... | " " |
| Charles Minnegerode | 1842...... | " " |
| J. Morgan Smead | 1848...... | " " |

CATALOGUE OF ALUMNI. 81

| NAMES. | DATE OF APPOINTMENT. | REMARKS. |
|---|---|---|
| Edwin Taliaferro | 1858 | Professor Latin and Latin Lit., and the Romance Languages. |
| Edward S. Joynes | 1858 | Prof. Greek & Greek Lit. & Ger. |
| Charles Bellini | 1779 | Professor of Modern Languages. |
| L. H. Gerardin | 1803 | " " " |
| C. de La Pena | 1829 | " " " |
| Thomas R. Dew | 18— | Professor of Political Economy. |
| George Frederick Holmes | 1846 | Prof. of History and Polit. Econ. |
| Henry A. Washington | 1849 | " " " |
| Robert J. Morrison | 1858 | " " " |
| Rev. William Dawson | 1729 | Prof. of Moral and Intel. Phil. |
| Rev. Richard Graham | 1749 | " " " |
| Jacob Rowe | 1758 | " " " |
| Rev. —— Johnson | 1767 | " " " |
| Rev. Samuel Henley | 1770 | " " " |
| Rev. Robert Andrews | 1777 | " " " |
| Archibald C. Peachy | 1847 | " " " |
| Rt. Rev. John Johns, D. D., LL. D. | 1849 | " " " |
| Rev. Silas Totten, D. D | 1849 | " " " |
| Rev. George T. Wilmer, D. D. | 1869 | " " " |
| Rt. Rev. James Madison | 1774 | Prof. of Nat. Phil. & Chemistry. |
| Dr. John McLean | 1812 | " " " |
| Dr. Thomas L. Jones | 1814 | " " " |
| Dr. Robert Hare | 1818 | " " " |
| Dr. P. K. Rogers | 1819 | " " " |
| William B. Rogers, LL. D | 1829 | " " " |
| Dr. John Millington | 1836 | " " " |
| William F. Hopkins | 1849 | " " " |
| Rev. Hugh Jones | 172- | Professor of Mathematics. |
| Alexander Irvine | 1729 | " " |
| Joshua Fry | 175- | " " |
| William Small | 1758 | " " |
| Rev. Thomas Gwatkin | 1770 | " " |
| George Blackburn | 1805 | " " |
| Ferdinand S. Campbell | 1811 | " " |
| Robert Saunders | 1833 | " " |
| Benjamin S. Ewell | 1848 | " " |
| Thomas T. L. Snead | 1869 | " " |
| Thomas P. McCandlish | 1869 | Professor of Latin, French and Roman, and French History. |
| Frank Preston | 1869 | Professor of Greek, German, and of Grecian and German History. |
| Rev. L. B. Wharton | 1870 | " " " |
| Benjamin S. Ewell | 1869 | Professor of Natural Philosophy. |
| Richard A. Wise, M. D | 1869 | Professor of Chemistry. |
| Rev. James Henderson | 1792 | Adjunct Professor of Humanity. |
| Robert Gatewood | 1851 | Adjunct Prof. of Mathematics. |
| James M. Wise | 1855 | " " " |
| Thomas T. L. Snead | 1856 | " " " |
| T. P. McCandlish | 1860 | Adjunct Prof. of Languages. |

6

## Names of Professors,

*The Departments in which they Instructed not being known.*

Joshua Fry ............................................. 1729
Rev. William Stith ................................... 1731
Edward Ford .......................................... 1738
John Græme ........................................... 1741
Rev. Thomas Dawson ............................... 1738
William Preston ...................................... 1752
Rev. John Camm ..................................... 1752

## Masters of the Grammar School.

Rev. William Robinson ............................. 1742
William Davis ......................................... 1758
Rev. Gronow Owen .................................. 1758
Rev. William Webb .................................. 1760
Rev. James Horrocks ................................ 1762
Wm. R. Garrett ....................................... 1866
T. J. Stubbs ............................................ 1868
J. Wilmer Turner .................................... 1869
Chas. S. Dod .......................................... 1873

## Masters of the Indian School.

John Fox ................................................ 1729
Robert Barrett ........................................ 1737
Rev. Emmanuel Jones .............................. 1755

# STUDENTS.

### Students at College before 1720.

| NAMES. | RESIDENCES. | REMARKS. |
|---|---|---|
| John Allen | Surry. | |
| William Bassett | New Kent. | |
| Richard Bland | Prince George. | |
| Georgè Braxton | King and Queen. | |
| William Brent | Stafford. | |
| Carter Burwell | Gloucester. | |
| Robert Burwell | " | |
| Lewis Burwell | " | |
| William Byrd | Charles City. | |
| Harwood Cary | Warwick. | |
| Henry Cary | " | |
| Henry Fitzhugh | Stafford. | |
| Peter Hegeman | " | |
| Thomas Lee | | |
| Carter Page | Rosewell, Glou. co...Son of Mann Page. | |
| John Page | " " " | |
| Matthew Page | " " " | |
| Mann Page | " " " | |
| Ralph Page | " " " | |
| Robert Page | " " " | |
| Edward Randolph | Turkey Island, Henrico county...Son of Wm. Randolph. | |
| Isham Randolph | " " " | Ad. Gen. of Col. |
| John Randolph | " " " | Treas. of Col. |
| Richard Randolph | " " " " " | |
| Thomas Randolph | " " " | |
| William Randolph | " " " | |
| Christopher Robinson | Middlesex. | |
| John Robinson | King and Queen. | |
| Ralph Wormley | Rosegill, Middlesex...Son of Ralph Wormley. | |

### Students at College from 1720 to 1735.

| | | |
|---|---|---|
| James Blair | Williamsburg | Son of Dr. A. Blair. |
| John Blair | " | Judge S. Court U. S. |
| Carter Burwell | James City. | |
| Archibald Cary | Ampthill. | |

| NAMES. | RESIDENCES. | REMARKS. |
|---|---|---|

Richard Cary..................York.
Wilson Cary..................Warwick..................Son of Miles Cary.
Miles Cary..................      "                                "         "
William Churchill..........Middlesex.
Bowler Cocke................Bremo, Henrico.
Richard Corbin.............Middlesex.
John Edloe....................Charles City.
Francis Lightfoot..........Sandy Point, Charles City.
Philip Lightfoot.............      "
Benjamin Harrison.........Berkeley, Ch. City...Son of Benj. Harrison, Signer Declaration Independence.
Richard Kennon............Charles City.
Bernard Moore...............King William.
Robert Carter Nicholas..Williamsburg.
Beverly Randolph..........Chatsworth, Hen......Son of Wm. Randolph, Gov. of Va
Peter Randolph...............      "           "      ......      "         "
William Randolph..........      "           "      ......      "         "
Beverly Randolph..........Williamsburg.............Son of Sir J. Randolph.
John Randolph...............      "          ............      "         "
Peyton Randolph............      "          ............      "     " First Presid'nt American Congress.
Richard Randolph..........Curls, Henrico..........Son of Richard Randolph.
William Randolph..........Tuckahoe, Gooch......Son of Thomas Randolph.
Benjamin Robinson........Caroline.
Christopher Robinson....Middlesex.
Robert Tucker................Norfolk.
Benjamin Waller............Williamsburg.
Ralph Wormley..............Middlesex.................Son of Ralph Wormley.
George Wythe................Elizabeth City..........Chancellor.
John Carter....................Corotoman...............Son of Robert Carter, (known as King Carter.)
Robert Carter.................Sabine Hall...............      "         "         "
George Carter................Nomini.......................      "         "         "
Landon Carter...............Cleve..........................      "         "         "
Edward Carter...............Blenheim...................      "         "         "

## From 1738 to 1752.

Alexander Champion......Jamestown.
Roscow Cole..................Gloucester.
Mordecai Cook...............Gloucester.
Thomas Dawson............Williamsburg.
Cole Digges....................Warwick.
Benjamin Edwards........Southampton.
Francis Fontaine...........Williamsburg.
John Ford......................
Alexander Græme.........
John Græme..................

CATALOGUE OF ALUMNI.                                      85

| NAMES. | RESIDENCES. | REMARKS. |

Matthew Hubard..........Williamsburg.
James Maury...............Albemarle.
William Skipwith..........Petersburg...............Son of Sir William Shipwith.
Peyton Skipwith...........      "       ..............    "         "         "

## 1752.

Charles Carter...............Lancaster county......Son of John Carter of Corotman.
Edward Carter.............      "          ......    "         "         "
Wilson Miles Cary.........Warwick.................Son of Wilson Cary.
Augustine Cooke..........Gloucester county.....
Severn Eyre..................Northampton co.
John Fox......................Gloucester.
James Bray Johnson......James City.
John Page....................Gloucester county.
Christopher Robinson....Middlesex county.
John Whiting...............Gloucester county.
Peter Beverly Whiting...      "
Edward Wilcox.............Charles City.

## 1753.

Jaquelin Ambler...........Jamestown.
James Armistead..........
Robert Armistead.........York county.
Vivion Brooking...........
Wilson Cary................Elizabeth City co......Son of Miles Cary.
Samuel Cobbs...............
Giles Hawkins..............
Rice Hooe....................King George co.
John Lomax.................      "
Lunsford Lomax...........      "
John Nelson.................York county.
George Plater...............Maryland.
William Row...............Hampton.
William Selden.............      "
Daniel Sweeny.............Elizabeth City.
John Turberville..........Westmoreland.
John Webb..................New Kent.

## 1754.

William Ballard............York county.
Peter Bland..................Prince George.
Theoderic Bland...........      "       .........Col. in Con. Army, and Member
                                                         of Congress.
James Whitall Bradby...Surry.
William Browne............James City..............Son of Gen. Browne.

## CATALOGUE OF ALUMNI.

| NAMES. | RESIDENCES. | REMARKS. |
|---|---|---|
| Walter Coles | Henrico. | |
| James Fontaine | Hanover. | |
| Carter Harrison | Berkeley, Ch City | Son of Benj. Harrison. |
| Henry Harrison | " | " " |
| Nathaniel Harrison | " | " " |
| Robert Harrison | " | " " |
| Richard Hewitt | | |
| James Hubard | Williamsburg. | |
| James Marye | Spotsylvania. | |
| Peter Marye | " | |
| John Matthews | | |
| William Meredith | Hanover. | |
| Clement Read | Williamsburg | Son of Thomas Read. |
| James Read | " | " " |
| Theoderic Munford | Charles City. | |
| Thomas Price | Hanover. | |
| Thomas Reade | | |
| William Russell | York. | |
| William Stith | Brunswick | Nephew of Rev. Mr. Stith, Pres. William and Mary College. |
| Richard Taliaferro | King George. | |
| William Taliaferro | " | |
| Henry Talman | | |
| John Tenant | Caroline. | |
| Robert Throckmorton | Gloucester. | |
| Charles Mynn Thruston | " | Officer in Con. Army. |
| John Tyler | James City | First Gov. of Va., Marshall under Col. Gov., U. S. District Judge, son of John Tyler. |
| Robert Tucker | Norfolk. | |
| James Wallace | Elizabeth City. | |
| Robert Wallace | " | |
| Foster Webb | New Kent. | |

### INDIANS AT THE INDIAN SCHOOL IN 1754.

William Cooke,  
John Langston,  
Charles Murphy,  
William Squirrel.  
Gideon Langston.  
John Montour.  
Thomas Sampson,

### 1755.

Bowles Armistead.........Gloucester.
John Armistead............ "
Edmund Berkeley.........Middlesex.
Henry Beverly...............Spotsylvania...........Son of Ro. Beverly.

## CATALOGUE OF ALUMNI. 87

| NAMES. | RESIDENCES. | REMARKS. |
|---|---|---|

Benjamin Bryan.
William Buckner..........Gloucester.
Nathaniel Burwell........    "        ..............Son of Col. R. Burwell.
John Esten.
Francis Meriwether.......Hanover.
Nicholas Meriwether......    "
Mathew Moody.............Williamsburg.
Richard Spann.
John Stringer.

### 1756.

Thomas Adams..............Henrico.
William Allen.................Surry ....................Son of John Allen.
William Armistead........Gloucester.
Carter Braxton.............King and Queen.......Son of Geo. Braxton, Signer of Declaration of Independence.
George Braxton............     "         "    .......Son of Geo. Braxton.
Lacky Collier...............Elizabeth City.
John Elliott.
Seaton Elliott.
Richard Gist.................Buckingham.
James Hardyman..........Charles City.
Daniel McCarty............King George.

### 1757.

Hudson Allen...............James City.
William Barrett............    "
Lawrence Battaile.........Caroline.
Lewis Burwell..............Gloucester ..............Son of Lewis Burwell, President of the Council.
Nicholas Collins.
Richard Eppes..............Chesterfield.
William Finnie.............Amelia.
Benjamin Harrison........Surry......................Son of Ben. Harrison of Wakefield.
Nathaniel Harrison........    "            "         "        "
Mathew Holt................Williamsburg.
Gronow Owen..............    "         ..........Son of Rev. Mr. Gronow Owen.
Robert Owen................    "         ..........    "         "         "
Robert Riddell..............    "
Francis Warrington.......Elizabeth City.........Son of Rev. John Warrington.
William Webb...............New Kent.

### 1758.

Robert Armistead.........Gloucester.
Starkey Armistead........Elizabeth City,
Westwood Armistead.....    "

| NAMES. | RESIDENCES. | REMARKS. |
|---|---|---|

John Aylett...............King William.
Charles Binns.
Richard Cary...............Warwick.
Dudley Digges..............Williamsburg............Son of Dudley Digges.
Arthur Emerson...........Norfolk.
Benjamin Harrison........Prince George..........Son Col. N. Harrison of Brandon
Stephen Mitchell...........York.
Hugh Nelson...............    "

## 1759.

Stirling Edmonds.........Brunswick.
Jesse Ewell..................Prince William.........Son of Bertrand Ewell.
Thomas W. Ewell.........    "
Benjamin Grymes.........Middlesex.
Charles Grymes............    "
James Grymes..............    "
Philip Ludwell Grymes..    "          ...............Son of Ph. Grymes, of Brandon.
Simon Hollier...............Elizabeth City.
Thomas Jefferson..........Albemarle...............President United States. Son of Peter Jefferson.
Warner Lewis...............Warner Hall, Glo......Son of Warren Lewis.
John Randolph.............Curls, Henrico.........Son of Col. R. Randolph.

## 1760.

Edward Bland..............Prince George.
James Bland.................    "
William Bland..............    "
George Byrd.
John Cary.....................Warwick.
William Cole.
William Digges.............Warwick.
John Doncastle.............Maryland.
Burr Harrison...............Prince William.
Charles Harrison..........Charles City............Gen'l in Rev. war. Son Benj. Harrison.
John Hubard................Williamsburg.
William Hubard............    "
Walter Jones.................Westmoreland.
Rodham Kenner...........    "
William Mallory............Elizabeth City.
William Massie.............New Kent.
Thomas Massie.............    "
Burgess Smith...............Northumberland.
Gerrard Smith...............    "
John Smith....................    "
Philip Smith..................    "

## CATALOGUE OF ALUMNI. 89

| NAMES. | RESIDENCES. | REMARKS. |

Robert Spotswood.........Orange................Grandson of Gov. Spotswood.
John Tazewell.............Williamsburg.
William West..............West Point, K'g Wm.
William Westwood.........Hampton.
William Whiting..........Gloucester.

### 1761.

William Brodnax..........Brunswick.
James Emerson............Norfolk.
Francis Eppes............Prince George.
Edward Hack..............Norfolk.
Charles Hansford.........Warwick.
Austin Moore.............King William.
Bernard Moore............     "
Benjamin Robinson........King & Queen.
Henry Robinson...........     "
John Robinson............     "
John Thompson............Petersburg.
Champion Travis..........Jamestown............Son of E. C. Travis.
Augustine Tabb...........Gloucester.

### 1762.

William Colson...........Berkeley.
John Edmonds.............Brunswick.
Edward Harwood...........Warwick.
Samuel Harwood...........     "
Dabney Carr..............Albemarle.
James McClung............Williamsburg.
Robert Moseley...........Norfolk.
Edward Moseley...........     "
John Nicholas............James City............Son John Nicholas, Seven Isl'd.
Edmund Pendleton.........Caroline..............Nephew of Judge Pendleton.
Edmund Ruffin............Prince George.
John Hyde Saunders.......Cumberland.
John Swann...............Gloucester.
Charles Tomkies..........     "
Bartholomew Yates........Middlesex.
Edm'nd Randolph Yates    "

### 1763.

Archibald Bolling........Chesterfield.
Edward Bolling...........     "
Beverly Dixon............Williamsburg.
William Fleming..........Chesterfield..........Judge Court of Appeals.
George Holden............                      Son of G. H. Holden.
William Moulston.........

7

| NAMES. | RESIDENCES. | REMARKS. |
|---|---|---|
| Thomas Nelson | York | Gov. and Son of Prest. Nelson of Council. |
| John Page | Rosewell, Glou | Son of Mann Page, Gov. of Va. |
| William Reynolds | York. | |
| Edward Smith | Gloucester | Son of John Smith. |
| John Walker | Orange. | |

### 1764.

| | | |
|---|---|---|
| William Clugh | | |
| Thomas Hughes | Gloucester | Son of Gab. Hughes. |
| William Leigh | King William | Son of Fer. Leigh. |
| Mann Page | Gloucester | Son of Hon. J. Page. |
| Mann Page | Mansfield, Spotsyl. | Son of Mann Page, of Rosewell, Gloucester. |
| John Perrin | Gloucester. | |
| Thomas Read | " | Son of Rev. Mr. Read. |
| Bathurst Skelton | Hanover. | |
| Henry Whiting | Goluecester | Son of Fran. Whiting. |
| William Yates | Williamsburg | Son of Rev. Wm. Yates. |
| John Sampson | | An Indian. |

### 1765.

| | | |
|---|---|---|
| John Tayloe Griffin | King & Queen. | |
| John Hughes. | | |
| William Marshall. | | |
| George Meredith | Hanover. | |
| Thomas Necks. | | |
| John Savage | Accomac. | |
| Gregory Smith. | | |
| William Thompson | | Son of Rev. Mr. Thompson. |
| John Wilcox | Charles City. | |
| Lewis Willis | Gloucester. | |
| John Tauhaw | | An Indian. |

### 1766.

| | | |
|---|---|---|
| Carter Burwell | Cart Grove, J. City | Son of Col. C. Burwell. |
| Nathaniel Burwell | " " | " " " |
| Walter King Cole | Williamsburg. | |
| Peter Lyons | Studley, Hanover | Son of Judge Peter Lyons. |
| Robert Carter Nicholas | Williamsburg | Son of the Treasurer. |
| Edmund Randolph | " | U. S. Att. Gen. and Sec. of State. Son of John Randolph. |
| William Shelden Sclater | York. | |
| Francis Scott | Prince Edward | Son of Col. Th. Scott. |
| Gustave Scott. | | |
| Charles Soyer. | | |
| Abner Waugh | Orange | Son of Alex. Waugh. |

## CATALOGUE OF ALUMNI. 91

### 1767.

| NAMES. | RESIDENCES. | REMARK |
|---|---|---|
| John Burwell. | | |
| John Eustace. | | |
| John Gregory | King and Queen | Son of R. Gregory. |
| Richard Gregory | " | " " |
| William Jennings. | Hampton. | |
| Edward Jones | Gloucester | Son of Richard Jones. |
| Strother Jones | Augusta | Son of G. Jones. |
| James Keith. | | |
| William Kennon | Charles City. | |
| George Mercer | Fredericksburg. | |
| James Mercer | " | |
| John Mercer. | | |

### 1768.

| | | |
|---|---|---|
| Joseph Bridger | Nansemond. | |
| David Boyd | Mecklenburg. | |
| Samuel Camp | James City. | |
| Isaac Coles | Richmond. | |
| Edward Convers. | | |
| Thomas Davis | Charles City. | |
| James Maury | Albemarle. | |
| Mathew Maury | " | |
| Robert Robinson | York. | |
| Starkey Robinson | " | |
| John Travis | Jamestown | Son of Ed. C. Travis. |
| Charles Tucker | Norfolk. | |
| Travis Tucker | " | |

### 1769.

| | | |
|---|---|---|
| John Byrd | Westover | Son of Hon. William Byrd. |
| Thomas Byrd | " | " " " |
| David Copland | Cumberland. | |
| Nicholas Cabell | Amherst | Son of William Cabell. |
| John Leigh | King William. | |
| David May | Prince George. | |
| Nathaniel Nelson | York | Son of Hon. William Nelson. |
| Robert Nelson | " | " " " |
| William Nelson | " | " " " |
| Clement Read | Middlesex | Son of Dr. Reade, of Urbana. |
| John Reade | " | " " " |
| Samuel Shield | York. | |
| Robort Mush | | An Indian. |
| George Sampson | | " |

## 1770.

| NAMES. | RESIDENCES. | REMARKS. |
|---|---|---|
| William Buckner | Gloucester. | |
| Maximilian Calvert | Norfolk | Son of Maximilian Calvert. |
| John Cocke | Surry | Son of Col. R. Cocke. |
| James Dudley | Warwick | Son of William Dudley. |
| Thomas Dixon | Williamsburg | Son of Rev. Mr. Dixon. |
| William Dixon | " | " " " |
| Thompson Mason | Fairfax. | |
| William Page | " | Son of Hon. J. Page. |
| Charles Read. | | |
| Thomas Smith | Gloucester | Son of Capt. John Smith. |
| John Taylor | Caroline | United States Senator and mover of resolutions 1798–9 in House of Delegates of Virginia. |
| James Walker | Orange. | |
| Benj. Carter Waller | Williamsburg | Son of Benjamin Waller. |
| John Waller | " | " " |

## 1771.

| | | |
|---|---|---|
| Richard Bland | Prince George | Son of Richard Bland, Jr. |
| Samuel Boush | Norfolk | Son of Samuel Boush. |
| William Boush | " | " " |
| Robert Brough | Hampton | Son of Robert Brough. |
| Jonathan Calvert | Norfolk | Son of Maximilian Calvert. |
| John Clayton | Gloucester | Son of Jasper Clayton. |
| Cole Digges | Warwick | Son of Col. W. Digges. |
| John Dixon | Williamsburg | Son of Rev. Mr. Dixon. |
| Dolphin Drew | Isle of Wight. | |
| Beverly Fitzhugh | King George | Son of Wm. Fitzhugh of Marmion |
| *Daniel Fitzhugh | " | " " " |
| *Theodoric Fitzhugh | " | " " " |
| John Gibbons | York | Son of Th. Gibbons. |
| James Innes | " | Attorney General of Virginia. |
| George Kendall | Accomac. | |
| James Madison | Augusta. | |
| Walker Maury | Williamsburg. | |
| Henry Montfort | North Carolina | Son of John Montfort. |
| *John Page | | Son of Hon. J. Page. |
| Thomas Peyton | Gloucester | Son of Sir John Peyton. |
| Beverly Randolph | Chatsworth, Hen | Governor of Virginia. Son of Col. Peter Randolph. |
| Peyton Randolph | Wilton, Henrico | Son of William Randolph. |
| Philip Rootes | Augusta | Son of Philip Rootes. |

---

Those whose names are marked thus * were the original members of the Phi Beta Kappa Society, organized December 15th, 1776.

| NAMES. | RESIDENCES. | REMARKS. |
|---|---|---|
| David Stewart | King George. | |
| William Stevenson | York | Son of W. W. Stevenson. |
| Griffin Stith | Northampton | Son of Griffin Stith. |
| Edward Tarry | Mecklenburg. | |
| Robert Throckmorton | Gloucester | Son of Robert Throckmorton. |
| John Thruston | " | |
| John Watson | " | Son of Major Watson. |
| John Whiting. | | |
| Mathew Whiting | Prince William | Son of Mathew Whiting, of Bull Run. |
| Willis Wilkinson | Nansemond | Son of Willis Wilkinson. |
| James Wormley | Middlesex | Son of Ralph Wormley. |
| John Nettles | | An Indian. |

## 1772.

| | | |
|---|---|---|
| Nathaniel Burwell | | Son of James Burwell. |
| Bobert Burton | Albemarle | Son of William Burton. |
| George Carter | Shirley | Son of Charles Carter. |
| John Hill Carter | " | " " |
| Landon Carter | Sabine Hall, in Richmond county | Son of Robert Carter. |
| Michael Christian | Northampton | Son of M. Christian. |
| Thomas Clay | Cumberland | Son of Charles Clay. |
| Langhorne Dade | King George | Son of Horatio Dade. |
| Joseph Eggleston | Amelia | Officer in Continental Army. |
| William Fontaine. | | |
| John Goodrich | Isle of Wight. | |
| James Heath | Northumberland. | |
| Randolph Jefferson | Albemarle | Son of Peter Jefferson. |
| John Leland. | | |
| William Nelson | York | Son of Th. Nelson, Jr. |
| George Nicholas | Williamsburg | Son of R. C. Nicholas, Treasurer of the Colony. |
| Carter Page | Gloucester | Son of Hon. J. Page. |
| William Smelt | King and Queen. | |
| William Steptoe | Middlesex. | |
| Thomas Tarpley. | | |
| William Tarpley. | | |
| —— Todd | Isle of Wight. | |
| St. George Tucker | Williamsburg | Son of Henry Tucker, Bermuda. Judge in State Court. |
| John Waddell. | | |
| John White | King William | Son of Rev. William White. |
| David Wright | Princess Anne | Son of Christ. Wright. |

## 1773.

| | | |
|---|---|---|
| Robert Baylor | Caroline | Aid to General Washington. |

CATALOGUE OF ALUMNI.

| NAMES. | RESIDENCES. | REMARKS. |
|---|---|---|
| Samuel Jordan Cabell | Amherst | Son of William Cabell, of Union Hill. |
| Thomas Evans | Eastern Shore | Judge State Court. |
| James Park Farley | Jamaica. | |
| Benjamin Harrison | Brandon | Son of Nathan'l Harrison. Member of first Ex. Council of Va. under its first Constitution. |
| Charles Hay | Williamsburg. | |
| Emanuel Jones | " | |
| John Lewis | Gloucester | Son of Warner Lewis. |
| *Alexander Mason | | |
| John Nelson | York | Col. in the Army during the Revolution. |
| Bret Randolph | Powhatan | Son of Bret Randolph. |
| Robert Randolph | Chatsworth | Son of Col. P. Randolph. |
| *Thomas Smith. | | |

## 1774.

| | | |
|---|---|---|
| Thomas Heath | Northumberland | Son of Thomas Heath. |
| John Mayo | Cumberland | Son of John Mayo. |
| William Mayo | " | " " |
| Robert Mitchell | Spotsylvania. | |
| Thomas Mitchell | " | |
| Geo. Viscount Fincastle | Williamsburg | Son of Earl of Dunmore. |
| Hon. Alexander Murray | " " | " " |
| Hon John Murray | " " | " " |
| Ryland Randolph | Curls, Henrico | Son of Richard Randolph. |
| James Roscow | Warwick. | |
| *John Starke | Westmoreland | Son of Mrs. Frances Starke. |

## 1775.

| | | |
|---|---|---|
| William Alexander | Fairfax. | |
| Booth Armistead | Elizabeth City. | |
| Henry Ashton | Caroline. | |
| John Bankhead | Westmoreland. | |
| *George Braxton | King William | Son of Carter Braxton. |
| Wilson Cary | Warwick | Son of Col. W. Miles Cary. |
| Michael King | Hampton | Son of Henry King. |
| *John Marshall | Fauquier | Chief Justice United States. |
| John Francis Mercer | Stafford | Governor of Maryland. |
| James McMillan. | | |
| William McMillan. | | |
| James Monroe | Westmoreland | President of the United States. |
| Thomas Nelson | York | Son of Gen'l Thomas Nelson. |
| John Stewart | King George. | |
| Johnson Tabb | Warwick | Son of John Tabb. |

CATALOGUE OF ALUMNI.  95

| NAMES. | RESIDENCES. | REMARKS. |
|---|---|---|
| Robert Wallace............ | " ................. | Son of James Wallace. |
| Ephraim Worthington... | Maryland. | |
| George Sampson........... | | An Indian. |
| Reubin Sampson........... | | " |

## 1776.

Robert Bolling............Petersburg.
Otway Byrd..................Westover..................Son of William Byrd.
Dandridge Claiborne.....King William.
Charles Carter..............Shirley......................Son of Charles Carter.
Charles Cocke...............Bremo, Henrico........Son of Col. B. Cocke.
*Hartwell Cocke............   "            .........   "      "
William Cocke.. ...........   "            .........   "      "
Edward Digges.
Joseph Eggleston..........Amelia......................Member of Congress.
Carter B. Harrison........Berkeley, Ch. City...   "      "
*Isaac Hill.
James Lyons..................Studley, Hanover......Son of Judge Lyons.
Robert Nicholson..........Yorktown.
Robert Page..................North End, Glou......Son of John Page, Major in the army during the Revolution.
John Roberts................Culpeper.
David Meade Randolph..Curls, Henrico........Son of Richard Randolph.
Richard Randolph.........   "            .........   "      "
Robert Saunders............Williamsburg...........Son of John Saunders.
Dennis Smelt.
Armistead Smith...........Gloucester............... Son of Capt. John Smith.
Granville Smith.............Louisa.
Mons. Baubee...............                                An Indian.
James Gunn..................                                "
Edmund Sampson..........                                "

*The following Students, as appears from the "Virginia Historical Register," left College during the Revolution to join the American Army:*

Robert Bolling,
Nathaniel Burwell,
Otway Byrd,
Charles Carter,
George Carter,
Dandridge Claiborne,
Charles Cocke,
William Cocke,
Langhorne Dade,
Edward Digges,
Joseph Eggleston,
Thomas Evans,
Carter B. Harrison,
John F. Mercer,
James Monroe,
William Nelson,
Robert Nicholson.
Carter Page,
Robert Page,
David Meade Randolph,
Edmund Randolph,
Peyton Randolph,
Richard Randolph,
John Roberts,
Robert Saunders,
Granville Smith,
James Lyons.

## 1777.

| NAMES. | RESIDENCES. | REMARKS. |
|---|---|---|

Philip Allen.
Joseph Billup.
Carter Braxton............King William.
Corbin Braxton............   "
John Briggs.
Frederick Bryan.
Archibald Campbell......Westmoreland.
Philip Fitzhugh.............Stafford.
Mordecai Gregory.........Gloucester.
Frederick Hearn.
*John Heath..................Northumberland.
*Thomas Lee.
Fielding Lewis.
Thomas Lewis.
Henry Nicholson.
Joseph Prentis..............Williamsburg...........State Judge.
James Ramsey.
James Ruffin.
—— Stalke.
*John Swann.
Peter Whiting...............          Son of Thomas Whiting.

## 1778.

John Dandridge.
Thomas Macon.
*John Morrison.
†Lewis Littlepage.........Hanover.
William Payne..............Fauquier.
William Starke.
John Stuart.
*Bushrod Washington...Westmoreland .........Judge S. Court United States.

## 1779.

John Crawley.
J. Hewlitt.
Isaac Hite..................... Winchester.
*John Nivison................Norfolk.
Thomas Rootes.............Augusta.
Daniel Scott.
Thomas Watkins.

## 1780.

Christopher Robinson....Virginia ....................Father of Chief Justice, Sir Jno.
  who left College to join                        Beverly Robinson.
  Col. Simcoe's regiment.

---

† Lewis Littlepage was attache to Spanish Mission, familiar at the French Court, sent on a mission to Russia, and became a favorite of the Empress Catharine.

## 1776 TO 1781.

| NAMES. | RESIDENCES. | REMARKS. |
|---|---|---|
| *John Allen | Surry. | |
| Richard Baker | Southampton. | |
| *Thomas W. Balendine. | | |
| *James J. Beckly. | | |
| Harden Burnley | Hanover. | |
| *Richard Booker | Amelia. | |
| *Paxton Bowdoin | Northampton. | |
| *Daniel Carroll Brent | Maryland. | |
| George Brent | Stafford. | |
| *John Brown. | | |
| Joseph Cabell | Amherst | Son of Col. Joseph Cabell. |
| *Landon Cabell | " | Son of William Cabell, Union Hill. |
| *William Cabell | " | " " |
| Robert Carter | Shirley | Son of Charles Carter. |
| Edward Carter | " | " " |
| *Thomas Clements. | | |
| Hartwell Cocke | Surry. | |
| *Thomas Cocke | Prince George. | |
| Littleton Eyre | Northampton. | |
| William B. Giles | Amelia | Governor of Virginia and United States Senator. |
| *Thomas Hall | Louisa. | |
| *Samuel Hardy. | | |
| *Henry Hill | King and Queen. | |
| *John Jones. | | |
| Thomas Lee | Westmoreland. | |
| *Richard Bland Lee | " | |
| *William Madison | Williamsburg | Son of Bishop Madison. |
| Stephen T. Mason | Fairfax. | |
| *John Moore. | | |
| William Nelson | Charles City | Professor of Law in William and Mary College, and Judge. |
| Elisha Parmele. | | |
| *William Pierce | James City. | |
| *Spencer Roane | King and Queen | Judge Court of Appeals. |
| *Thomas Savage | Accomac. | |
| Peyton Short | Surry | Son of Col. Short. |
| *William Short | " | " " |
| Armistead Smith. | | |
| Thomas Smith. | | |
| *Archibald Stewart | | Judge and Member of Congress. |
| *John Stewart | King George. | |
| *William Stewart. | | |
| *William Stith | Brunswick. | |

## 1783.

| NAMES. | RESIDENCES. | REMARKS. |

Ludwell Lee, A. B........  Son of Richard Henry Lee.
John Barrett.
Paul Carrington............  Judge Court of Appeals.

## 1785.

William Harwood.......... Warwick.
Thomas Hubard............ Williamsburg.
Charles Leland.
John Minor................ Hanover.
Francis Preston........... Montgomery.
Merit M. Robinson......... Isle of Wight.
Richard N. Venable....... Prince Edward.
John Wickham............. Williamsburg.

## 1787.

Mathew Page.

## 1785 TO 1790.

P. Baker................ Southampton.
James Breckinridge....... Botetourt................ Member of Congress, U. S. Senator, and Attorney General.
Alexander Campbell...... Richmond .............. United States District Attorney.
Peter Carr............... Albemarle.............. Son of Dabney Carr.
Turner Dixon............. Westmoreland.
Nicholas Faulcon......... Surry.
Benjamin Harrison........ Mt. Airy, Pr. Geo.
William Marshall......... Fauquier.
Hugh Nelson.............. York.................. Member of Congress.
Thomas Newton............ Norfolk................      "           "
William S. Peachy........ Amelia.
William Tyler............ Prince William.

## 1790.

Richard Goode.
John Griffin.................  Son of Judge Cyrus Griffin. U. S. Judge.
Thomas Randolph........ Goochland.............. Son of Thomas Isham Randolph.
Richard H. Yancey....... Louisa.

## 1791.

John Bracken............... Williamsburg.......... Son of Rev. J. Bracken.
Lit. W. Tazewell, A. B...James City.............. Governor of Virginia and United States Senator.

## 1792.

| NAMES. | RESIDENCES. | REMARKS. |

Robert Bannister............Dinwiddie.
Carter Burwell...............James City..............Son of Armistead Burwell.
Edwin Burwell............ .      "          ...............     "                "
Nathaniel Harrison........Prince George.
Humphrey Harwood......Warwick.
John Page.
John Randolph..............Roanoke, Charlotte...Son of John Randolph. United States Senator.
John Stith......................King George.
John Thompson.............Petersburg..................Author of Curtius.

## 1793.

*Wm. H. Cabell, L. B......Amherst..................Son of Col. Nicholas Cabell and Governor of Va., and President Court of Appeals.
Samuel Carr....................Albemarle..................Son of Dabney Carr.
John Dangerfield............Essex.
Phil Grymes....................Middlesex.
John Hancock.
George Keith Taylor......Dinwiddie ..............Appointed Judge by Jno. Adams
Robert B. Taylor........ Norfolk....................General in war of 1812.

## 1794.

John Alison.....................Petersburg.
William Crawford.
Henry Hook.
Lewis Warrington.........Williamsburg............Commodore in U. S. Navy.

## 1795.

Jerman Baker................Chesterfield.
William B. Banks..........Stafford.......................Judge in State Court.
John W. Foushee..........Richmond.
George Greenhow.........Williamsburg.
Joseph Hornsby.............         "
Hugh Mercer..................Fredericksburg.
John Norfleet..................Southampton.
Thomas Ruffin...............King William.
Miles Selden...................Henrico.
Peyton Southall.............Warwick.
John D. Watkins............New Kent.
John Wyatt....................Charlotte.

---

* The names of those Students on whom Academic Degrees have been conferred, will, together with the Degrees, be hereafter put first in the different years.

## 1790 TO 1795.

| NAMES. | RESIDENCES. | REMARKS. |
|---|---|---|

John Allay.
Nathaniel Bannister......Dinwiddie.
George Cabell..............  Son of Colonel Nicholas Cabell.
Henry Calloway............Amherst.
Robert Calloway...........Amherst.
John Campbell.
Fortunatus Corley.........  District Attorney.
Hume Field................Brunswick.
Edmund Hankins..........James City.
David Holmes...... ........Winchester..............Judge Court of Appeals.
Archibald Magill...........   "
John Mercer................Fredericksburg.........Son of General Hugh Mercer.
James Murdaugh...........Nansemond.
James P. Preston..........Montgomery ............Governor of Virginia.
Archibald Robertson.....Richmond ...............Son of W. Robertson.
Thos. Bolling Robertson,   "      ...............    "         "    Moved to Louisiana, and was its first representative in U. S. Congress, Governor and U. S. Judge.

Bennet Taylor...............Isle of Wight.
William Tennant...........Westmoreland.
Lewis Wolfe.

## 1796.

Carter B. Harrison, A. B.Cumberland.
David Yancey, A. B......Louisa.

## 1797.

Ellyson Currie, A. B.....  Son of Rev. D. Currie. Judge in State Court.
—— Risque......... ........Lynchburg.
George Tucker, A. B.....Bermuda ................Prof. at University of Virginia.
David Watson, A. B......Louisa.

## 1798.

Nathaniel Burwell, A. B.Carter's Grove, J. C.
Joseph C. Cabell, A. B...Amherst.
Isaac A. Coles, A. B.......Albemarle.
Wills Cooper, A. B........North Carolina.
Josiah Deane, A. B........Gloucester.
Roswell Johnson, A. B..Louisa.
William Lewis, A. B......Fredericksburg.
Thos. M. Maury, A. B...Albemarle.
Jas. W. Morris, A. B.....Louisa.

## CATALOGUE OF ALUMNI.

| NAMES. | RESIDENCES. | REMARKS. |
|---|---|---|
| Robert Nelson, A. B. | York | Son of Gen. Nelson. Chancellor. |
| Mann Page, A. B. | Mansfield, Spotsyl. | Son of Mann Page. |
| Thos. Whitefield, A. B. | Eastern Shore. | |
| Stewart Bankhead. | Westmoreland. | |
| George Banks. | Stafford. | |
| Norborne Beale. | Williamsburg. | |
| Wm. Brockenborough. | Tappahannock | Judge Court of Appeals. |
| William A. Burwell. | Franklin. | Member of Congress. |
| Bernard M. Carter. | Shirley. | Son of Charles Carter. |
| Robert S. Chew. | Fredericksburg. | |
| John H. Cocke. | Surry. | General in war of 1812. |
| Isaac Cole. | Halifax. | |
| Isaac H. Cole. | | |
| J. M. Tomlin. | Hanover. | |
| John Walker Fontaine. | | |
| Robert Gibson. | Prince Edward. | |
| Peachy R. Gilmer. | Albemarle. | |
| Lewis Harvie. | Richmond. | |
| Baily Johnson. | Hanover. | |
| Boswell Johnson. | Louisa. | |
| Arthur Lee. | Norfolk. | |
| William Lewis. | Fredericksburg. | |
| John Tayloe Lomax. | Caroline. | Judge of District Court. |
| Robert Michie. | Hanover. | |
| Garret H. Minor. | Louisa. | |
| Horatio Gates Moody. | Williamsburg. | |
| Thomas Nelson. | Hanover. | |
| William Nelson. | York. | |
| William D. Nevison. | Norfolk. | |
| William Nimmo. | " | |
| John C. Pryor. | Gloucester. | |
| Peyton Randolph. | Richmond | Son of Edmund Randolph. |
| Armistead Selden. | Henrico. | |
| John B. Seawell. | Gloucester. | |
| Thomas G. Smith. | King and Queen. | |
| Edw'd Carter Stanard. | Spotsylvania. | |
| Robert Stannard. | " | Judge Court of Appeals. |
| George W. Tenant. | Caroline. | |
| Richard Turner. | King George. | |
| George Turner. | " | |
| Joseph Watson. | Louisa. | |

### 1799.

| | | |
|---|---|---|
| H. St. Geo. Tucker, A. B. | Williamsburg. | Son of Judge St. George Tucker. Chancellor—Judge of Court of Appeals. |
| John Boyer. | Augusta | Son of Mich. Boyer. |

| NAMES. | RESIDENCES. | REMARKS. |

John Edmunds..............Sussex.
John H. Smith..............King and Queen.
David Trimble..............Kentucky.

## 1800.

William Archer..............Powhatan.
William Brent.................   Chargé at Buenos Ayres.
John M. Conway.
George Carter.
George Goosley..............York.
John Augustine Smith...King and Queen.......President of William and Mary College.
James Taylor.

## 1795 TO 1800.

William Armistead........Nottoway.
William Aylett..............King William.
George M. Bibb..............Prince Edward..........United States Senator, Chancellor of Kentucky, and Secretary of the Treasury United States.
Samuel Stewart Griffin...Williamsburg...........Son of Judge Cyrus Griffin.
James Johnson..............Isle of Wight...........Member of Congress.
Thomas L. Lomax..........Caroline.
Charles K. Mallory........Elizabeth City.
William Munford..........Richmond.
Tully Robinson...............Accomac.

NOTE.—Charles Carter, Champ Carter, Edward Carter, Robert Carter, John Carter, Hill Carter, and Landon Carter, sons of the second Edward Carter, of Blenheim, and grandsons of John, of Corotoman, were educated at the College of William and Mary.

## 1801.

Nicholas Cabell..............Amherst.................Son of Col. Nicholas Cabell.
Francis Carr..................Albemarle..............Son of Dabney Carr.
Williams Carter............Shirley..................Son of Charles Carter.
James Powell Cocke......Amelia.
Grandison Field............Mecklenburg.
William Foushee..........Richmond.
Miles King...................Norfolk.
Roger Jones..................Westmoreland.........Adjt. Gen'l United States Army.
Thos. Ap Catesby Jones..      "         .........Commodore United States Navy.
Richard H. Lee..............Norfolk.
William Lindsay............      "         .........Col. United States Army.
Richard Randolph.........Curls, Henrico.........Son of David Meade Randolph.
Griffin Stith..................Brunswick..............Judge in District Court.
Joseph Prentiss............Williamsburg.
Peter Randolph.............Nottoway..............Judge in State Court.

| NAMES. | RESIDENCES. | REMARKS. |
|---|---|---|
| N. Beverly Tucker | Williamsburg | Son of Judge St. George Tucker. United States Judge. Prof. at William and Mary College. |

## 1802.

| | | |
|---|---|---|
| Chapman Johnson, A. B. | Louisia. | Member of Convention of 1829. |
| Bnj. Watkins Leigh, A. B. | Chesterfield | Son of Rev. Wm. Leigh. United States Senator. |
| John Dandridge | Williamsburg. | |
| James B. Gilmer | Albemarle. | |
| Mann P. Lomax | Caroline. | |
| Thomas Preston | Montgomery. | |
| Ballard Smith | Greenbrier | Member of Congress. |
| John Yates | Jefferson. | |

## 1803.

| | | |
|---|---|---|
| William O. Allen | James City. | |
| Edward Ambler | Jamestown. | |
| Samuel B. Archer | Norfolk. | |
| J. M. Bannister | Williamsburg. | |
| William Barrett | James City. | |
| William T. Barry | Kentucky | Postmaster General. |
| John T. Bowdon | Northampton. | |
| Joseph C. Breckinridge. | | |
| William Brown | James City | Chancellor, and Judge in State Court. |
| Wilson Jefferson Cary | | Son of Wilson Cary. |
| Miles Cary | | " " |
| William Chapman | Prince William. | |
| S. Coke | Williamsburg. | |
| Tucker Coles | Albemarle. | |
| Thomas Croly. | | |
| Henry A. Dearborn | Massachusetts | Son of Gen'l Dearborn. Secretary of War. |
| John Douglass | New Kent. | |
| William P. Edrington. | | |
| A. B. Hooe | King George. | |
| William C. Holt | Norfolk | Speaker of Senate. |
| John W. Jones | Chesterfield | Speaker House Representatives. |
| William Johnson | Hanover. | |
| A. W. C. Logan | Kentucky. | |
| John Madison | Williamsburg | Son of Rt. Rev. Bishop Madison. |
| W. T. T. Mason | Fairfax. | |
| Richard A. Maupin | Williamsburg. | |
| Francis T. Maury | Spotsylvania. | |
| Joseph H. Mayo. | | |
| Peter Mayo | Richmond. | |

## CATALOGUE OF ALUMNI.

| NAMES. | RESIDENCES. | REMARKS. |
|---|---|---|
| Robert Mayo | Powhatan. | |
| William Minitree | James City. | |
| George Newton | Norfolk. | Son of Thomas Newton. |
| Robert Nicholas. | | |
| George D. Nicholson | York | Son of Dr. Robert Nicholson. |
| Edmund Penn | Amherst. | |
| B. Williams Payor | Charles City | Captain in war of 1812. |
| Daniel Scott. | | |
| John Shelton. | | |
| Thomas Tabb | Amelia. | |
| John Yelverton Tabb | " | |
| Allen Taylor | Botetourt | Judge in State Court. |
| William Waller | Williamsburg | Son of Benj. C. Waller. |
| George Watson | Louisa. | |
| Samuel Wyatt | | Son of Col. John Wyatt. |

## 1800 TO 1803.

| | | |
|---|---|---|
| Philip P. Barbour | Orange | Speaker of House of Representatives, and Judge S. Court U. S. |
| William C. Hett. | | |
| William Osborne Sprigg | Maryland. | |
| Henry E. Watkins | Prince Edward. | |
| Abraham Venable | | Son of Richard N. Venable. |
| Nathaniel Venable. | | |

## 1804.

| | | |
|---|---|---|
| Richard C. Anderson | Kentucky | First Minister to Colombia, South America. |
| B. Archer | Powhatan | Son of P. F. Archer. |
| Richard C. Archer | " | Secretary of War, Texas. |
| Nathaniel Balson. | | |
| John Bentley | " | |
| George Blow | Portsmouth. | |
| Samuel P. Bolling. | | |
| George Booker | Hampton. | |
| Peter Brown | James City. | |
| Charles Carter | Corotman | Son of Charles Carter. |
| Robert Cocke | Surry. | |
| John Cornick | Princess Anne. | |
| Benja. Crowninshield | Boston | Son of Secretary of Navy. |
| Samuel Davis. | | |
| John Demoville | Charles City. | |
| G. J. Devenish. | | |
| Peyton Doswell. | | |
| William Goodwyn | Dinwiddie. | |
| Archibald Hackett. | | |

CATALOGUE OF ALUMNI. 105

| NAMES. | RESIDENCES. | REMARKS. |
|---|---|---|
| John Hayes | Richmond. | |
| J. Smith Hollins | Baltimore. | Mayor of Baltimore. |
| William S. Hollins | " | |
| J. J. Howell. | | |
| Edward J. Johnson. | | |
| Catesby Jones | Westmoreland. | |
| Joseph Jones | Petersburg. | |
| Samuel Jones. | | |
| Antony Lawson | James City. | |
| William Leigh | Chesterfield. | Son of Rev. W. Leigh. Judge in State Court. |
| Robert Mallory | Hampton. | |
| Peter Minor. | | |
| John G. Moseby | Powhatan | Son of Col. Wade Moseby. |
| Henry Page | Cumberland | Son of Carter Page. |
| Thomas Pearson. | | |
| William Radford | Richmond. | |
| William Ragland | Louisa. | |
| William H. Roane | Hanover | United States Senator. |
| John Robertson | Richmond | Judge in State Court. |
| Winfield Scott | Dinwiddie | Lieut Gen. United States Army. |
| Joseph Selden | Henrico | Major United States Army, and Judge in Missouri. |
| Charles H. Smith | Norfolk | Son of Lar. Smith. Paymaster United States Army. |
| J. Speed Smith | Baltimore | Son of Gen'l Sam. Smith. |
| Peter F. Smith | Chesterfield. | |
| John S. Stiles | Baltimore. | |
| G. W. T. Wright | Maryland. | Son of Governor Wright. |
| Watt H. Tyler | Charles City. | Son of Governor Tyler. |

## 1805.

| | | |
|---|---|---|
| Arthur Smith, A. B. | Isle of Wight. | |
| Albert Allmand | Norfolk. | |
| Richard Becke. | | |
| Thomas Boswell | Petersburg. | |
| Robert Butler | Isle of Wight. | |
| Reverdy Cooke. | | |
| Mordecai Cookey | Norfolk. | |
| John J. Crittenden | Kentucky | Governor of Kentucky and Senator and Attorney General U. S. |
| William Macklin. | | |
| John Marks | Prince George. | |
| J. Parkinson. | | |
| Edward Randolph | Charles City. | |
| Benjamin Watkins | New Kent. | |
| Delaware West | King William. | |

8

## 1806.

| NAMES. | RESIDENCES. | REMARKS. |
|---|---|---|
| John T. Barraud, A. B... | Norfolk. | |
| Benj. Harrison, A. B..... | Berkeley | Son of Benjamin Harrison. |
| Barthol. D. Henley, A. B.. | James City. | |
| Benjamin Pollard, A. B.. | Norfolk. | |
| William S. Archer......... | Amelia............ | United States Senator. |
| Linn Banks................. | Rappahannock | Member of Congress. |
| Richard Batte.............. | Prince George. | |
| Henry A. Claiborne....... | King William. | |
| John Cooke. | | |
| William Crump............ | Powhatan | United States Minister to Chilli. |
| William F. Mercer........ | Norfolk. | |
| William Giles.............. | Henrico. | |
| Stephen Glasscock........ | Fauquier. | |
| John Godall................ | James City. | |
| William Harrison. | | |
| John M. Jeffries........... | King & Queen | State's Attorney. |
| William H. Jackson. | | |
| John F. May................ | Petersburg | Judge in State Court. |
| Hodijah Meade............. | Amelia........... | Son of Gen'l E. Meade. |
| William T. Nevison....... | Norfolk. | |
| Nathaniel Nelson.......... | Malvern Hills, Hen.. | Son of Robert Nelson. |
| John Page................... | Rosewell......... | Son of Governor Page. |
| Francis Ridley............. | Southampton. | |
| John Roane................. | Dinwiddie. | |
| Charles Russell............ | Warwick. | |
| Linneus Smith............. | Goochland. | |
| William Stiles............. | Baltimore. | |
| Henry W. Tucker.......... | Bermuda......... | Brother of George Tucker. |
| John Tyler.................. | Charles City | Son of Governor Tyler, and second Governor of the name. President of the United States. |
| J. B. Wilkinson............ | | Son of Gen'l Wilkinson, United States Army. |

## 1807.

James Boisseau, A. B.... Chesterfield.
William Crawford, A. B.
Ed'd O. Goodwyn, A. B.. Dinwiddie.
Brook Hill, A. B............ King & Queen.
Armis'd T. Mason, A. B. Loudoun ................ United States Senator.
John B. Patterson, A. B.. Mathews.
John D. Royall, A. B.... Nottoway.
Briscoe G. Baldwin........ Augusta ............... Judge Court of Appeals.
James Ball.

CATALOGUE OF ALUMNI. 107

| NAMES. | RESIDENCES. | REMARKS. |
|---|---|---|
| Edward Coles | Albemarle | Son of John Coles. Governor of some Territory. |
| Benjamin Dabney | Gloucester. | |
| William Edmonds | Dinwiddie. | |
| John Gibson | Prince William | State Senator. |
| Henry T. Harris | Albemarle. | |
| J. Hawkins | Kentucky | Succeeded Clay in Congress. |
| Thomas Hayes. | | |
| Joseph J. Hill | Dinwiddie. | |
| Thomas Hodges | Norfolk | Major United States Army. |
| John O. McAlister | Winchester. | |
| George McCarty | Loudoun. | |
| John Madison | Orange | Son of Gen'l William Madison. |
| John W. Page | Hanover | Son of Robert W. Page, Broad Neck. |
| Andrew Reid | Livington. | Son of Andrew Reid. |
| John Speed | Mecklenburg. | |
| William Smith. | | |
| William Stuart. | | |
| G. LaFayette Washington | Valley of Virginia. | |
| Charles Washington. | | |
| John Wood. | | |

## 1808.

| | | |
|---|---|---|
| Fred'k Campbell, A. B. | Westmoreland. | |
| George Loyall, A. B. | Norfolk. | Member of Congress. |
| John T. Mason, A. B. | Loudoun. | |
| Robert Wash, L. B. | Kentucky | Judge in Missouri. |
| Robert Yeatman, A. B. | Mathews. | |
| R. H. Bailey | Sussex. | |
| David Beaseley | Petersburg. | |
| Lewis Berkeley | Loudoun. | |
| John Tayloe Burwell | Clarke | Son of Col. Nathaniel Burwell. |
| Abner Calloway | Bedford. | |
| Wm. Fitzhugh Carter | Shirley | Son of Charles Carter. |
| Lewis Carr | Albemarle. | |
| Richard Cary | Gloucester. | |
| William B. Cowan | Lunenburg. | |
| Peter Graves | Caroline. | |
| George Hord. | | |
| Jesse Hughes | Powhatan | Son of David Hughes. |
| Henry Lee | Stratford, Westm. | Son of Gen'l H. Lee and Major United States Army. |
| Thomas T. Mayo. | | |
| Francis Mettauer | Prince Edward. | |
| Augustine Monroe | | Nephew of President Monroe. |
| J. G. Mosby | Powhatan. | |

## CATALOGUE OF ALUMNI.

| NAMES. | RESIDENCES. | REMARKS. |
|---|---|---|
| Robert D. Murchie | Chesterfield. | |
| Samuel Patterson | Mathews. | |
| John L. Peyton | Winchester. | |
| Alexander Pope. | | |
| John C. Ragland. | | |
| | | |
| Nathaniel Smith | Kentucky. | |
| Peyton Smith. | | |
| Thomas O. Taylor. | | |
| William B. Tomlin | King William. | |
| Charles Washington | Westmoreland. | |

### 1809.

| | | |
|---|---|---|
| Gerard Brandon, A. B. | Manchester. | |
| John Croghan, A. B. | Kentucky. | |
| John Gaines, A. B. | King and Queen. | |
| Samuel Myers, A. B. | Norfolk. | |
| Charles Todd, A. B. | Kentucky. | United States Minister to Russia. |
| Alfred Alston | South Carolina. | |
| Robert Andrews | Williamsburg. | Son of Rev. Robert Andrews. |
| John S. Barbour | Culpeper. | Member of Congress. |
| Daniel Cary Barraud | Norfolk. | |
| Wilson Bond. | | |
| Aaron Booker | Amelia. | |
| Richard Booker | Chesterfield. | |
| Jesse Cole | Williamsburg. | Son of Jesse Cole. |
| Thomas T. Crittenden | Kentucky. | |
| Gabriel Galt | Norfolk. | |
| Jacquelin B. Harvie | Richmond | Son of John Harvie. |
| Andrew H. Holmes | Winchester | Killed in war of 1812. |
| Charles S. Henry. | | |
| William Irvine | Chesterfield. | |
| William W. Linton | Prince William. | |
| Littlebury Mosby | Powhatan. | |
| Thomas Nelson | York. | |
| William Old | Powhatan | State Senator. |
| John Page | | Son of Robert Page. |
| William C. Rives | Albemarle. | United States Senator and Minister to France. |
| B. D. Russell | Warwick. | |
| William Somerville | Maryland. | |
| Augustine Smith | | Colonel in United States Army. |
| Robert P. Waller | Williamsburg | Son of Benjamin C. Waller. |

### 1810.

| | | |
|---|---|---|
| Dabney Browne, A. B. | James City | Professor in William and Mary College. Son of J. Browne. |

## CATALOGUE OF ALUMNI. 109

| NAMES. | RESIDENCES. | REMARKS. |
|---|---|---|
| Ferd. S. Campbell, A. B. | Westmoreland | Professor in William and Mary. |
| George Croghan, A. B. | Kentucky | Colonel in United States Army, defender of Fort Sandusky, afterwards Adjutant General United States Army. |
| Francis W. Gilmer, A. B. | Albemarle. | |
| Inman Horner, A. B. | Fauquier. | |
| William B. Page, L. B. | Gloucester | Son of Governor Page. |
| William W. Taylor, A. B. | | Son of John Taylor. |
| J. Bowen. | | |
| Carter Braxton | Chericoke, K. Wm. | Son of George Braxton. |
| Warren Christian | Charles City. | |
| Walker Fontaine | Hanover. | |
| John Harrison | Charles City. | |
| J. M. Hite. | | |
| Charles Hoge. | | |
| Robert Hunter. | | |
| Philip Jones. | | |
| John W. King | Dinwiddie. | |
| William Lamb | James City. | |
| Miles Macon | New Kent. | |
| Alfred Madison | Orange. | |
| John Maury | Albemarle. | |
| William Meriwether | " | |
| William Moody | Williamsburg. | |
| William B. Page | Frederick | Son of John Page. |
| Walker Y. Page | Broadneck, Han. | Son of Robert Page. |
| Christopher Roane | Charles City. | |
| Edmund Ruffin | Prince George | Son of Ed. Ruffin. |
| Charles Sewell | Gloucester. | |
| Overton Sewell | " | |
| Robert G. Scott | Georgia. | |
| Richard Stoddert | Maryland | Son of Benjamin Stoddert, the first Secretary of the Navy. |
| G. W. Stribling | Staunton. | |
| George Vashaw | Goochland. | |
| M. S. Watkins | Chesterfield. | |
| James Wills. | | |

## 1811.

| | | |
|---|---|---|
| George Avery, L. B. | Sussex. | |
| Benjamin Jones, L. B. | Nottoway. | |
| Robt. McCandlish, L. B. | James City. | |
| William Greenhill, L. B. | Nottoway. | |
| Richard Povall, L. B. | Powhatan. | |
| Francis McAuley, A. B. | York. | |
| John Nelson, A. B. | Baltimore | Minister to Naples and Attorney General United States. |

## CATALOGUE OF ALUMNI.

| NAMES. | RESIDENCES. | REMARKS. |

Richard Pollard, L. B...Alta Vista, Albe.
J. Augustine Smith,L. B.King & Queen.
H. L. Wilson, A. B.
Thomas Ambler...............Jamestown.
John Andrews................Williamsburg.
William Boswell...............Matthews.
James Bowdoin...............Northampton.
William Burwell...............Carter's Hall, Clk.....Son of N. Burwell.
Colin Clarke......................Powhatan.
John Cocke.......................Surry.
John Cutler.......................North Carolina.
Temple Demoville.............Charles City.
Lewis Dunn......................Warwick.
Richard Field...................Mecklenburg.
Theophilus Field..............     "
John Field........................     "
William H. Fitzhugh.....Ravensworth, Fair....Member of Convention of 1829. Son of W. Fitzhugh.
James Gilliam..................Petersburg................Son of Dr. Gilliam.
C. H. Harrison................Clifton, Cumberl'd...Son of R. Harrison.
R. B. Hunter...................King George.
Jesse Irvine.
George Mayre.................Fredericksburg.
William Mason................Fairfax.
Edward Mosby..............Powhatan.
Gregory Page..................Gloucester.................Son of Governor Page.
Robert E. Randolph......Eastern View, Fau...Son of Col. R. Randolph.
J. F. Robinson.
Thomas Tabb..................Amelia.
William C. Taylor.
Joseph Watkins..............Dover, Goochland.....Son of J. Watkins.
George Wyche................Sussex.

## 1812-13.

James S. Gilliam, A. B..Petersburg.
Carter Harrison, A. B...Maycox, Pr. Geo......Son of C. B. Harrison.
Wade Mosby, A. B........Powhatan.
Thos. G. Peachy, A. B...Williamsburg.
James Prentiss, A. B.....Petersburg.
Edward Terry, A. B.....Mecklenburg.
William B. Tyler, A. B..Prince William.........Son of William Tyler, Judge State Court.
Jacob Blake....................Charles City.
William Boswell.............Hanover.
Archibald M. Harrison...Clifton, Cumberl'd.
Nathaniel Miller............Goochland.
Wilson Nicholas.

CATALOGUE OF ALUNNI. 111

NAMES. RESIDENCES. REMARKS.

Samuel Pest.
Lewis Rogers............……Albemarle.
Willis B. Vick…………Princess Anne.
William A. Winston……Hanover.

## 1813-14.

Edward Boisseau, A. B..Chesterfield.
William Brodnax, A. B..Brunswick.
James Brown, A. B.......
Rob. T. Thompson, A.B..
Lewis C. Tyler, A. B.....Williamsburg...........Son of Chancellor Samuel Tyler.
Archibald Atkinson.......Isle of Wight...........Member of Congress.
George Booth...............Gloucester.
Hill Carter....................Shirley....................Son of Robert Carter.
William Christian.........Charles City.
John Coke....................Williamsburg.
John Dandridge…………Prince George.
Powhatan Ellis ………….Amherst………..……...United States Senator and Minister to Mexico.
Patrick Galt..................Williamsburg...........Col. in United States Army.
Richard Galt………....….. "
Thomas Henderson........ " Son of J. Henderson.
William Henley………..... "
Edward Jones.
Merrit Jordan.................Isle of Wight.
William H. Logan.
Howard McCarty..........Loudoun.
John M. McCarty.......... "
Wm. Mason McCarty..... "
John Page.....................Shelly, Gloucester.......Son of Mann Page.
Robert Page................. " ....... " "
William S. Peachy........Williamsburg.
Samuel Pete.
Henry Shield.................Yorktown.
Machen Seawell............Gloucester.
.Robert Thompson.........Norfolk.
William Thornton.........Gloucester.
James Wilson................Isle of Wight.

## 1814-15.

Eliezar Black, A. B.
Richard Coke, A. B......Williamsburg.............Member of Congress.
J. K.Hornsborough, A.B. "
Howard Shield, A. B.....Yorktown.
John Anderson..............Chesterfield.

## CATALOGUE OF ALUMNI.

| NAMES. | DATE OF APPOINTMENT. | REMARKS. |
|---|---|---|
| Fontaine Briggs | Gloucester. | |
| Lloyd Briggs | " | |
| John Bryan | York. | |
| Dandridge Claiborne | King William. | |
| William Dew | King & Queen. | |
| George Mason. | | |
| Jackson Morton | Culpeper | U. S. Senator from Florida. |
| Thomas Montgomery. | | |
| William Randolph. | | |
| George Robinson | Amelia. | |
| James Semple | Williamsburg | Son of Judge Semple. |
| John Semple | " | " " |

### 1815–16.

| | | |
|---|---|---|
| Edward Cabell | Lynchburg | Son of George Cabell. |
| William Finch | Charles City. | |
| Cary S. Jones. | | |
| Warner Lewis. | | |
| Collier Minge | Charles City | Son of John Minge. |
| John Minge | " | " " |
| Mann Page. | | |
| Pryor Richardson | James City. | |
| Powhatan Roberts | Richmond. | |
| William Van Bibber | Mathews. | |

### 1816–17.

| | | |
|---|---|---|
| Stephen Archer | Amelia. | |
| William Armistead | New Kent | United States Marshall. |
| William Baskerville | Mecklenburg. | |
| Linneus Bolling | Powhatan. | |
| Junius Burk | Petersburg | Son of Historian. |
| John Burwell. | | |
| Nicholas C. Cabell | Amherst. | |
| Landon R. Cabell | " | |
| P. H. Cabell | " | |
| John B. Christian | New Kent | Judge in State Court. |
| Edward Cocke. | | |
| John Coleman. | | |
| John Coles. | | |
| Augustine Dabney | Gloucester. | |
| Robert Douthat | Richmond City. | |
| Francis Eggleston. | | |
| Alexander Fernando. | | |
| Alexander Fleet | King & Queen. | |
| Christopher Fleet. | ' | |

## CATALOGUE OF ALUMNI. 113

| NAMES. | RESIDENCES. | REMARKS. |
|---|---|---|
| Charles Goodwyn | Dinwiddie. | |
| Robert Greenhow | Williamsburg. | |
| Ezra Halsted. | | |
| Warner Jones | Gloucester. | |
| William Jones | " | |
| James Jordan. | | |
| John Kerr. | | |
| E. H. Lundy | Sussex. | |
| James Lyle | Chesterfield. | |
| William H. Macfarland | Lunenburg | President Farmers Bank of Va. |
| John G. Miller | Goochland. | |
| Mann P. Nelson | Gloucester. | |
| Washington Nelson | York | Son of Th. Nelson. |
| Robert Carter Nicholas | Richmond city. | |
| Robert Pickett | " | |
| John H. Pleasants | Goochland | Editor of Richmond Whig. Son of Governor Pleasants. |
| John Plunkett | Williamsburg. | |
| John Prentiss | " | |
| Robert Quarles. | | |
| William Riddick | Suffolk. | |
| Henry Rives | Nelson | Son of Robert Rives. |
| Robert Rives | " | " " |
| Moncure Robinson | Richmond city. | |
| William E. B. Ruffin | Prince George. | |
| George W. Smith. | | |
| Mutins Spark. | | |
| Thomas L. Stewart. | | |
| Joshua Storrs | Henrico. | |
| Edward Stratton | Eastern Shore. | |
| John N. Stratton | " | |
| Daniel Turner | Greensville. | |
| John Urquhart | Southampton. | |
| Bobert Ware | Richmond county. | |
| Willis H. Woodley | Southampton. | |

## 1817–18.

| | | |
|---|---|---|
| John Ambler | Jamestown | Son of John Ambler. |
| Richard Archer | Amelia. | |
| John Boyken | Surry. | |
| Cary Breckinridge | Botetourt | Son of Hon. Jas. Breckinridge. |
| Alexander Brodnax | Brunswick. | |
| Paul Carrington | Halifax | Son of Gen. G. Carrington. |
| J. Gregory Claiborne. | | |
| J. B. Clopton | New Kent | Judge in State Court. Son Hon. John Clopton. |
| Robert L. Crawford. | | |

9

## CATALOGUE OF ALUMNI.

| NAMES. | RESIDENCES. | REMARKS. |
|---|---|---|
| George C. Dromgoole | Brunswick | Member of Congress. |
| Carter H. Edloe | Prince George | Son of John Edloe. |
| William O. Goode | Mecklenburg | Member of Congress. |
| Peterson Goodwyn | Dinwiddie. | |
| Carter C. Harrison | Sussex. | |
| Alexander Jones | Gloucester. | |
| John D. Leland. | | |
| James Lyons | Richmond city | Son of Dr. James Lyons. |
| James McLaurine | New Kent. | |
| Thomas Mann | King and Queen. | |
| George Morton | Culpeper. | |
| Richard H. Mosby | Powhatan. | |
| Thomas F. Nelson | Clarke | Son of Philip Nelson. |
| H. N. Pendleton | Caroline | Son of E. Pendleton. |
| George S. Philips. | | |
| Nathaniel Piggott | James City. | |
| T. C. Quinlam. | | |
| David Meade Randolph | Curls, Henrico | Son of D. M. Randolph. |
| Newman Roane | King William. | |
| William Sheppard | Richmond. | |
| John R. Steed | Norfolk. | |
| Henley Taylor | James City. | |
| Robert E. Taylor. | | |
| Richard Turner | King George. | |
| S. W. Washington. | | |
| W. T. Washington. | | |
| J. M. White. | | |
| H. Willis. | | |

## 1818-19.

Archibald Taylor, A. B..Norfolk.
John Mason, L. B.
William B. Allison.........Petersburg.................Son of John Allison.
Thomas F. Barnes.
William E. Boisseau......Chesterfield.
Thomas Botts.
Philip A. Branham.
Abraham J. Cabell.........Amherst ................Son of Judge Cabell.
Charles J. Cabell..........                        Son of Joseph Cabell.
Edward A. Cabell..........                        Son of Col. William Cabell.
Robert H. Cabell...........                        Son of Landon Cabell.
Cassius Carter................Prince William.........Son of Ed. Carter.
John C. Carter..............Blenheim, Albm.......Son of Robert Carter.
Robert Copeland.
Gawin L. Corbin...........York.......................Son of Gawin L. Corbin.
Oliver M. Fowle............Alexandria.
Minor Gibson.

CATALOGUE OF ALUMNI.  115

| NAMES. | RESIDENCES. | REMARKS. |

Robert Gilliam............ ......Petersburg.
William H. Glasscock.....Fauquier.
Archibald Govan.. .........Hanover.
Atcheson Gray.
Peter Guerrant.
George Hankins....... .......James City.
Robert C. Harrison.
Tipton B. Harrison.
William Hutnall.
William B. Irby............ ...Mecklenburg............ ...Son of William Irby.
Montfort Jones.
Edward Mallory.
James Mann.. ...............King & Queen.
William Marshall.
William M. Maxwell.
Jeremiah Morton............Culpeper . ............ ......Member of Congress.
Antony Pennington.
George Perkinson.........Amelia.
Thomas J. Perkinson..... "
William P. Pierce.........James City.
Albert Read ............ .......Charlotte.
Samuel T. Sawyer.........North Carolina........Member of Congress.
Daniel Slaughter. ..........Culpeper.. ............ .......State Senator.
James M. Smith.
James Southgate.
Pendleton Strother........Orange.. ............ .........Son of John Strother.
Samuel Williamson.
William Winston...........Hanover.
John Woolfolk.. ............Caroline.

## 1819-20.

Otway B. Barraud, A. B..Norfolk............ ..........Son of Dr. P. Barraud.
George W. Bassett .......Hanover............ ...........Son of John Bassett.
Peter F. Boisseau ...▲.....Amelia.
James Brown.
Richard K. Cralle.........Lunenburg.
Francis Gildark.
Ralph Graves............ .....James City.
Edmund Harrison.........Charles City.
Thomas King.
William Langhorne.......King William.
Peter Lyons.. ............ ......Hanover.
John Magill......... ..........Frederick.
Nathaniel Magill.
James M. Mason ...........Winchester ............ ......U. S. Senator.  Son of General
                                                                    Mason, of Georgetown, D. C.

CATALOGUE OF ALUMNI.

NAMES. RESIDENCES. REMARKS.

James Murdaugh..........Nansemond.
John Murdaugh.:..........      "
John B. Peachy............Williamsburg.
Richard G. Pegram........Brunswick.
Philip Grymes Randolph.Ben Lom'd, Gooch'd..Son of A. C. Randolph.
George Rives...................Nelson...................Son of Robert Rives.
Douglas Wilkins.

## 1820–21.

Thomas R. Dew, A. B...King & Queen..........President of William and Mary College.
Benjamin Stewart, A. B.
Orris A. Brown .............James City.
Samuel Bockius...............Richmond.
Robert Carver.
Philip Claiborne..............King William............Son of Dr. Claiborne.
Randolph Corbin.........:...King's Creek, York...Son of Gawin L. Corbin.
John A. Dabney ..........Gloucester.
John S. Davidson..........Frederick.
John A. G. Davis..........King & Queen..........Professor of Law at the University of Virginia.
Thomas Hawes.
William Mason...............Brunswick.
William Nelson .............York............................Son of William Nelson.
Wyndham Robertson.....Richmond....................Governor of Virginia. Son of W. Robertson.
James W. Rogers .........Williamsburg ............Professor. Son of Professor P. K. Rogers.
William B. Rogers..........       "        ............Professor in William and Mary and University of Virginia. Son of Prof. P. K. Rogers.
John N. Scott.
Robert M. Tidball.

## 1821–22.

Thos. E. Burfort, A. B...Chesterfield...............District Attorney United States. Son of Lawson Burfort, State Treasurer.
Richmond T. Lacy, A. B..New Kent.
Frederick Marx, A. B....Richmond.................Son of Joseph Marx. Distinguished physician.
R. Barnes.
Peter P. Batte...............Prince George.
John J. Chew................Fredericksburg.
William Cocke..............Powhatan.
John Douglas................New Kent.
John N. Faulcon...........Surry.
J. M. Harrell................Nansemond.
George E. Hines.

## CATALOGUE OF ALUMNI. 117

| NAMES. | RESIDENCES. | REMARKS. |

Lunsford Lomax.
George W. McCandlish..Williamsburg.
Henry W. Moncure........Richmond ...............Son of William Moncure.
John O. Trueheart............ "
Daniel G. Tucker...........Winchester..............Son of George Tucker. United
                                                                States Congress from Ohio.
John J. Van Meter........Hardy county.
Littleton T. Waller........Williamsburg...........Son of John Walker Waller.
Thomas P. Watkins......Goochland.

### 1822–23.

William S. Scott, A. B.
Alex. W. Tennant, A. B..King George.
James Watson, A. B......Louisa.
Joseph D. White, L. B...             Governor of Florida and Member
                                            of Congress.

Richard Baylor..............Essex..
Alexander Bryant.........Prince George.
Richard Byrd................Isle of Wight.
John Cargill..................Sussex.
Robert M. Garrett.........Williamsburg.
John M. Hankins..........James City.
John P. Harrison..........Richmond.
Samuel Hawkins...........Maryland.
Lewis Holliday.............Louisa.
H. W. Johnson.
William H. Moncure......Stafford.....................Judge of Court of Appeals.
Robert Page.................Page Brook, Clark...Son of John Page.
Levin M. Powell...........Loudoun.
Albert H. Prosser.........Henrico ....................Son of Thomas Prosser.
Edwin Redd.
William H. Roy............Mathews.
Charles Selden.............Powhatan.
John A. Selden.............Henrico.....................Son of Miles Selden.
Thomas J. Smith.
Thomas Walker.........🌑.....Charles City.
Conway Whittle...........Norfolk.
Thomas H. Wilcox........Charles City.
Gabriel G. Williamson...Norfolk ...................Son of Thomas Williamson.

### 1823*–24.

Elias T. Bartle, A. B.....Maryland.
Richard Baylor, A. B.....Essex.
John Morris, A. B.........Louisa.

---

*The number of students attending the College from the year 1786 to the year 1823 taken from the book of matriculation (since lost) by the late Robt. McCandlish, Rector of the College—1,645—an average of about 45 students each year.

## CATALOGUE OF ALUMNI.

| NAMES. | RESIDENCES. | REMARKS. |
|---|---|---|

Robert Saunders, A. B...Williamsburg...........Son of Robert Saunders.
Otway B. Barraud, L. B..Norfolk.
Benj. F. Dabney, L. B...King & Queen.
George Wythe Munford,
    L. B.........................Richmond ................Secretary of the Commonwealth.
                                                                   Son of William Munford.
Willoughby Newton,L.B.Westmoreland.........Member of Congress.
C. J. D. Pryor, A. B. &
    L. B..........................Hampton.
Orville Allen..................James City.
H. J. Banks.
James Beale..................Richmond .................Distinguished physician.
George Booker...............Hampton.
Beverly B. Brown..........James City.
Thomas H. Burwell........Carter's Hall, Cl'k...Son of Col. N. Burwell.
Theophilus Field............Mecklenburg.
John George...................Henrico.
Joshua H. Harrell..........Nansemond.
Alexander Knox.............Mecklenburg.
Alexander J. Marshall...Fauquier.
James Marshall..............    "
Lucian Minor.................Hanover....................Prof. of Law at William and
                                                                Mary College.
Henry Myers..................Richmond.
R. Ryland Randolph......Culpeper..................Son of Bret Randolph.
William Simkins...........Eastern Shore.
Cornelius C. Taylor.......Norfolk....................Son of Richard Taylor.

## 1824-25.

Thomas R. Dew, A. M...              President of College of William
                                                          and Mary.
John H. Cocke, A. B......Fluvanna................Son of Gen. J. H. Cocke.
Philip St. Geo. Ambler...Fauquier.................Son of Col. John Ambler.
Richard Anderson.........Chesterfield.
Thomas Barclay.
J. W. Brockenborough...Hanover..................Son of Judge W. Brockenbo-
                                                             rough. United States Judge.
Wilson M. Cary.............Fluvanna & Balt......Son of Wilson Jefferson Cary.
J. W. C. Catlett.............Gloucester.
Samuel Garland............Amherst.
William R. Hackley.
John Hall.
William Overton...........Hanover.
D. F. Randolph.
George A. Smith.
Gerard B. Stewart.........King George.

CATALOGUE OF ALUMNI. 119

| NAMES. | RESIDENCES. | REMARKS. |

Henry Tazewell............Norfolk...................Son of Littleton W. Tazewell.
John S. Wilkins..............Lunenburg.

## 1825-26.

Wm. H. Garland, A. B...Amherst ...............Son of Samuel Garland.
Beverly B. Brown, L. B.
Richmond T. Lacy, L. B.
C. Anthony........................Campbell.
John Bird............................Williamsburg.
William B. Boyd...............King and Queen.
J. Powell Byrd..................Gloucester.
William Christian.
James S. French...............Petersburg.
Alexander Price................Richmond.
William Radcliffe..............Williamsburg.
Augustine Robbins...........Gloucester.
Baylor Semple..................Fredericksburg.
Thomas Smith....................Williamsburg.
John Speed.........................Amherst.
Alexander H. H. Stuart...Augusta.....................U. S. Secretary of the Interior.
John G. Williamson........Norfolk ....................Son of Th. Williamson.
Edward Wilkinson...........Charles City.

## 1826-27.

Walker Hawes, A. B.
George C. Ball.
A. Blair.
Spotswood Christian......Charles City.
Richard C. Crump............New Kent.
William R. C. Douglas...     "
John M. Galt.....................Portsmouth.
James P. Henderson........Williamsburg.
James M. Jeffries..............King and Queen.
George Southall...............Yorktown ............... Son of Peyton Southall.
George W. Syme..............Petersburg................Son of Andrew Syme.
Leonard Taylor.

## 1827-28.

Philip A. Dew, A. B......King and Queen.
Robert C. Jones, A. B...Gloucester................Son of William Jones.
A. G. Taliaferro, A. B...     "          ...............Son of Dr. Wm. Taliaferro.
Richard H. Adams..........Charles City.
John Y. Archer.................Amelia......................Son of Jno. R. Archer.
Euclid Borland.................North Carolina.
Richard B. Boyd..............King William.

| NAMES. | RESIDENCES. | REMARKS. |
|---|---|---|
| Edward J. Bullock | Richmond | Son of Col. David Bullock. |
| Charles W. Byrd | Isle of Wight. | |
| G. J. Byrd | " | |
| Thomas R. Campbell | Clarkeston. | |
| John J. Clarke | Charles City. | |
| Edwin Cunliffe | Manchester. | |
| J. L. Deans | North End. | |
| Thomas H. Edwards | Portsmouth | Son of Th. Edwards. |
| John G. Hatton | " | |
| Charles L. Henshaw | King and Queen. | |
| B. Hunter | South Quay. | |
| A. S. Jones | Mecklenburg, Va | Son of John Jones. |
| Edward W. Marks | Petersburg. | |
| David Minge | Charles City | Son of John Minge. |
| James Minge | " | " " |
| R. T. Moffat | Portsmouth | Son of C. W. Moffat. |
| F. D. Piggot | James City | Son of F. Piggot. |
| Richard H. Riddick | Suffolk | Son of Col. Jos. Riddick. |
| George Ruffin | | Son of |
| William A. Selden | Richmond | Son of John A. Selden. |
| John B. Somerville | North Carolina. | |
| S. S. Stubbs | Gloucester. | |
| Thomas Y. Tabb | Amelia | Son of Yelverton Tabb. |
| C. Taylor | Manchester. | |
| James B. Thornton | Caroline | Son of J. B. Thornton. |
| Wm. B. Todd | King and Queen | Son of Wm. Todd. |
| Richard Tunstall | Caroline. | |
| James M. Tyre | Manchester. | |
| Logan Waller | King William. | |
| Curtis Waller | Spotsylvania. | |
| S. Wilson | Surry | Son of Samuel Wilson. |
| R. R. Wilson | " | Son of James Wilson. |
| Robert Yates | Gloucester. | |

## 1828–29.

| Richard Blow, Jr., A. B. | Sussex | Son of George Blow. |
|---|---|---|
| Jas. C. Eggleston, A. B. | Amelia | Son of Ed. Eggleston. |
| Joseph Hobson, A. B. | Richmond | Son of Joseph Hobson. |
| A. W. Robins, L. B. | Gloucester. | |
| Benj. E. Anderson | Richmond | Son of R. Anderson. |
| John F. Archer | " | |
| John B. Butler | Smithfield | Son of Dr. Robert Butler. |
| Robert G. Cabell | Richmond | Son of Wm. A. Cabell. Distinguished physician. |
| Bassett S. Claiborne | King William | Son of George Claiborne. |
| William A. Clark | Manchester | Son of Wm. B. Clark. |
| Benedict Crump | New Kent | Son of Beverly Crump. |

## CATALOGUE OF ALUMNI. 121

| NAMES. | RESIDENCES. | REMARKS. |
|---|---|---|

Thomas S. Dabney........King William..........Son of Benj. F. Dabney.
Samuel J. Douglass.......Petersburg.
Thos. W. R. Edmunds...Surry.
Edward M. Eggleston....Amelia.......................Son of Wm. F. Eggleston.
George L. Fauntleroy....Gloucester................Son of Wm. E. L. Fauntleroy.
R. F. Hannon..................Petersburg...............Son of B. F. Hannon.
John W. Haskins............Powhatan.................Son of John Haskins.
P. W. Kemp....................Gloucester................Son of M. W. Kemp.
Newton C. King.............Norfolk....................Son of Miles King.
John W. Jarvis...............Mathews...................Son of John D. Jarvis.
James Johnson..............King William............Son of Christopher Johnson.
Benj. F. Jones...............     "                       ...........Son of Thomas Jones.
Anderson Jones.............Mathews....................     "            "
Orlando S. Jones...........     "            ..................Son of John Jones.
John C. Mann................King & Queen..........Son of John Mann.
Thomas Martin ...........Powhatan..................Son of Thomas Martin.
George F. Morrison.......Williamsburg............Son of George Morrison.
Robert Rodgers..............     "
James M. Scott..............Richmond.................Son of Robert G. Scott.
Edward Simmons .........Petersburg...............Son of Robert Simmons.
Frederick W. Southgate..Norfolk....................Son of John Southgate.
A. G. Southall.
James B. Southall.
Richard Taliaferro.........York.
Edwin A. Teagle...........Williamsburg............Son of Edward Y. Teagle.
George K. Taylor .........Surry.
John T. Turner..............King George.............Son of Richard Turner.
Richard H. Turner........Williamsburg.............     "            "
Edward Turner.............     "            ..................     "            "
William Whiting...........King & Queen.
William E. Winfree......Chesterfield...............Son of Wm. Winfree.

## 1829-30.

Morean Bowers, A. B....Williamsburg.
Jno. R. Chambliss, L.B..Sussex......................Son of Lewis H. Chambliss. General C. S. A. Killed in battle.
Richard R. Garrett, A. B..Williamsburg..........State Senate.
John M. Gregory, L. B...James City...............Governor of Virginia and State Judge.
John B. Jarvis, A. B.....Mathews....................Son of John D. Jarvis.
Wm. A. Lyle, L. B........Rockbridge...............Son of William Lyle.
Edwin Shield, A. B.......York...........................Son of Samuel Shield.
Wm. Taliaferro, A. B...Gloucester..................Son of Dr. William Taliaferro.
James Minge, L. B.
D. C. Topp, L. B..........Tennessee..................Son of John Topp.
John Willison, A. B......Petersburg.

10

## CATALOGUE OF ALUMNI.

| NAMES. | RESIDENCES. | REMARKS. |
|---|---|---|
| William Bishop | Williamsburg. | |
| E. M. Cabell | Buckingham | Son of Frederick Cabell. |
| George W. Crump | Norfolk. | |
| George W. Chisman | York. | |
| H. S. Christian | Charles City | Son of Turner Christian. |
| Thomas H. Daniel | Petersburg. | |
| William T. Galt | Williamsburg. | |
| Thomas R. Gregory | Dinwiddie | Son of Francis Gregory. |
| Thomas A. Harrison | Charles City. | |
| Walter Henderson | Williamsburg. | |
| William B. Lightfoot | Fredericksburg. | Son of Philip Lightfoot. |
| William H. Jones | Williamsburg | Son of William M. Jones. |
| John H. Marshall | Fauquier | Son of Thomas Marshall. |
| William McCandlish | Williamsburg | Son of William McCandlish. |
| John S. Parker | Northampton | Son of S. E. Parker. |
| Eustace Robinson | Richmond | Son of John Robinson. |
| William L. Savage | Northampton. | |
| Ferdinand C. Stewart | Williamsburg | Son of F. S. C. Stewart. |
| Carolinus Turner | Fredericksburg. | |
| Thomas Turner | " | |
| Frederick A. Wingfield | Williamsburg | Son of C. T. Wingfield. |
| John H. Wright | North Carolina. | |

### 1830-31.

George Blow, A. B........Sussex ...................Son of George Blow. State Judge and General.
Thomas Daniel, A. B....Petersburg ..............Son of Thomas Daniel.
Cyrus A. Griffin, A. B....Williamsburg............Son of Dr. S. S. Griffin.
Alfred Johns, L. B........Buckingham..............Son of Glover Johns.
Thomas Martin, A. B.....James City...............Son of Dr. Thomas Martin.
Jas. D. McPherson, L. B. North Carolina.........Son of William McPherson.
John D. Munford, L. B..Richmond ..............Poet and scholar.
Edmund P. Oliver, A. B..Nottoway ................Son of Isaac Oliver.
Robert Ridley, L. B......Southampton.
George W. Semple, A. B..Williamsburg............Son of Judge Semple.
Edward Simmons, L. B..Petersburg...............Son of Robert Simmons.
James B. Watts, A. B...Botetourt.................. Son of Edward Watts.
W. W. Wingfield, A. B..Norfolk.
C. Q. Tompkins, A. B....Mathews ....... .........Son of Col. C. Tompkins. Capt. U. S. A—Col. C. S. A.
E. J. Young, A. B........Northampton........... Son of Thomas Young.
John T. E. Ambler........Richmond...............Son of Edward Ambler.
William M. Ambler........ "
Leroy H. Anderson........Williamsburg............Son of Leroy Anderson. Distinguished physician.
William M. Armistead...Hampton.
J. B. Browne ................ "

## CATALOGUE OF ALUMNI. 123

| NAMES. | RESIDENCES. | REMARKS. |
|---|---|---|
| George C. Eaton | Williamsburg | Son of John Eaton. |
| Mallory T. Dickson | Norfolk. | |
| T. R. Friend | Charlotte Gap. | |
| J. C. Friend | Petersburg | Son of Nathaniel Friend. |
| J. Faulcon | Warrenton. | |
| Richard H. Gregory | Lombardy Grove | Son of William O. Gregory. |
| William O. Gregory | Richmond. | |
| John Jones | Charles City. | |
| H. L. Jones | " | |
| Allen Jones | Williamsburg | Son of William M. Jones. |
| R. Morris | " | Son of Robert Morris. |
| E. C. Outlaw | North Carolina. | |
| Joseph H. Pendleton | Williamsburg. | |
| William S. Pryor | Hampton. | |
| William Robinson | Petersburg | Son of Thomas Robinson. |
| Albert Southall | Gloucester. | |

### 1831-32.

Ro. H. Armistead, L. B..Williamsburg.
Lemuel J. Bowden, L.B.. "
Samuel H. Early A. B...Virginia.
Robert R. Irving, L. B...Buckingham.
Wm. J. Macklin, L. B....Greenesville.
Wm. Martin, A. B.........Williamsburg.
Jno. D. Murdaugh, A. B..Williamsburg.
R. B. Somerville, A. B....North Carolina.
John S. Stubbs, A. B......Gloucester.
T. Wallace, A. B., L. B...Petersburg.
Wm. H. Wright, A. B.....North Carolina.
J. W. Burfoot...............Richmond .............Son of Lawson Burfoot.
Wm. Broaddus..............Williamsburg.
Mayo B. Carrington........Cumberland............Son of Benjamin Carrington.
R. E. Dejarnette..........Caroline...................Son of D. Dejarnette.
J. W. Eppes. ...............Cumberland.
J. W. Greenhow............Richmond ..............Son of Robert Greenhow.
Thomas B. Giles............Amelia...................Son of Governor Wm. B. Giles.
*Robert C. Harrison.......Williamsburg.
Robert C. Jones............Gloucester...............Son of William Jones.
John H. Jones..............Charles City.
P. C. Lightfoot.............Buckingham.
William B. Miller..........Mt. Airy.
R. Martin....................Richmond.
Frederick Proctor..........Elizabeth City.
A. Robinson.................Richmond.
H. M. Tennant..............Philadelphia.
*Robert Saunders, Jr......Williamsburg.

---

* Resident Graduates.

## CATALOGUE OF ALUMNI.

| NAMES. | RESIDENCES. | REMARKS. |
|---|---|---|
| William Smith | Baltimore. | |
| L. H. Trigg | Abingdon. | |
| Samuel Wills | Williamsburg. | |

### 1832–33.

| | | |
|---|---|---|
| J. W. Dew, A. B. | King & Queen. | |
| Jas. S. C. Griffin, A. B. | Williamsburg. | Son of Dr. S. S. Griffin. |
| J. B. Lord, A. B. | North Carolina. | |
| John Payne, A. B. | Port Conway. | |
| A. G. Taliaferro, A. B. | Gloucester. | Son of Dr. W. T. Taliaferro. |
| E. A. Tatem. | Norfolk. | |
| Wm. S. Thruston, A. B. | Gloucester. | Son of Robert Thruston. |
| Wm. G. Young, A. B. | Denbigh, Warwick. | Son of John Young. |
| William B. Clayton. | New Kent. | |
| John J. Empie. | Williamsburg. | Son of Rev. Dr. Empie. |
| Peter Eppes. | Prince George. | |
| William R. Galt. | Norfolk. | Son of Alexander Galt. |
| Thomas J. Gresham. | King & Queen. | |
| Richard J. Harrison. | Sussex. | Son of William Harrison. |
| William J. Harrison. | " | Son of Benjamin Harrison. |
| Richard W. Jeffrey. | Norfolk. | |
| Joseph W. Mason. | Sussex. | Son of Joseph Mason. |
| Seth Mason. | Frederick. | Son of S. Mason. |
| Thomas R. Swift. | Portsmouth. | |
| John James Thweatt. | Petersburg. | |

### 1833–34.

| | | |
|---|---|---|
| Humph. H. Wynne, A.B. | Yorktown. | |
| William Browne. | Williamsburg. | Son of Dabney Browne. |
| William Carter. | Hanover. | Son of William Carter. |
| Thomas H. Dickinson. | Amelia. | |
| Walter F. Jones. | Gloucester. | |
| Charles F. Kennedy. | Norfolk. | Son of Capt. E. P. Kennedy. |
| Philip L. Lee. | Williamsburg. | |
| Thomas D. Warren. | " | |
| Charles Washington. | Frederick county. | Son of Geo. F. Washington. |

### 1834–35.

| | | |
|---|---|---|
| Robert Taylor, A. B. | Gloucester. | |
| J. R. Armistead. | Petersburg. | |
| Robert J. Banister. | Richmond. | |
| Thomas A. Burfoot. | Petersburg. | |
| Henry H. Burwell. | Mecklenburg. | Son of P. R. Burwell. |
| S. C. L. Burwell. | Frederick county. | |
| Thomas B. Camp. | Norfolk. | |

## CATALOGUE OF ALUMNI. 125

| NAMES. | RESIDENCES. | REMARKS. |
|---|---|---|
| Robert F. Cole | Williamsburg. | Son of Dr. Jesse Cole. |
| William Crafford | Warwick. | |
| John Crargin | Massachusetts. | |
| George H. Crump | Surry | Son of John C. Crump. |
| Walter Davies | Gloucester | Son of A. L. Davies. |
| Samuel G. Fauntleroy | King & Queen. | |
| Archibald F. Foster | Williamsburg. | |
| Joseph Foster | " | |
| William T. French | Prince William. | |
| Charles Friend | Petersburg | Son of Nathaniel Friend. |
| Alexander D. Galt | Gloucester. | |
| William W. Gwathmey | Richmond | Son of G. W. Gwathmey. |
| Charles B. Hayden | Smithfield. | |
| John A. Henley | Williamsburg. | |
| Daniel Jones | " | Son of Allen Jones. |
| Josiah N. Jones | Smithfield. | |
| B. J. Johnson | South Carolina | Son of Wm. Johnson. |
| L. A. Lamb | Charles City | Son of John Lamb. |
| James Motley. | | |
| James Rempty | Lewisburg, Va. | |
| James E. Ruffin | King William. | |
| John J. Scott | South Carolina. | |
| Richard B. Segar | Urbanna | Son of Richard M. Segar. |
| James Sheppard | Hanover | Son of J. M. Sheppard. |

## 1835-36.

| | | |
|---|---|---|
| Wm. A. Christian, A. B. | New Kent | Son of Robert Christian. |
| Walter D. Leake, L. B. | Goochland | Son of Josiah Leake. |
| John Shelton, L. B. | Louisa. | |
| Marcus Armistead | Petersburg | Son of M. A. Armistead. |
| W. H. Armistead | " | " " |
| W. H. I. Anson | Petersburg | Son of M. D. I. Anson. |
| Jasper W. Bell | Lunenburg | Son of Adam Bell. |
| James G. Bosher | Richmond | Son of James Bosher. |
| George H. Cabaniss | Williamsburg | Son of James Cabaniss. |
| Henry Christian | New Kent. | |
| Thomas E. Cox | Richmond | Son of Edward Cox. |
| R. Cousins | Southampton. | |
| Lewis S. Dortch | Philadelphia, Pa. | |
| Robert French | Norfolk. | - |
| William D. Gurley | Southampton. | |
| Frederick G. Gregory | King William | Son of T. W. S. Gregory. |
| William N. Gregory | " | " " |
| Straughan Henley | Walkerton, Va. | |
| W. R. Hollman | Surry. | |
| John J. Jones | Lunenburg. | |
| R. S. Jones | Gloucester | Son of S. Jones. |

| NAMES. | RESIDENCES. | REMARKS. |
|---|---|---|
| Edward Lorraine | Richmond | Distinguished civil engineer. |
| Thornton McCarty | Alexandria. | |
| Edmund C. Murdaugh | Williamsburg. | Episcopal Clergyman. |
| R. Nelson | Gloucester | Son of P. R. Nelson. |
| N. Nicolson | Middlesex | Son of P. W. Nicolson. |
| James Olham | Tennessee. | |
| F. W. Power | York. | |
| Edmund Randolph | Amelia. | |
| Benjamin Robinson | Shacklesford, Va. | |
| Edward S. Russell | York | Son of Thomas C. Russell. |
| James A. Semple | Williamsburg | Son of John F. Semple. |
| Edward A. Semple | " | " " |
| S. R. Sheild | " | |
| S. J. C. Stewart | Philadelphia | Son of F. S. A. Stewart. |
| A. K. Taylor | North Carolina. | |
| Henry S. Taylor | " | |
| Jacob Tinsley | Hanover. | |
| C. J. Waller | " | Son of Benjamin Waller. |
| William Wynne | Petersburg. | |

## 1836-37.

| | | |
|---|---|---|
| William R. Bland, A. B. | Nottoway | Son of Edward Bland. |
| A. C. Jones, A. B. | Isle of Wight. | |
| F. J. Mettauer, A. B. | Prince Edward | Son of Dr. J. P. Mettauer. |
| W. S. Peachy, L. B. | Williamsburg | Son of Dr. Thomas G. Peachy. |
| Edward P. Pitts, L. B. | Northampton | Son of W. G. Pitts. |
| John M. Speed, L. B. | Lynchburg | Son of John Speed. |
| Robert Tyler, L. B. | Charles City | Son of President Tyler. |
| John Tyler, A. B. | " | " " |
| E. W. Allen | Hanover | Son of William Allen. |
| Francis Armistead | Hampton. | |
| Monro Banister | Amelia. | |
| John Barksdale | " | Son of W. J. Barksdale. |
| William P. Bayly | Accomac | Son of Thos. Bayly. |
| Benjamin Blake | Essex. | |
| A. C. Browne | King & Queen. | |
| E. C. Carrington | Halifax | Son of Walter C. Carrington. |
| George C. Carrington | " | " " |
| James Carroll | Isle of Wight. | |
| John B. Cary | Hampton | Principal Hampton Mil. A. |
| George P. Coleman | Williamsburg | Son of Thos. Coleman. |
| Benjamin Curtis | Richmond | Son of H. Curtis. |
| J. C. Davis | Waynesborough. | |
| Edwin H. Edmunds | Brunswick | Son of N. S. Edmunds. |
| John M. Eppes | Sussex. | |
| John Finney | Powhatan | Son of B. W. Finney. |
| N. B. Foreman | Norfolk county. | |

## CATALOGUE OF ALUMNI.   127

| NAMES. | RESIDENCES. | REMARKS. |
|---|---|---|
| John J. Gravatt | Port Royal. | |
| R. S. Hamilton | Fredericksburg | Son of George Hamilton. |
| John T. Harris | Buckingham. | |
| John P. Harrison | Charles City | Son of Benjamin Harrison. |
| John B. Hendrin | New Kent. | |
| R. T. Holstead | Norfolk. | |
| William H. 'I. Anson | Petersburg. | |
| William Lambert | Richmond | Son of William Lambert. |
| John W. Lane | Amelia. | |
| Charles K. Mallory | Hampton | Son of Francis Mallory. |
| R. McCandlish | Williamsburg. | |
| William J. McGowan | Petersburg | Son of Wm. McGowan. |
| Robert Meade | Brunswick | Son of David Meade. |
| Nicholas Mills | Richmond | Son of Nicholas Mills. |
| W. C. Moody | Williamsburg | Son of William Moody. |
| T. H. Morris | Baltimore. | Son of John B. Morris. |
| William P. Munford | Richmond | Son of William Munford. |
| Wilson Nicholas | " | Son of P. N. Nicholas. |
| John Page | Clarke | Son of John E. Page. |
| W. R. Pierce | Williamsburg | Son of John R. Pierce. |
| W. C. Pegram | Dinwiddie. | |
| A. H. Perkins | Yorktown. | |
| George Rawlings | Richmond | Physician. |
| George W. Richardson | Kentucky. | |
| W. J. Richardson | New Kent | Son of John Richardson. |
| John A. Robinson | Richmond | Son of A. Robinson. |
| Powhatan Robinson | Petersburg. | |
| T. B. Russell | York. | |
| John D. Scellen | Williamsburg. | |
| James E. Scott. | | |
| R. A. Shield | Yorktown | Son of Robert Shield. |
| W. R. S. Skipwith | Richmond. | |
| Thomas F. Spady | Northampton. | |
| W. M. Sutton | Hanover | Son of James T. Sutton. |
| J. R. Sydnor | Lynchburg. | |
| L. W. Tazewell | Richmond | Son of William Tazewell. |
| P. M. Thompson | Richmond | Son of Garland Thompson. |
| B. S. Tompson | Kanawha | Son of Philip R. Tompson. |
| William W. Townes | Petersburg | Son of John D. Townes. |
| William W. Tyler | Richmond. | |
| Cornelius Tyree | Amherst. | |
| A. D. Upshur | Northampton. | |
| B. D. Watkins | Cumberland. | |
| John B. Wilkinson | Petersburg. | |
| George Wilson | Norfolk | Son of George Wilson. |
| George Wingfield | " | |
| Richard B. Wright | " | Son of William Wright. |

## 1837-38.

| NAMES. | RESIDENCES. | REMARKS. |
|---|---|---|

Herb. A. Claiborne, A. B..Richmond ............Son of H. A. Claiborne.
James A. Clopton, A. B..New Kent................Son of J. Clopton.
Elias Dodson, A. B.......Halifax.
Benjamin F. Dew, A. B..King and Queen......Son of Thomas Dew.
Thos. B. Donnelly, A. B..Williamsburg.
John Finney, A. B..........Powhatan ...............Son of Benjamin W. Finney.
John M. Galt, A. B........Williamsburg ..........Son of Dr. A. D. Galt. Superintendent E. L. Asylum.
Edward Gresham, A. B..King and Queen......Son of Thomas Gresham.
Samuel S. Henley, A. B..     "            ......Son of T. M. Henley.
Wm. L. Henley, L. B.....Williamsburg...........Son of Richard Henley.
Arch'd C. Peachy,A. B...     "            ............Son of Dr. T. G. Peachy. Professor College William & Mary.
G. L. C. Salter, L. B......York....................... Son of G. L. C. Salter.
Robt. G. Scott, A. B......Richmond ................Son of Robt. G. Scott. U. S. Consol to Brazil.
John O. Steger, A. B.....Amelia ...................Son of H. Steger. Prominent lawyer.
John Addison...................Northampton.
William H. Armistead...Petersburg.
John B. Ball.....................Lancaster.
D. J. Beasley.................Petersburg.
William Blankenship....Chesterfield.
Thomas G. Blewitt........Mississippi.
T. J. Chambliss ...........Sussex .....................Son of William O. Chambliss.
William A. Christian.....Charles City.
James L. Clarke ..........Gloucester................Son of Colin Clarke.
N. C. Cocke...................Prince George ........Son of Thomas Cocke.
William Cole.....................     "
Robert E. Cutler...........Nelson....................Son of Robert E. Cutler.
A. D. Dickinson............Prince Edward.........State Senator. State Judge.
John S. Edwards.......... Mathews..................Son of Thomas Edwards.
Jacob Faulcon...............Surry ......................Son of John A. Faulcon.
Charles G. Field............Mecklenburg.
Thomas J. Field............     "
John H. Fox...................Yorktown.
William H. Gwathmey...King William...........Son of Richard Gwathmey.
Leonard Henley............Williamsburg...........Physician.
John W. Irby.................Nottoway ................Son of W. B. Irby.
Andrew L. Jarvis..........Mathews..................Son of John D. Jarvis.
Robert W. Johnson........Cumberland.
Edmund W. Jones.........North Carolina.
Timothy H. Lasslter......     "
William A. Littlejohn....     "
Henry Lindsey..............Williamsburg.

## CATALOGUE OF ALUMNI.

| NAMES. | RESIDENCES. | REMARKS. |
|---|---|---|
| Duncan McRae | North Carolina | Colonel in Southern army. |
| Charles P. Moncure | Richmond. | |
| Charles W. Montague | Gloucester. | |
| Thomas B. Montague | " | |
| A. T. Page | Cumberland | Son of John C. Page. |
| William G. Pollard | King William | Son of Robert Pollard. |
| John Pratt | Caroline. | |
| Powhatan Robertson | Richmond | Son of Judge John Robertson. |
| Moore Robinson | " | Son of John Robinson. |
| William Robinson | King and Queen | Son of William Robinson |
| John W. Rochelle | Southampton. | |
| Joseph T. Royall | Nottoway | Son of John D. Royall. |
| William H. Sims | Halifax | Son of John Sims. |
| P. S. Smith | Nottoway | Son of Kennon Smith. |
| William B. Smith | Cumberland. | |
| Philip B. Tankard | Northampton. | |
| John A. Taylor | Norfolk. | |
| William B. Taylor | Surry. | |
| William A. Thom | Culpeper | Son of John Thom. Prominent physician. |
| W. N. Waller | Williamsburg. | |
| James R. Warren | James City | Son of M. S. Warren. |
| William P. Wood | North Carolina. | |
| J. J. Wright | Essex | Son of George Wright. |
| Joseph H. Wyatt | King & Queen. | |
| William B. Wynne | West Florida. | |
| William H. Yerby | Lancaster. | |

### 1838–39.

| | | |
|---|---|---|
| Thomas Blackwell, A.B. | Lunenburg. | |
| John B. Cary, A. B. | Hampton | Son of A. Cary. Col. C. S. A. |
| Herb. A. Claiborne, L.B. | Richmond | Son of H. A. Claiborne. |
| John A. Coke, A. B. | Williamsburg | Son of John Coke. |
| R. Ivanhoe Cocke, L.B. | Powhatan | Son of John F. Cocke. |
| Wm. W. Crump, L. B. | Richmond | Son of S. J. Crump. Judge in State Court. |
| Thos. B. Donnelly, L. B. | Williamsburg. | |
| Benj. F. Garrett, A. B. | " | |
| Wash'n Greenhow, L. B. | Richmond | Son of Robert Greenhow. |
| Edward Gresham, L. B. | King & Queen. | |
| John W. Grigsby, L. B. | Rockbridge. | |
| Wm. H. Fitzhugh, A. B. | Prince William | Son of W. H. Fitzhugh. |
| Henry Harrison, A. B. | Charles City | Son of Benjamin Harrison. |
| Alex. Jones, A. B. | Petersburg | Son of John W. Jones. |
| James B. Jones, A. B. | " | " " |
| Benj. B. Minor, L. B. | Spotsylvania | Son of H. J. Minor. |
| Chas. W. Montague, A. B. | Gloucester. | |

## CATALOGUE OF ALUMNI.

| NAMES. | RESIDENCES. | REMARKS. |
|---|---|---|
| Wm. M. Overton, A. B. | Lunenburg | Son of W. G. Overton. |
| John Poindexter, L. B. | Louisa. | |
| Edm'd Randolph, A. B. | Amelia | Son of Peyton Randolph. |
| Julian C. Ruffin, A. B. | Petersburg | Son of Edmund Ruffin. |
| Austin M. Trible, L. B. | Essex | Son of John Trible. State Senator. |
| F. M. Baker | Richmond | Son of Hilary Baker. Episcopal Clergyman. |
| Joseph G. Banks | Georgia. | |
| F. L. Barziza | Williamsburg | Son of P. J. Barziza. |
| B. E. Booth | Surry | Son of Samuel Booth. |
| James E. Brooks | Richmond | Son of James Brooks. |
| James Buchanan | Tennessee. | |
| Thomas H. Bullock | Lynchburg | Son of James Bullock. |
| G. P. Carrington | Cumberland | Son of B. M. Carrington. |
| C. A. Clarke | Halifax. | |
| Daniel A. Daly | Mecklenburg. | |
| L. W. Edloe | Williamsburg | Son of William Edloe. |
| John F. Edmunds | Brunswick. | |
| Charles C. Field | Gloucester. | |
| Charles S. Fox | King & Queen. | |
| W. W. Glenn | Baltimore | Son of Judge John Glenn. |
| Frederick Hall | Portsmouth. | |
| James Hamilton | North Carolina. | |
| T. E. Harding | Northumberland. | |
| James H. Harrison | Sussex. | |
| H. J. Hartwell | Brunswick | Son of Harrison Hartwell. |
| W. J. Hankins | North Carolina. | |
| A. Hill | Petersburg. | |
| James M. Jackson | King & Queen. | |
| W. B. Johnson | Fredericksburg. | |
| James F. Jones | Frederick | Son of William S. Jones. |
| John B. Kercheval | Hampton | Son of Samuel Kercheval. |
| Thomas H. Leary | North Carolina. | |
| John W. McKessach | Tennessee. | |
| C. McLaurin | Mississippi. | |
| D. E. Meade | Dinwiddie. | |
| J. C. Medley | Halifax | Son of J. Medley. |
| John E. Moore | Brunswick. | |
| S. W. Morris | Louisa | Son of Thomas Morris. |
| J. H. Nottingham | Northampton. | |
| A. S. Pegram | Dinwiddie | Son of Edward J. Pegram. |
| John D. Pierce | James City | Son of J. R. Pierce. |
| Daniel W. Pitts | Alabama. | |
| William C. Pratt | Caroline | Son of J. P. Pratt. |
| Winston Radford | Lynchburg | Son of William Radford. |
| John R. Reins | Richmond | Son of Richard Reins. |
| William H. Scott | Georgia. | |

## CATALOGUE OF ALUMNI.   131

| NAMES. | RESIDENCES. | REMARKS. |
|---|---|---|
| H. C. Semple | James City | Son of Judje James Semple. |
| Jabez S. Smith | Petersburg | Son of Jabez Smith. |
| Orlando M. Smith | Surry. | |
| William M. Sneed | North Carolina. | |
| Waddy Street | Lunenburg | Son of David Street. |
| Edwin Taylor | Caroline | Son of John Taylor. |
| John B. Taylor | Roanoke. | |
| George Turner | King George. | |
| James B. Turner | North Carolina. | |
| Corbin G. Waller | Williamsburg | Son of Dr. Robert P. Waller. |
| Charles C. Waller | " | Son of Benjamin Waller. |
| A. Watson | Accomac. | |
| J. Willis | Mississippi. | |
| L. J. Winder | Yorktown. | |
| William R. Young | Caroline. | |

### 1839–40.

W. E. Blankenship, L. B.. Chesterfield.
Jas. M. Carrington, L.B..Richmond ............Son of L. Carrington.
L. W. Carter, A. B........Shirley.................Son of Hill Carter.
Wm. E. Clarke, L. B.....Alabama.
Benj. F. Dew, A. M......King and Queen......Son of Thomas Dew.
John H. Dillard, L. B....North Carolina.
Geo. R. Dupuy, A. B....Petersburg.
John Finney, L. B.........Powhatan.
Wm. H. Gwathmey, A.B. King William.
Thos. H. Harrison, A. B..Sussex...................Son of William Harrison.
Alex. Jones, L. B. .........Chesterfield............Son of J. W. Jones.
Edmund W. Jones, L. B..North Carolina.
Jas. B. Jones, L. B.........Chesterfield............Son of J. W. Jones.
Warn. T. Jones,
    A. B., L. B...Gloucester.............Judge of Gloucester county.
David E. Meade, A. B...Dinwiddie.
John Minge, A. B. .........Charles City............Son of Dr. John Minge.
G. W. Nottingham, A.B..Northampton.
Wm. Old, L. B..............Powhatan ..............Son of Wm. Old. Capt. C. S. A.
A. C. Peachy, A. M.......Williamsburg...........Son of Dr. Thomas G. Peachy.
J. H. Rawlings,
    A. B., L. B...Spotsylvania ............Son of Lewis Rawlings.
G. W. Richardson,
    A. B., L. B...Hanover.
M. B. Seawell, L. B......Gloucester...............Son of B. Seawell. Prominent lawyer.
William H. Sims, A. B...Halifax....................Son of John Sims.
Tristham L. Skinner,
    A. B...North Carolina.........Major C. S. A.  Killed at Seven Pines.

| NAMES. | RESIDENCES. | REMARKS. |
|---|---|---|
| John B. Stanard, | A. B...Fredericksburg. | |
| Thos. S. Watson, | A. B...Louisa. | Son of David Watson. |
| Wm. Waller, | L. B.........Williamsburg. | Son of Col. W. Waller. |
| Lloyd W. Williams, | L. B..Norfolk. | |
| Wm. C. Williams, | A. B...Richmond. | |
| Wm. Allen. | ...Hampton. | |
| E. A. Barziza | Williamsburg. | Son of P. J. Barziza. |
| W. L. Barziza | " | " |
| James Beatty | Baltimore. | |
| Norborne Blow | Sussex. | Son of Col. George Blow. |
| Wm. N. Blow | " | " |
| N. R. Cary | Hampton. | Son of G. A. Cary. |
| D. A. Claiborne | Brunswick. | |
| T. L. Clanton | North Carolina. | |
| B. Cosnahan. | South Carolina. | |
| J. F. Dilley | Maryland. | |
| Robert Doles | Southampton. | Son of Patrick Doles. |
| E. D. Farrar | Mississippi. | |
| John Ferguson | Shenandoah. | Son of R. F. Ferguson. |
| Thomas W. Field | Gloucester. | |
| B. S. Foster | North Carolina. | |
| B. J. Gouldin | Caroline. | |
| Wm. D. Gresham. | King & Queen. | Prominent lawyer. |
| Wm. Hancock | Richmond. | Son of M. W. Hancock. |
| John A. Hannon | Petersburg. | Son of R. F. Hannon. |
| J. Harrison | Prince George. | |
| John T. Hatcher | Norfolk. | Son of Charles Hatcher. |
| T. P. Holcombe | Richmond. | Son of T. N. Holcombe. |
| Daniel C. Holliday | New Orleans. | |
| B. Howes | New York city. | |
| A. G. Jones | New Kent. | Son of Chesley Jones. |
| John A. Jones | Hampton. | |
| Walker F. Jones | Gloucester. | Son of Walker Jones. |
| J. D. Lyle | Richmond. | Son of J. Lyle. |
| C. T. Mason | Brunswick. | Son of Nathaniel Mason. |
| L. W. Mason | Sussex. | Son of Henry Mason. |
| T. J. McKenzie | Richmond. | |
| Peyton Meade | Amelia. | Son of Hodijah Meade. |
| Thomas G. McGehee | North Carolina. | |
| John S. Miller | Buckingham. | Son of W. A. Miller. |
| B. Owen | Alabama. | |
| James Pendleton | King & Queen. | Son of Philip B. Pendleton. |
| Lewis W. Pitts | Alabama. | |
| F. C. Riddick | Suffolk. | Son of Burwell Riddick. |
| Wm. G. Riley | Accomac. | Son of Wm. Riley. State Judge. |
| James M. Robertson | Lynchburg. | |
| L. B. Rose | Fredericksburg. | |
| A. H. G. Sands | Williamsburg. | Son of Thomas Sands. |

## CATALOGUE OF ALUMNI. 133

| NAMES. | RESIDENCES. | REMARKS. |

Thomas F. Scott............Campbell.
S. Semple....................James City.
E. B. Shelton..............Louisa..................Son of William Shelton.
C. E. Smith..:..............Missouri..............Son of Gen. Thomas A. Smith, U. S. A.
John H. Taylor............Mecklenburg.
Wm. M. Towler............       "        ..........Son of W. Towler.
Wat H. Tyler................Hanover..............Son of Dr. W. H. Tyler.
Mat P. Waller...............Williamsburg........Son of Dr. Robert P. Waller.
Thomas R. Williams......Nottoway.............Son of D. G. Williams.
A. A. Whitehead...........Smithfield.............Son of J. B. Whitehead.
George T. Wright..........Essex....................Son of George Wright.
John R. Wright............King & Queen........Son of William Wright.

### 1840-41.

Jas. A. C. Clopton, A.M..New Kent.............Son of James Clopton.
Wm. W. Coke, A. B.......Williamsburg..........Son of John Coke.
Jas. W. Cook,
          A. B., L. B...Greensville............Son of James W. Cook.
John P. Dickinson, L. B..Caroline...............Son of S. C. Dickinson.
Wm. R. Drinkard, A. C..Petersburg..............Son of Beverley Drinkard.
Alex. C. Garrett, A. B... Williamsburg.
B. F. Garrett,
          A. M., L. B...Williamsburg.
Geo. F. Harrison, A. B...Cumberland ...........Son of Carter H. Harrison.
Daniel C. Holliday, A.B..New Orleans.
Benjamin Irby, A. B......Nottoway...............Son of Edmund Irby.
·Alex. Jones, A. M.........Chesterfield.
Jas. B. Jones, A. M.......      "
L. W. Mason, L. B.........Sussex....................Son of Henry Mason.
Jessie S. Miller, A. B.....Buckingham.
John E. Moore, A. B....Brunswick.
W. M. Overton,
          A. M., L. B...Lunenburg ............Son of Wm. G. Overton.
Jno. W. H. Parker,
          L. B...Accomac ...............Prominent lawyer.
Arch. C. Peachy, L. B....Williamsburg.
Wm. B. Taliaferro, A. B..Gloucester.............Son of W. T. Taliaferro. Major Gen'l C. S. A.
Wm. A. Temple, L. B...Sussex.
John S. Trueheart, A. B..Richmond.
John D. Warren, A. B...     "     ..............Capt. C. S. A.
Wm. F. Wood,
          A. B., L. B...Tennessee.
John T. Wootten, L. B...Henry.
Selden S. Wright, L. B...Essex ....................Son of Thomas Wright.
Wm. H. Anderson.........Alabama.

| NAMES. | RESIDENCES. | REMARKS. |
|---|---|---|
| H. A. Budham | North Carolina. | |
| Thomas Blankenship | Chesterfield. | |
| Samuel J. Booker | Buckingham | Son of George Booker. |
| C. J. Cabaniss | Dinwiddie. | |
| George Caroll | Isle of Wight. | |
| Wm. C. Clement | Franklin | Son of G. W. Clement. |
| S. P. Christian | New Kent | Son of John F. Christian. |
| W. A. Cocke | Powhatan. | |
| O. A. Crenshaw | Fluvanna. | |
| D. C. Dejarnette | Caroline | Son of Daniel Dejarnette. Member of Congress. |
| L. C. Dew | King & Queen | Son of Thomas Dew. |
| O. B. Finney | Accomac | State Senator. |
| Fayette Griffin | Williamsburg | Son of Dr. S. S. Griffin. |
| A. F. Haymond. | | |
| W. W. Jacob | Northampton. | |
| John W. Johnson | Petersburg | Son of Ashton Johnson. |
| John T. King | Alabama. | |
| W. J. Leary | North Carolina. | |
| John B. Lemoine | Petersburg | Son of John C. Lemoine. |
| John H. Lewis | Tappahannock. | |
| S. W. Mapp | Accomac. | |
| Marion T. Mayo | Fluvanna | Son of Wm. Mayo. |
| Edward W. Morris | Hanover | Son of Richard Morris. |
| R. Neblett | Lunenburg | Son of Dr. S. Neblett. |
| Charles Old | Powhatan | Son of William Old. |
| Francis Patterson | North Carolina. | |
| James W. Preston | Washington county | Son of John M. Preston. |
| Joseph Royall | Nottoway. | |
| Thomas F. Scott | Louisana. | |
| J. W. Sheppard | Hanover | Son of Joseph M. Sheppard. |
| Crawford E. Smith | Missouri | Son of Gen. T. A. Smith, U. S. A. |
| Reuben Smith | " | " " " |
| Richard K. Smith | Nottoway | Son of Kennon Smith. |
| Samuel G. Staples | Patrick | Son of Abraham Staples. |
| R. H. Tatum | Chesterfield | Son of Henry W. Tatum. |
| Isaac Vaiden | Williamsburg. | |
| W. E. Walker | Greensville. | |
| Wm. L'Fayette Watkins | Brunswick | Son of Stephen D. Watkins. |
| Wm. M. Weems | Louisiana. | |
| John G. Williams | Richmond | Prominent lawyer. |
| Samuel White | Tennessee | Son of Judge Hugh L. White. |

## 1841–42.

James Boisseau, A. B..... Dinwiddie.
George W. Caroll, A. B.. Isle of Wight.
Gideon Christian, A. B... Charles City.

## CATALOGUE OF ALUMNI. 135

| NAMES. | RESIDENCES. | REMARKS. |
|---|---|---|
| Wm. W. Coke, L. B. | Williamsburg. | |
| Peter G. A. Evans, L. B. | North Carolina. | |
| John H. Fox, A. B. | Yorktown. | |
| Joseph W. Kay, A. B. | Essex | Son of James Kay. |
| Joseph H. Lewis, A. B. | " | Son of Warner Lewis. |
| Robt. L. Montague, L.B. | Middlesex | Son of Lewis B. Montague. Lt. Governor of Virginia. |
| John S. Moon, L. B. | Albemarle | Son of S. D. Moon. |
| Eaton Nance, A. B. | Charles City | Son of Zachariah Nance. |
| Robert Ould, L. B. | Georgetown | U. S. District Attorney. Prominent lawyer. |
| J. J. Poval, L. B. | Powhatan. | |
| Francis Ruffin, A. B. | Surry | Son of Francis Ruffin. |
| John R. Stith, L. B. | Northumberland. | |
| Littleton Tazewell, L.B. | Richmond. | |
| John G. Williams, A. B. | " | Prominent lawyer. |
| P. A. Atkinson | North Carolina. | |
| George C. Ashton | King George | Son of D. Ashton. |
| James F. Batte | Greensville. | |
| Edmund W. Bayly | Northampton. | |
| Wm. C. Clement | Franklin | Son of J. W. Clement. |
| John R. Copeland | Petersburg. | |
| John T. Custis | Accomac. | |
| William S. Custis. | " | |
| R. S. Dobson. | Hanover. | |
| Stratton B. Downing. | Southampton | Son of E. W. Downing. |
| S. B. Evans | North Carolina. | |
| Hilliard Fort | " | |
| T. W. Goodrich | Greensville | Son of Robert H. Goodrich. |
| D. Harmanson | Northampton. | |
| D. W. Harris. | Georgia. | |
| Benjamin Harrison | Charles City | Son of Benjamin Harrison. |
| John B. Hatchett | Lunenburg | Son of Haynie Hatchett. |
| M. T. Hankins | North Carolina. | |
| Charles B. Hubbard | Richmond. | |
| Henry B. Hunter | North Carolina. | |
| Edwin B. Jones | Brunswick. | |
| James F. Jones | Northampton. | |
| John P. Jones | Hampton | Son of John Jones. |
| Wm. H. Jones | Fluvanna | Son of Charles W. Jones. |
| Wilson W. Jones | Northampton. | |
| E. R. Leatherbury | " | Son of John W. Leatherbury. Prominent physician. |
| J. R. McQuire | Suffolk. | |
| William S. Merrit | Goochland. | |
| R. H. Power | Yorktown | Son of F. B. Power. State Senator. |
| Walter G. Randle | Georgia. | |

## CATALOGUE OF ALUMNI.

| NAMES. | RESIDENCES. | REMARKS. |
|---|---|---|
| Washington L. Riddick | Suffolk | Son of Mills Riddick. |
| L. J. Rose | Brunswick | Son of Henry Rose. |
| F. T. Vail | Yorktown | |
| W. B. Thompson | South Carolina | Son of Hon. Waddy Thompson. |
| Mathew Whitaker | North Carolina | Son of Hon. W. Whitaker. |
| John F. Wooten | " | |

### 1842–43.

| | | |
|---|---|---|
| F. L. Barziza, L. B. | Williamsburg | Son of P. J. Barziza. |
| Seneca M. Conway, L. B. | Northumberland. | |
| Beverly B. Douglas, N.B. | New Kent | Major C. S. A. State Senator. |
| Wm. F. Fitchett, L. B. | Northampton | Son of Daniel Fitchett. |
| Alex. C. Garrett, L. B. | Williamsburg. | |
| Geo. F. Harrison, L. B. | Cumberland. | |
| Daniel Hatcher, A. B. | Powhatan | Son of Seth Hatcher. |
| H. H. Land, L. B. | Princess Anne. | |
| W. A. Leigh, L. B. | Prince Edward | Son of Paschal J. Leigh. |
| William S. Morris, A. B. | Hanover | Son of Richard Morris. |
| W. J. Neblett, L. B | Lunenburg | Son of Dr. S. Neblett. |
| Pleasant P. Peace, L. B. | North Carolina. | |
| Jno. B. Peachy, L. B. | Williamsburg | Son of Dr. Thomas G. Peachy. |
| J. P. Pierce, L. B | Charles City | Son of John R. Pierce. |
| L. J. Rose, A. B. | Brunswick | Son of Henry Rose. |
| Wash. L. Watkins, A.B. | Petersburg | Son of D. Watkins. |
| Thos. M. Wilson, A. B. | Norfolk | Son of George Wilson. |
| H. T. Banister | Amelia. | |
| A. W. Battle | Georgia. | |
| G. G. Bird | South Carolina. | |
| William Carter | Williamsburg. | |
| Charles Coleman | Williamsburg | Son of William Coleman. Physician. |
| R. D. Gale | Alabama. | |
| E. J. Harrison | Cumberland. | |
| John M. Hodges | Halifax. | |
| E. W. Keesee | Richmond. | |
| A. Lewis | North Carolina. | |
| R. Miller | Norfolk | Son of B. M. Miller. |
| B. C. Perkins | " | |
| Wm. J. Seymour | Brunswick | Son of William Seymour. |
| John E. Smaw | Northampton. | |
| L. M. Spratley | Surry | Son of P. T. Spratley. |
| S. B. Spratley | " | " " |
| Walter Taylor | Mecklenburg. | |
| W. J. Weeks | Louisiana. | |
| Edmund T. Wilkins | Tennessee | Son of Dr. Benj. Wilkins. Distinguished physician. Superintendent California Lunatic Asylum. |

## CATALOGUE OF ALUMNI. 137

| NAMES. | RESIDENCES. | REMARKS. |
|---|---|---|

S. P. Wilson..................Pittsylvania..............Son of Robert Wilson.
W. R. Wilson..................Surry..........................Son of James Wilson.
Chastain White..............Son of William L. White. State Senator.
J. W. White....................Hanover.

### 1843-44.

A. C. Garrett, A. M......Williamsburg.
Edmund Berkeley, A. B.Loudoun ..................Son of Lewis Berkeley. Colonel
                                C. S. A.
Thos. H. Campbell, L. B.Nottoway..............Son of A. A. Campbell. State
                                Senator.
E. G. Canthan, L. B......Essex.
Geo. W. Field, L. B......Brunswick..............Son of R. W. Field.
Richard Gatewood, A. B.Norfolk ..................Son of Richard Gatewood.
Thos. R. Gresham, A. B.King and Queen.
Jas. M. Mathews, L. B...Tappahannock.
Lyttleton Nock, L. B.....Accomac ..................Son of William Nock.
Francis C. Riddick, L. B.Suffolk...................Son of Burwell Riddick.
Francis Ruffin, L. B......Surry.........................Son of Francis Ruffin.
Miles Selden, A. B.........Charles City............Son of John A. Selden.
Sydney Smith, A. B......York .........................Son of Henry Smith.
Henry M. Vaiden, A. B..Williamsburg...........Son of Isaac Vaiden.
Wm. G. Walker, A. B...North Carolina.
S. Decatur Whittle, L. B.Mecklenburg.
Thos. M. Wilson, L. B...Norfolk.
Edw'd T. Wingo, L. B..Cumberland.
Hunter Woodis, L. B.....Norfolk....................Mayor of Norfolk.
H. S. Belt........................Richmond.
E. F. Blair......................    "
R. H. Brookes................North Carolina.
W. P. Byrd.....................Williamsburg...........Son of Addison L. Byrd.
John F. Carter................    "
Benjamin L. Christian...New Kent.
William Christian .........Richmond.
T. R. Dew......................King & Queen .........Son of William Dew.
F. L. Douthat.................Charles City.
Wm. A. Durfey..............Williamsburg...........Son of William Durfey.
Richard Eppes...............Prince George.
James W. Field .............Mecklenburg.
Wm. S. Field..................Gloucester.
Lucian Fletcher.............Lynchburg.
A. A. Hughes.................Richmond................Son of A. Hughes.
J. C. Mann.....................King & Queen .........Son of William Mann.
Louis H. Russell............North Carolina.
F. H. Smith.
James E. Smith.............Alabama.
L. D. Spragins...............Halifax....................Son of T. D. Spragins.

138          CATALOGUE OF ALUMNI.

| NAMES. | RESIDENCES. | REMARKS. |
|---|---|---|
| Thomas Tinsley | Richmond | Son of T. G. Tinsley. |
| M. S. Valentine | Richmond | Son of M. S. Valentine. |
| Bernard Wiley | Savannah. | |
| F. C. Williams | Nottoway | Son of D. G. Williams. |
| J. M. Willis | Hampton | Son of J. M. Willis. |

## 1844-45.

| | | |
|---|---|---|
| Rob. B. Armistead, A.B. | Alabama | Son of Wm. Armistead. Major C. S. A. Killed at Shiloh. |
| W. N. Berkeley | Loudoun | Son of L. Berkeley. Major C. S. A. |
| Jas. S. Christian, A. B. | Williamsburg | Son of Judge John B. Christian. |
| Josiah Harris, A. B. | Georgia. | |
| Robt. Hutchinson, A. B. | Essex. | |
| Tiberius G. Jones, A. B. | Buckingham. | |
| Abrah. H. McLaws, A.B. | Georgia | Major C. S. A. |
| Joseph C. Mayo | Norfolk | Son of P. P. Mayo. |
| Bernard Peyton, A. B. | Richmond | Son of Gen. B. Peyton. |
| Geo. G. Thompson, A. B. | Culpeper | Captain C. S. A. |
| Wm. R. Cocke, L. B. | Powhatan | Son of John F. Cocke. |
| Thos. R. Gresham, L. B. | King & Queen. | |
| Robert Hord, L. B. | Caroline. | |
| Waller Massie, L. B. | Nelson. | |
| Christopher C. Peace, L. B. | North Carolina. | |
| Rufus S. Rennolds, L. B. | Essex. | |
| Henry Thorp, L. B. | Alabama. | |
| Henry M. Vaiden, L. B. | New Kent. | |
| Wm. J. Widgen, L. B. | Northampton. | |
| G. G. Williams, L. B. | Norfolk. | |
| William F. Avent. | Greensville | Son of Tomline Avent. |
| C. Barbour | Culpeper | Son of Hon. J. S. Barbour. |
| J. L. Burwell | Clarke | Son of G. Burwell. |
| E. Christian | Richmond. | |
| John R. Coupland | Petersburg | C. S. A. |
| J. F. Flewellen | Georgia. | |
| Charles J. Fox | Yorktown. | |
| J. C. Garlick | King William. | |
| John L. Jones | Gloucester. | |
| Thomas Latane | Essex' | Son of Henry Latane. |
| Benjamin Lewis | Mecklenburg. | |
| Bev. St. Geo. T. Peachy. | Williamsburg | Son of Dr. T. G. Peachy. Surgeon C. S. A. |
| Charles L. Scott | Richmond | Son of Rob't G. Scott. Member Congress from California and Major C. S. A. |
| N. M. Slaughter | Georgia. | |

| NAMES. | RESIDENCES. | REMARKS. |

W. R. Staples..............Patrick county.........Son of A. Staples. Judge Court of Appeals.
P. Montagu Thompson...Richmond...............Son of Garland Thompson.

## 1845-46.

Wm. H. Campbell, A. B..Hanover...................Son of Hugh Campbell.
Richard M. Cary, A. B...Hampton.
Jos. S. Dejarnette, A. B.Caroline..................Son of Elliott Dejarnette.
R. P. Fauntleroy, A. B..King & Queen.........Son of M. G. Fauntleroy.
John F. Jones, A. B......Warwick ..................Son of Wm. S. Jones.
Robt. L. Madison, A. B..Petersburg.
Sterling Neblett, A. B...Lunenburg ...............Son of Dr. S. Neblett.
John P. Nelson, A. B.....Alabama.
Thos. G. Peachy, A. B...Williamsburg...........Son of Dr. T. G. Peachy.
Charles H. Shield, A. B..Norfolk....................Son of Charles H. Shield.
Joel A. Billups, L. B.....Georgia.
Daniel H. Foster, L. B..Mathews..................Son of R. Foster.
James F. Jenkins, L. B...Suffolk.
John W. King, L. B......Mecklenburg.
Joseph H. Lewis, L. B...Essex ......................Son of Warner Lewis.
Bernard Peyton, L. B...Richmond................Son of Bernard Peyton.
Sydney Smith, L. B......Williamsburg.
J. N. B. Thomas, L. B...Isle of Wight............Son of Josiah Thomas.
Geo. G. Thompson, L. B..Culpeper.
Richard A. Barker.........Richmond.
Arthur Brown...............Westmoreland.
Henry B. Brown..........Richmond.
C. C. Chalmers.............Isle of Wight..........Son of James Chalmers.
J. L. Claiborne............Pittsylvania.............Son of Leonard Claiborne.
William H. Curtis.........Warwick..................Son of Dr. D. P. Curtis.
William A. Durfey.........Williamsburg..........Son of W. Durfey.
John R. Jameson..........Lunenburg.
Anderson W. Kercheval..Hampshire.
C. R. McAlpine............Portsmouth.
James D. McEvery........Louisiana.
James E. McFarland......Petersburg.
John F. Miller..............Greenbrier.
James M. Pasteur..........Alabama.
John L. Scott...............Dinwiddie............Son of Wm. B. Scott.
William A. Scott...........     "          .........     "          "
Walter Scott.................Richmond.............Son of Robert G. Scott.
John A. Selden ............Charles City.........Son of John A. Selden.
J. P. Taylor.................Nottoway.
F. J. Thompson.............Culpeper .............Son of F. J. Thompson.
T. H. Urquhart.............Southampton........Son of C. F. Urquhart.
William R. Vaughan......Hampton...............Son of James M. Vaughan.

## CATALOGUE OF ALUMNI.

| NAMES. | RESIDENCES. | REMARKS. |
|---|---|---|
| William J. Waller | Williamsburg | Son of Benj. Waller. |
| Wm. R. Wood | Amelia | Son of Alfred Wood. |

### 1846-47.

| | | |
|---|---|---|
| James S. Christian, A. M. | Williamsburg | Son of Judge John B. Christian. |
| Joseph A. Lewis, A. M. | | |
| John B. Christian, A. B. | " | Son of Judge John B. Christian. |
| Robert Christian, A. B. | " | " " |
| Peyton S. Coles, A. B. | Albemarle | Son of Col. John Coles. |
| Miles K. Crenshaw, A. B. | Fluvanna. | |
| J. Henry Earnest, A. B. | Hanover | Son of J. H. Earnest. |
| W. J. Haile, A. B. | | |
| Julian Harrison, A. B. | Goochland | Son of Randolph Harrison. Col. C. S. A. |
| Archi. McCandlish, A. B. | Williamsburg | Son of Robert McCandlish. |
| Vinc. D. Markham, A. B. | Powhatan | Son of Vincent Markham. |
| Simon B. Marye, A. B. | Mississippi. | |
| Hugh M. Waller, A. B. | Williamsburg | Son of Dr. Robert P. Waller. Capt. C. S. A. |
| Thos. N. Watson, A. B. | Richmond | Son of Dr. G. Watson. |
| Robt. B. Armistead, L. B. | Alabama. | |
| Jos. S. R. Clarke, L. B. | Williamsburg. | |
| Saml. H. Hairston, L. B. | Mississippi. | |
| Jas. Barron Hope, L. B. | Norfolk | Editor and Poet. Major C. S. A. |
| William B. Jones, L. B. | Warwick | Son of W. S. Jones. Capt. C. S. A. |
| Woodson C. Moody | Williamsburg. | |
| John Motley, L. B. | King & Queen | Son of John Motley. Capt. C. S. A. |
| Eaton Nance, L. B. | Richmond. | |
| A. S. Norment, L. B. | Hanover | Son of Joseph Norment. |
| Jesse T. Bernard | Portsmouth | Son of Overton Bernard. |
| John S. Burwell | Clarke | Son of George H. Burwell. |
| John M. Chevers | Old Point | Son of Rev. M. L. Chevers. |
| William J. Councill | Suffolk. | |
| Charles Dabney | Mississippi. | |
| Thomas M. Fleming | Goochland | Son of Tarlton Fleming. C. S. A. |
| John E. Friend | Chesterfield. | |
| G. W. Harrison | Brunswick. | |
| John Henderson | Georgia. | |
| Reuben B. Hicks | Brunswick | Son of Thomas Hicks. |
| B. C. Houston | Georgia. | |
| Samuel Hulston | Henry county. | |
| George B. Jones | Hampton | Son of John Jones. |
| James Kent | Petersburg | Son of Charles Kent. |
| William H. Mitchell | Richmond | Son of William Mitchell. |

| NAMES. | RESIDENCES. | REMARKS. |

J. J. Moody..................Essex.
George W. Shields...........Norfolk .........Son of William C. Shields.
Philip E. Tabb................Gloucester...........Son of Philip E. Tabb.
P. A. Taliaferro...............    "        ............Son of W. T. Taliaferro. Surgeon C. S. A.
Thomas W. Upshur...........Norfolk ............Son of George P. Upshur.
Joseph Vaiden.................New Kent...........Son of H. D. Vaiden.
B. H. Walker...................Greensville ..........Son of W. F. Walker.
James C. Walton..............Brunswick...........Son of R. H. H. Walton.
Junius L. Weisiger............Goochland............C. S. A.

## 1847–48.

Richard S. Eubank, A. B...Essex ....................Son of William Eubank.
C. W. Murdaugh, A. B......Portsmouth..........Son of James Murdaugh.
Richard Coke, L. B...........Williamsburg.......Son of John Coke. Governor of Texas 1874. Capt. C. S. A.
S. A. Goodwynn, L. B......Greensville.
A. J. Henshaw, L. B.........Alabama.
R. L. Kent, L. B...............Charlotte.
R. J. Lackey, L. B............Northumberland ...Son of John T. Lackey.
H. J. Lee, L. B..................Lunenburg...........Son of Rev. H. Lee.
Joseph E. N. Lewis, L. B.Jefferson ...............Son of John H. Lewis.
G. C. W. Palmore, L. B.....Cumberland .........Son of John L. Palmore.
St. George Tucker, L. B.....Winchester...........Son of H. St. George Tucker. Lt. Col. C. S. A.
W. Armistead.....................Alabama.............Son of William Armistead.
B. B. Botts.........................Richmond............ Son of John Minor Botts.
James T. Bowyer...............Botetourt..............Son of H. W. Bowyer.
Tucker S. Coles..................Albemarle.............Son of John Coles.
S. H. Davies......................Greensville.
W. A. Dudley....................Petersburg.
Joseph Edwards................Surry.
R. E. Harris.......................Nelson.
John T. Lyle.....................Richmond.............Son of James Lyle.
W. H. Lyons.....................    "        ............Son of James Lyons. Judge Hustings Court, Richmond city.
A. T. Mason.....................Dinwiddie ............Son of William Mason.
Jesse A. Parker................ Isle of Wight.
W. H. Priddy...................Hanover.
R. Randolph.....................Alabama.............Son of Carter Randolph.
Leroy H. Redwood...........    "        ............Son of W. H. Redwood.
• Robert W. Starke............Richmond............Son of Joseph Starke.
J. P. Taliaferro.................Baltimore.............Son of B. G. Taliaferro.
Langdon C. Taylor..........Williamsburg........Son of E. D. Taylor.
A. B. Tucker....................Winchester...........Son of Henry St. George Tucker.

## CATALOGUE OF ALUMNI.

| NAMES. | RESIDENCES. | REMARKS. |
|---|---|---|
| James G. Tyler | Hanover | Son of Dr. W. H. Tyler. |
| Tully R. Wise | Washington city | Son of T. R. Wise. |

### 1848*–49.

John R. Bland, L. B.
Richard S. Eubank, L. B...Essex ............Son of William Eubank.
Joel Hayes, L. B..............Gloucester............Son of Joel Hays.
Cassius Lee, L. B............Alexandria.
Edwin T. Mapp, L. B......Accomac.
Wm. C. Nash....................Powhatan............Son of Judge Nash.
H. Tinker..........................Alabama.

### 1849–50.

J. B. Christian, A. M., L.B.Williamsburg........Son of Judge John B. Christian.
Robert Christian, A. M.....      "                "
A. McCandlish, A. M., L.B.      "        ........Son of Robert McCandlish.
H. M. Waller, A. M...........      "        ........Son of Dr. Robert P. Waller.
                Capt. C. S. A.
Ambrose S. Lee, L. B......Lunenburg ............Son of Rev. H. Lee.
J. A. Jones, L. B..............Hampton ..............Son of W. W. Jones.
George Mason, L. B.........Winchester.............Son of Hon. J. W. Mason.
Talbot Sweeny, L. B........Williamsburg.
John S. Coles....................Albemarle.
S. D. Dickinson................Georgia.
William H. Fauntleroy.....King and Queen.
H. B. Hammond...............Maine.
Randolph Harrison............Goochland...........Son of Randolph Harrison. Col.
                C. S. A.
O. D. McCarty..................Richmond county..Son of J. B. McCarty.
Robert B. Martin...............North Carolina.
W. R. Mason.....................King George.........Son of W. R. Mason.
Colin Neblett.....................Lunenburg ..........Son of Dr. S. Neblett.
Henry J. Porter.................Georgia.
Tazewell Tyler..................Charles City.........Son of Hon. John Tyler. Surgeon C. S. A.

### 1850–51.

William Blane, L. B.........Halifax..................Son of Jacob Blane.
Isaac H. Christian, L. B...Charles City.........Son of I. H. Christian.
Lemuel Napier, L. B........Alabama.
Wm. E. Atkinson..............Lunenburg ..........Son of R. B. Atkinson.
A. J. Brent........................Northumberland.

---

* There were no exercises in any but the Law Department during this year.

CATALOGUE OF ALUMNI. 143

| NAMES. | RESIDENCES. | REMARKS. |
|---|---|---|
| William W. Douglas | Williamsburg | Son of Wm. R. C. Douglas. Surgeon. C. S. A. U. S. Consul. |
| William R. Fleming | Goochland | Son of Tarlton Fleming. Lieut. C. S. A. |
| C. A. Harrison | Cumberland. | |
| Caspar McElfresh | Maryland. | |
| E. H. Pollard | Albemarle | Son of Richard Pollard. |
| John S. Prout | Washington city | Prof. Medical College, Brooklyn, N. Y. |
| J. Speed Rudd | Fredericksburg | Son of Capt. Rudd. |
| W. F. Shield | Norfolk | Son of Charles H. Shield. |
| J. F. Tucker | Mississippi. | |
| William H. Urquhart | Isle of Wight. | |
| William A. Washington | Westmoreland | Son of Lawrence Washington. |
| Benjamin T. Williamson | Richmond | Son of D. G. Williamson. |

## 1851-52.

| | | |
|---|---|---|
| Robert H. Bush, B. P* | James City | Son of William Bush. |
| Walter Gwynne, B. P | Richmond | Son of Walter Gwynne. |
| John H. Ivy, A. B | North Carolina | Son of Benjamin W. Ivy. |
| Philip A. Johnson, A. B | Illinois. | |
| W. M. Pendleton, B. P | Norfolk | Son of E. Pendleton. |
| W. Y. Peyton, A. B | Williamsburg. | |
| A. G. Tinsley, B. P | Richmond | Son of Thomas G. Tinsley. |
| W. A. Todd, A. B | Norfolk | Son of Mallory M. Todd. |
| Chann. M. Williams, A. M. | Williamsburg | Episcopal Bishop to China. |
| John B. Amiss | Rappahannock | Son of E. Amiss. |
| T. J. Barham | Sussex. | |
| John Bolling | Richmond. | |
| S. Brooks | Chesterfield | Son of T. H. Brooks. |
| John W. Clowes | Williamsburg | Son of Peter Clowes. C. S. A. |
| Benjamin F. Denmead | Baltimore, Md. | Son of Adam Denmead. |
| Edward Denmead | " | |
| William T. Fisher | Northampton | Son of Thomas Fisher. |
| John T. Fitchett | " | Son of George P. Fitchett. |
| John Fontaine | Georgia | Son of John Fontaine. |
| Thomas T. Galt | Fluvanna | Son of William Galt. |
| John K. Johns | Baltimore | Son of Henry D. Johns. |
| E. E. Kellam | Accomac. | |
| Samuel S. Kirkland | North Carolina | Son of J. W. Kirkland. Capt. C. S. A. |
| G. E. Labby | Lynchburg. | |
| E. G. Lee | Jefferson | Son of E. J. Lee. |
| William E. Lively | Williamsburg | Son of Charles Lively. |

* Bachelor of Philosophy.

# CATALOGUE OF ALUMNI.

| NAMES. | RESIDENCES. | REMARKS. |
|---|---|---|
| John W. Nottingham....... | " | ........Son of A. T. Nottingham. |
| J. R. Purnell.................. | Worcester ......... | Son of Jonn S. Purnell. |
| John W. Scott................ | Fauquier. | |
| Edward Smith............... | Warren county. | |
| L. W. Smith................... | Norfolk............. | Son of A. S. Smith. |
| William T. Snead........ ...... | Accomac............. | Son of Charles Snead. |
| G. L. Thrift................... | Norfolk. | |
| L. Whelan..................... | Louisiana. | |
| John T. Williams.............. | Prince William...... | Son of John Williams. |
| Walter Winn.................. | Louisiana. | |

## 1852-53.

W. M. A. Brodnax, L. B...Alabama...............Son of J. W. Brodnax.
C. L. McCrae, B. P..........Prince William......Son of Dr. J. W. F. McCrae.
D. McChichester, B. P......Fairfax................Son of J. E. McChichester.
John B. Donovan, L. B.....Gloucester............Son of Cornelius Donovan. C. S. A.
C. F. Goodwynn, L. B......Greensville.
W. Gwynn, L. B..............Richmond ...........Son of Walter Gwynn.
Jno. S. Hansborough, A.M.Orange. ...............Episcopal Clergyman.
S. G. Harris, A. B............Mecklenburg.........Surgeon C. S. A.
George K. Hart, L. B........Baylesburg.
E. H. Henry, A. B...........Fauquier ....... ......Son of Dr. E. H. Henry.
J. B. Jett, B. P...............Westmoreland ......Son of James Jett. Judge State Court.
George W. Stone, A. M.....Brunswick...........Son of George Stone.
A. Stubblefield, L. B.........Charles City.........Son of J. S. Stubblefield.
W. W. Trent, B. P............Cumberland ........Son of C. Trent.
James M. Wise, A. M........Washington, D. C..Son of Tully R. Wise. Capt. C. S. A.
George D. Wise, A. B.......Accomac ..............Son of John J. Wise. Capt. C. S. A. Killed before Petersburg.
Obadiah J. Wise, L. B....... " ...............Son of Henry A. Wise, Governor of Virgina. Editor "Richmond Enquirer." Capt. C. S. A. Killed at battle Roanoke Island.
Robert E. Wynne, L. B.....Williamsburg........Son of Thomas Wynne.
George G. Atkins............. "
C. F. Berkeley ................Loudoun .............Son of Lewis Berkeley. Capt. C. S. A.
E. F. Bowyer..........................Fincastle ............Son of H. W. Bowyer.
F. E. Buford.....................Brunswick............Son of Wm. P. Buford.
John H. Clark..................Halifax...............Son of John T. Clark.
George H. Coke ...............Williamsburg .......Son of John Coke. Surgeon C. S. A.

CATALOGUE OF ALUMNI.     145

| NAMES. | RESIDENCES. | REMARKS. |
|---|---|---|
| John W. Custis | Accomac. | |
| N. H. Fisher | Northampton | Son of M. W. Fisher. |
| W. Green | Warrenton | Son of E. F. Green. |
| R. Gregory | King William. | |
| E. L. Hooff | Jefferson. | |
| D. F. May | Petersburg | Son of David May. Surgeon C. S. A. |
| James May | " | Son of David May. Officer C. S. A. |
| J. Michie | " | Son of Dr. W. G. Michie. |
| S. H. Newman | Baltimore. | |
| John K. Nichols | Georgia | Son of S. W. Nichols. |
| R. Nottingham | Northampton | Son of L. B. Nottingham. |
| A. A. O'Neel | Monroe. | |
| T. C. Parramore | Accomac | Judge State Court. |
| John M. Pettitt | Williamsburg | Son of William M. Pettitt. C. S. A. |
| W. H. Shield | York | Son of William H. Shield. Surgeon C. S. A. |
| G. H. Shorter | Georgia. | |
| P. T. Sutton | Hanover | Son of James Sutton. Capt. C. S. A. |
| Watkins Warren | Williamsburg | Son of Dr. M. S. Warren. |
| H. M. Washington | Brentsville | Son of J. M. Washington. |
| Charles Wilkinson | Norfolk | Son of J. Wilkinson. |
| W. G. Williams | Orange | Son of L. B. Williams. |
| Wm. Williamson | " | |
| W. N. J. Winder | Northampton. | |
| J. H. D. Wingfield | Portsmouth | Son of Rev. J. H. Wingfield. Episcopal clergyman. |
| H. A. Wise | Accomac | Son of Hon. Henry A. Wise. Episcopal clergyman. |

## 1853-54.

| | | |
|---|---|---|
| A. Ashton, B. P | King George. | |
| M. D. Ball, A. B | Fairfax | Son of S. M. Ball. Col. C. S. A. |
| Wm. H. Burroughs, L. B. | Princess Anne | Son of J. J. Burroughs. |
| A. Coke, B. P | Williamsburg | Son of John Coke. Capt. C. S. A. |
| C. R. Grandy, A. B. | Norfolk | Son of C. W. Grandy. |
| J. S. Gilliam, A. M | Petersburg | Surgeon C. S. A. |
| William Lamb, B. P | Norfolk | Son of William W. Lamb. Col. C. S. A. |
| B. T. Tayloe, B. P | Prince George | Son of E. T. Tayloe. Officer C. S. A. |
| T. G. Wynne, A. B. | Williamsburg | Son of R. C. Wynne. |
| R. P. Alexander | Mecklenburg | Son of M. Alexander. |
| H. M. Ashby | Fauquier | Col. C. S. A. |
| J. E. Bland | King & Queen | Son of Robert Bland. |

12

## CATALOGUE OF ALUMNI.

| NAMES. | RESIDENCES. | REMARKS. |
|---|---|---|
| Roderick Bland | " | Son of Roderick Bland. |
| R. E. Bland | City Point | Son of J. B. Bland. |
| R. T. Bland | Middlesex | Son of A. Bland. |
| Edward F. Brodnax | North Carolina | Son of R. Brodnax. |
| Cassius Carter | Prince William. | |
| H. E. Coleman | Halifax | Son of John Coleman. Col. C. S. A. |
| J. Cushing Dame | Danville | Son of Rev. George W. Dame. |
| Wm. P. Dixon | Alexandria | Son of Turner Dixon. |
| Joseph W. Glover | Prince George | Son of Archibald Glover. |
| James T. Harris | Mecklenburg. | |
| Washington Hunt | Northampton. | |
| J. J. Lampkin | Kinsale, Va. | |
| W. T. Lipscombe | Williamsburg | Son of Roscow Lipscombe. |
| T. L. Lomax | King George | Son of M. S. Lomax. Officer C. S. A. |
| D'Arcy Paul | Norfolk | Son of S. W. Paul. |
| William Pettis | Williamsburg. | Episcopal clergyman. |
| George T. Scarburgh | " | Son of Judge G. P. Scarburgh. Surgeon C. S. A. |
| W. S. O. Slade | Washington, D. C. | Son of William O. Slade. Capt. C. S. A. |
| W. W. Strachan | Petersburg | Son of F. F. Strachan. |
| Van Taliaferro | Lynchburg | Son of B. B. Taliaferro. |
| Henry A. Tayloe | Richmond | Son of W. H. Tayloe. C. S. A. |
| M. J. White | Mississippi | Son of Franklin White. |
| Thomas G. Williamson | Portsmouth | Son of Lieut. G. G. Williamson. Capt. C. S. A. |
| W. D. Winston | Hanover | Son of W. D. Winston. |
| George D. Wise' | Washington, D. C. | Son of T. R. Wise. Capt. C. S. A. |
| Andrew F. Withers | Fauquier | C. S. A. |

### 1854–55.

| | | |
|---|---|---|
| Charles R. Grandy, A. M. | Norfolk | Son of C. W. Grandy. |
| Wm. J. Morrisett, A. M. | Williamsburg. | |
| R. McPhail Smith, A. M. | North Carolina | Son of L. L. Smith. |
| Walker W. Vest, A. M. | Williamsburg | Son of W. W. Vest. C. S. War Department. |
| Wm. D. Bloxham, L. B. | Florida | Son of William Bloxham. |
| John A. Clark, L. B. | Charles City | Son of J. J. Clark. C. S. A. |
| J. B. Jett, L. B. | Westmoreland | Son of James Jett. C. S. A. |
| Wm. Lamb, L. B., B. P. | Norfolk | Son of William W. Lamb. Col. C. S. A. |
| S. J. Pendleton, L. B. | Williamsburg | Son of William Pendleton. |
| Wm. Y. Peyton, L. B., A. B. | " | |
| T. W. Thompson, L. B. | Moundsville | Son of Col. John Thompson. |

## CATALOGUE OF ALUMNI. 147

| NAMES. | RESIDENCES. | REMARKS. |
|---|---|---|
| Geo. D. Wise, L. B., A. B. | Accomac | Son of John J. Wise. Capt. C. S. A. Killed before Petersb'g. |
| A. Taylor Bell, A. B. | Norfolk | Son of Alexander Bell. Surgeon C. S. A. |
| Hill Carter, Jun., A. B. | Shirley | Son of Hill Carter. Officer C. S. A. Killed at Wilderness. |
| Claudius R. Hains, A. B. | South Carolina | Son of C. R. Hains. Episcopal clergyman. |
| Wm. F. M. Jacobs, A. B. | Martinsburg | Son of B. L. Jacobs. Episcopal clergyman. |
| John N. Murphy, A. B. | Westmoreland. | |
| R. H. Murphy, A. B | Old Point Comfort. | Son of J. W. Murphy. Episco- clergyman. |
| Alfred M. Randolph, A. B. | Fauquier | Son of Robt. L. Randolph. Epis- copal clergyman. |
| J. R. Robertson, A. B. | Petersburg | Son of James Robertson. C. S. A. |
| Chas. S. Stringfellow, A.B. | " | Son of Rev. H. Stringfellow.— Maj. C. S. A. |
| Cyrus W. Grandy, B. P. | North Carolina. | |
| Henry Gwynn, B. P. | Raleigh | Son of Walter Gwynn. Officer C. S. A. |
| F. C. S. Hunter, B. P. | King George | Son of Dr. Thomas L. Hunter. Officer C. S. A. |
| A. W. C. Nowlin, B. P. | Wytheville | Son of B. W. Nowlin. State Senator. |
| John M. Adams | Alabama | Son of R. H. Adams. |
| Thomas Ball | Richmond county. | C. S. A. |
| Robert A. Bright | Williamsburg | Son of Samuel F. Bright. Capt. C. S. A. |
| E. B. Challener | James City. | |
| John R. Chilton | Lancaster. | |
| John A. Clarke | Charles City | Son of J. J. Clarke. C. S. A. |
| A. S. Davidson | Louisiana | Son of Dr. J. P. Davidson. |
| Richard A. Davis | Gloucester | Son of R. A. Davis. |
| Riddick Gatling | | Son of Riddick Gatling. |
| E. C. Gee | Brunswick. | |
| J. P. Gilliam | Dinwiddie. | |
| Edward M. Harris | Brunswick | Son of John S. Harris. |
| W. L. Henderson. | | |
| Parke Jones | James City | Son of William M. Jones. |
| Edward H. Lively | Williamsburg | C. S. A. |
| Junius E. Marks | Prince George | Son of E. A. Marks. C. S. A. |
| E. Morrissett | Chesterfield | Son of T. E. Morrissett. C. S. A. |
| John T. Perrin | Gloucester | Son of William K. Perrin. Maj. C. S. A. |
| John H. Sands | Williamsburg | Son of Johnson Sands. Capt. C. S. A. |

| NAMES. | RESIDENCES. | REMARKS. |

T. E. Shands............... ..........Prince George.
A. S. Smith.................. ..........Norfolk............. ......Son of Rev. A. S. Smith. C. S. A.
J. R. Smith................... .........   "          ...............Son of Rev. A. S. Smith. C. S. A.
A. H. Smyth............. ..........Alexandria.
Joseph W. Southall.......... ..Amelia...... ............Son of Dr. P. T. Southall.
John S. Sullavan............ ......Lancaster ..........C. S. A.
Edwin Sully.. ..................Alexandria .........C. S. A.
Douglas W. Trower.........Northampton.
H. B. Warren................. ..........James City... ..........Son of M. S. Warren. C. S. A.

## 1855-56.

Henry E. Clark, A. M......Halifax.............. ......Son of J. T. Clark.
A. D. Payne, A. M......... Fauquier..... ..........Son of R. Payne. Col. C. S. A.
Henry C. Slaughter, A. M..Pittsylvania..........Son of C. D. Slaughter.
P. Bell Smith, A. M..........Fauquier............. ...Son of Hon. Wm. Smith. Capt. C. S. A.
Thomas P. Smith, A. M....     "      ...............Son of Hon. Wm. Smith. Col. C. S. A.
Thos. T. L. Snead, A. M...Accomac...............Son of George F. Snead. Prof. Mathematics William and Mary College. Capt. C. S. A.
W. Talbot Walke, A. M....Norfolk............. ........Son of Richard Walke. Officer C. S. A.
Alexander Coke, L. B......Williamsburg........Son of John Coke. Capt. C. S. A.
Edgar B. Montague, L. B..Middlesex ..........Col. C. S. A.
James B. Pannill, L. B.... Pittsylvania..........Son of William L. Pannill. C. S. A.
James H. Barnes, A. B.....James City............Son of William H. Barnes. C. S. A.
Robt. J. Graves, A. B......Albany, N. Y.......Presbyterian clergyman.
Wm. H. Graves, A. B......Wythe.................. ..........Capt. C. S. A.
Wm. W. Payne, A. B......Fauquier.............. ......Son of R. Payne. Surgeon C. S. A.
Samuel J. Hough, B. P.....Baltimore............ ..Son of S. H. Hough. C. S. A.
D. S. Baldwin............... ..........Richmond ............Son of O. P. Baldwin.
Woodville Bowyer............Fincastle............. ......Son of H. W. Bowyer.
Julian R. Beckwith..........Prince George.......Son of Dr. T. S. Beckwith. C. S. A.
P. G. Breckinridge........... .........Botetourt.......... ......Son of Cary Breckinridge. Capt. C. S. A.
Wm. H. Clay........... ..........Amelia ......... ......C. S. A.
J. C. Dame................. ........Danville............. ......Son of Rev. G. W. Dame.
Samuel D. Davies............Prince George.......Son of John B. Davies.
J. E. S. Delk................. ..........Isle of Wight.........Son of Jeremiah Delk.

## CATALOGUE OF ALUMNI. 149

| NAMES. | RESIDENCES. | REMARKS. |
|---|---|---|
| S. D. Delk | Isle of Wight | Son of Jeremiah Delk. |
| R. R. Gaines | Alabama | Son of W. D. Gaines. |
| W. K. Gatewood | Middlesex | Son of Dr. W. L. Gatewood. C. S. A. |
| Jno. W. Green | Culpeper | Son of William Green, Esq. C. S. A. Killed in battle. |
| John Jerdone | Orange | Son of Francis Jerdone. C. S. A. |
| Geo. W. Johnston | Norfolk | Son of James H. Johnston. |
| Roswell Lindsay | Williamsburg | Son of William T. Lindsay. C. S. A. |
| William E. Lively | " | Son of Charles Lively. C. S. A. |
| Goodrich Mitchell | Fauquier | Son of Dr. R. T. Mitchell. C. S. A. |
| R. W. Nottingham | Northampton. | |
| Richard M. Page | Gloucester | Capt. C. S. A. |
| William H. Pettitt | Williamsburg | Son of Wm. M. Pettitt. C. S. A. Died in service. |
| Robt. M. Spencer | Greensville | Son of D. W. Spencer. C. S. A. |
| Isaiah H. White | Accomac | Son of S. C. White. Surgeon C. S. A. |
| Thomas G. Williamson | Caroline | Son of G. G. Williamson. Capt. C. S. A. |

## 1856-57.

| | | |
|---|---|---|
| D. U. Barziza, A. M. | Williamsburg | Son of P. J. Barziza. Capt. C. S. A. |
| R. W. Lamb, A. M. | Norfolk | Son of W. W. Lamb. Capt. C. S. A. |
| T. P. McCandlish, A. M. | Williamsburg | Son of Colonel R. McCandlish. Capt. C. S. A. |
| Richard Walke, A. M. | Norfolk | Son of Rich'd Walke. C. S. A. |
| Philip J. Barziza, L. B. | Williamsburg | Son of P. J. Barziza. |
| Paul C. Edmunds, L. B. | Halifax | Son of J. R. Edmunds. Officer C. S. A. |
| W. H. Graves, A. B., L. B. | Wytheville | Capt. C. S. A. |
| R. McPhail Smith, A. M., L. B. | North Carolina | Son of L. L. Smith. |
| G. W. Stone, A. M., L. B. | Brunswick | Son of George Stone. C. S. A. |
| Philip M. Arnold, A. B. | King George | Son of John Arnold. C. S. A. |
| Thomas T. Arnold, A. B. | " | " " C. S. A. |
| Edward L. Baptist, A. B. | Mecklenburg | Son of R. H. Baptist. C. S. A. |
| W. I. Clopton, A. B. | Williamsburg | Son of Judge J. B. Clopton.—Capt. C. S. A. Judge State court. |
| Joseph G. Griswold, A. B. | Richmond | Son of C. G. Griswold. Maj. C. S. A. |

150 CATALOGUE OF ALUMNI.

| NAMES. | RESIDENCES. | REMARKS. |

Jesse S. Jones, A. B.........Hampton ............Lieut. C. S. A.
Edmunds Mason, A. B.....Greensville............Son of Dr. George Mason. Surgeon C. S. A.
Wm. C. Parham, A. B......Brunswick............Son of Dr. E. H. M. Parham. Capt. C. S. A.
John H. Barlow...............Williamsburg........Son of J. H. Barlow. Officer C. S. A.
Josiah L. Bayly..............Accomac.............Son of J. J. Bayly. Captain C. S. A.
Robert A. Bowry.............Williamsburg........C. S. A.
Thomas E. C. Curtis.........Accomac.
V. H. Fauntleroy............Middlesex.............Son of Dr. R. B. Fauntleroy.
William M. Feild.............Dinwiddie............Son of Dr. Hume Feild.
Henry M. Isham..............New York............Son of A. H. Isham.
J. C. P. Kellam................Accomac.
John W. Lawson..............Williamsburg........Surg'n C. S. A. State Senator.
John S. Lindsay...............Williamsburg........Son of Thomas Lindsay. Episcopal clergyman.
J. J. H. Newman..............Baltimore.
R. A. Owens....................Williamsburg.
B. G. Smith......................North Carolina.....Son of William R. Smith.
J. S. Spencer....................Greensville..........Son of Thomas R. Spencer. C. S. A.
Charles W. Thomas.........Williamsburg........Son of William Thomas.
T. H. Thompson ..............      "          ........Son of Willis Thompson.
R. R. Weisiger..................Goochland.

## 1857-58.

William R. Garrett, A. M.Williamsburg........Son of Dr. R. M. Garrett. Capt. S. A.
B. St. George Tucker,A.M..       "          ........Son of Judge B. Tucker. Surgeon C. S. A.
James Monroe, L. B.........New York............Son of A. Monroe, and nephew of ex-President Monroe.
Joseph W. Stone, L. B......Mississippi............Son of J. H. Stone.
William R. Sullivan, L. B..Williamsburg.
Robert G. Taylor, L. B.....Gloucester............C. S. A.
Wm. J. H. Ballard, A. B...Orange.
John H. Beale, A. B.........Fredericksburg......C. S. A.
A. S. Furcron, A. B..........Chesterfield..........Son of Thomas Furcron. C. S. A.
Thomas W. Mason, A. B...Greensville ..........Son of Dr. G. Mason. C. S. A.
S. W. Murphy, A. B..........Maryland.............Son of J. W. Murphy. Episcopal clergyman.
H. M. Stringfellow, A. B...Hanover...............Son of Rev. H. Stringfellow.— Capt. C. S. A.
John C. Ames, B. P.........Washington, D. C..Son of George C. Ames.

## CATALOGUE OF ALUMNI.

| NAMES. | RESIDENCES. | REMARKS. |
|---|---|---|
| Wm. R. Taliaferro, B. P. | Orange | Son of E. P. Taliaferro. C. S. A. |
| Charles S. Wools, B. P. | Vicksburg | Lieut. C. S. A. |
| W. A. Bragg | Petersburg | Son of William A. Bragg. |
| Charles E. Clay | Bedford | Son of P. A. Clay. C. S. A. |
| Octavius Coke | Williamsburg | Son of John Coke. Capt. C. S. A. |
| C. W. Foreman | Princess Anne | Son of John F. Foreman. C. S. A. |
| W. J. Garnett | Richmond | Son of Jas. M. Garnett. C. S. A. |
| P. Hamilton | Halifax | Lieut. C. S. A. |
| Henry Hunton | Prince William | Son of Charles H. Hunton. C. S. A. |
| R. W. James | Williamsburg | Son of J. T. James. C. S. A. |
| George E. Mann | Gloucester | Son of C. Mann. C. S. A.—Judge, Galveston, Texas. |
| William Marshall | Fauquier | Grandson of Chief Justice. Capt. C. S. A. |
| Benjamin H. May | Petersburg | Son of Dr. David May. C. S. A. |
| R. A. Parker | Sussex | Son of J. H. Parker. C. S. A. |
| John Pierce | Williamsburg | Son of William Pierce. C. S. A. |
| Charles W. Snead | Accomac | Son of Charles Snead. |
| L. L. Snead | " | " " |
| George W. Stone. | | |
| A. D. Tapscott | Lancaster. | |

## 1858-59.

| | | |
|---|---|---|
| R. T. Armistead | Williamsburg | Son of R. H. Armistead. C. S. A. |
| Edmund R. Bagwell | Onancock | Son of Dr. Thomas P. Bagwell. Lieut. C. S. A. Gen'l Virginia Militia. |
| Thomas J. Barlow | Williamsburg | Son of John H. Barlow. Lieut. C. S. A. |
| James W. Belvin | Yorktown | Son of James Belvin. Surgeon C. S. A. |
| T. R. Bowden | Williamsburg | Son of L. J. Bowden. |
| E. Camm | " | Son of Dr. Edward Camm. C. S. A. |
| Thomas C. Carrington | " | C. S. A. |
| S. S. Chevers | Old Point Comfort. | Son of Rev. M. L. Chevers. Episcopal clergyman. |
| F. G. Claiborne | Halifax | C. S. A. |
| W. S. Davis | Brunswick | Son of T. S. Davis. C. S. A. |
| T. K. Forniss | Alabama | Son of P. D. Forniss. C. S. A. Killed in battle. |
| Thomas Clayton Frame | Delaware. | |
| A. S. Furcron | Chesterfield | C. S. A. |
| S. W. Gary | Norfolk | C. S. A. |
| W. Galt | Fluvanna | Son of James Galt. C. S. A. |

CATALOGUE OF ALUMNI.

| NAMES. | RESIDENCES. | REMARKS. |
|---|---|---|
| T. R. Harrison | Richmond | Son of William M. Harrison.— Lieut. C. S. A. |
| R. T. Hurt | Petersburg | Son of B. T. Hurt. C. S. A. |
| M. Hurst | Nortumberland | Son of W. Hurst. |
| W. R. Hargrove | Surry. | |
| R. H. Jones | Hampton. | |
| Wickliffe Kincheloe | Virginia | Son of B. Kincheloe. C. S. A. Killed in battle. |
| George W. Lindsay | Richmond | Son of J. M. Lindsay. C. S. A. |
| George H. May | Petersburg | Son of Dr. David May. C. S. A. |
| H. S. McCandlish | Williamsburg | Son of Col. Rob't McCandlish. C. S. A. |
| Norman M. Neblett | Lunenburg | Son of Sterling Neblett. C. S. A. |
| George H. Poindexter | Richmond | Son of J. H. Poindexter. C. S. A. |
| D. R. Phifer | North Carolina | Son of C. Phifer. C. S. A. |
| T. V. Robinson | Richmond. | C. S. S. |
| L. H. Smith | North Carolina. | C. S. A. |
| T. S. B. Tucker | Williamsburg | Son of Judge B. Tucker. Capt. C. S. A. |
| R. Totten | " | Son of Silas Totten. Episcopal clergyman. |
| James E. Worthen | Richmond | Son of John Worthen. C. S. A. |
| Bobt. E. Wynn | Petersburg | Son of John M. Wynn. C. S. A. |
| W. G. Wynn | " | " " C. S. A. |
| William L. Young | Warwick | C. S. A. |

## 1859-60.

Walter E. Weir, A. M......Prince William......Son of William J. Weir. Capt. C. S. A.

Frank H. Alfriend, A. B...Richmond............Son of Thomas M. Alfriend. C. S. A.

J. Filmer Hubbard, A. B...James City...........Son of Dr. C. M. Hubbard. C. S. A.

T. Jefferson Stubbs, A. B..Gloucester............Son of T. J. Stubbs. C. S. A.

William Tayloe, B. P........King George..........Son of Col. E. T. Tayloe. C. S. A.

Robt. C. Atkinson.............Smithfield.............Son of Hon. A. Atkinson. C. S. A.

R. A. Brister......................Berlin...................Son of T. J. Brister. C. S. A.

W. N. Causey....................Hampton..............Son of William Causey. C. S. A.

A. T. Clarke......................Willcox................Son of J. J. Clarke. C. S. A.

W. H. Day........................Grove Hill............W. C. Clanton, Guardian. C. S. A.

H. S. Dix..........................Williamsburg........Son of John S. Dix. C. S. A.

Sterling H. Gee................Weldon, N. C.......Son of Charles J. Gee. Capt. C. S. A. Killed at Five Forks.

## CATALOGUE OF ALUMNI. 153

| NAMES. | RESIDENCES. | REMARKS. |
|---|---|---|
| M. R. Harrell, Jr. | Williamsburg | Son of M. R. Harrell. C. S. A. |
| G. B. Harrison | Cabin Point | Son of William B. Harrison.— C. S. A. |
| J. R. Hubard | Norfolk | Episcopal clergyman. C. S. A. |
| H. T. Jones, Jr | Williamsburg | Son of H. T. Jones. C. S. A. |
| Wm. Ap. C. Jones | Gloucester C. H. | Mrs. M. A. B. Montague, G'n. C. S. A. |
| R. B. Lewis | Oak Grove | Son of Geo. Lewis. C. S. A. |
| J. S. Lindsay | Williamsburg | Son of Thos. Lindsay. Chaplain C. S. A. |
| Thomas H. Mercer | " | Son of Dr. J. C. Mercer. Lieut. C. S. A. |
| Wm. H. E. Morecock | " | Officer C. S. A. |
| John D. Myers | Lexington | Son of J. H. Myers. C. S. A. |
| N. C. Newton | Norfolk | Son of C. W. Newton. C. S. A. |
| W. D. Peachy | Williamsburg | Son of William S. Peachy. C. S. A. |
| Geo. Wilmer Robertson | Petersburg | Son of James Robertson. C. S. A. |
| Wm. Sherwell | Williamsburg | C. S. A. |
| L. P. Slater | " | Son of P. Slater. C. S. A. |
| John Southgate | Norfolk | Tazewell Taylor, Guardian. C. S. A. |
| J. H. Tucker | San Marino | Son of Col. E. B. Tucker. C. S. A. |
| R. B. Tunstall, Jr | Norfolk | Son of Dr. R. B. Tunstall. C. S. A. |
| P. T. Warren | Onancock | Son of Rev. P. Warren. Methodist clergyman. |
| John Wilkinson | Hallsboro' | Son of Richard Wilkinson. C. S. A. |
| J. H. Williams | Northampton | L. B. Nottingham, Guardian. Episcopal minister. |
| Richard A. Wise | Norfolk | Son of Henry A. Wise. Capt. S. A. Prof. of Chemistry of William and Mary College. |
| F. M. Wyman | Vicksburg, Miss. | Son of Geo. Wyman. C. S. A. |

### 1860-61.*

John Archer Coke, A. B...Williamsburg........Son of John Coke. Capt. C. S. A.
Charles S. Harrrison, A. B..Brandon, Pr. Geo..Son of Wm. B. Harrison. Capt. C. S. A.
B. H. B. Hubbard, A. B...Lancaster ...........Son of Wm. Hubbard. C. S. A.

---

* From 1861 to 1865, the College was closed because of the war.

## CATALOGUE OF ALUMNI.

| NAMES. | RESIDENCES. | REMARKS. |
|---|---|---|
| George Mason, A. B | Greensville | Son of Dr. George Mason. C. S. A. |
| Charles Poindexter, A. B. | Richmond | Son of J. H. Poindexter. C. S. A. |
| James N. Stubbs, A. B | Gloucester | Son of T. J. Stubbs. C. S. A. |
| John G. Williams, A. B | Orange | Son of S. B. Williams. C. S. A. |
| Peyton N. Page, B. P | Gloucester | Major C. S. A. |
| Thomas R. Argyle | Goochland C. H. | Son of T. R. Argyle. C. S. A. |
| Richard J. Ayres, Jr | Accomac | Son of R. J. Ayres. |
| Jos. V. Bidgood | Williamsburg | Son of Dr. R. W. Bidgood. Lt. C. S. A. |
| Wm. O. Browne | Hicksford | C. S. A. |
| John W. Bush | Burnt Ordinary | Son of William Bush. C. S. A. |
| J. H. Chandler | Westmoreland | H. Bush, Guardian. C. S. A. |
| J. H. Deans | Gloucester | Son of J. L. Deans. C. S. A. |
| John G. Dix | Williamsburg | Son of John S. Dix. C. S. A. |
| James H. Dix | Accomac | Judge Geo. P. Scarburg, Guar'n. C. S. A. Died in service. |
| Geo. Benj. Fosque | Onancock | Son of John M. Fosque. C. S. A. |
| Worth O. Gwynn | Norfolk | Son of Major T. P. Gwynn. C. S. A. |
| James Hardy | " | Son of Wm. J. Hardy. C. S. A. |
| Gresham Hough | Baltimore, Md | Son of W. D. Hough. C. S. A. |
| Wm. Hoxton | Washington, D. C. | Dr. King, U. S. A., Guardian. Officer C. S. A. Episcopal clergyman. |
| H. E. Jordan | Richmond | Son of B. J. Jordan. C. S. A. |
| Fred. C. A. Kellam, Jr | Accomac | Son of F. C. A. Kellam. |
| Jas. S. Lawson | James City | A. W. Hankins, Guardian. |
| A. L. Lippitt | Alexandria | Son of E. R. Lippitt. |
| M. A. Macmurdo | Hanover | Son of C. W. Macmurdo. C. S. A. |
| Henry J. Meade | Bedford | Jno. A. Wharton, Guardian. C. S. A. |
| Geo. S. Miller | Mathews | Son of S. G. Miller. C. S. A. |
| H. D. Ponton | Weldon, N. C | Son of W. H. Ponton. C. S. A. |
| Wm. A. Reese | Greensville | J. R. Chambliss, Guardian. C. S. A. |
| Wm. Reynolds, Jr | Baltimore, Md | Son of William Reynolds. |
| H. T. Sharp | Norfolk | Son of W. W. Sharp. C. S. A. Episcopal clergyman. |
| E. W. Spratley | Greensville | Son of W. H. Spratley. C. S. A. |
| W. C. Stubbs | Gloucester | Son of J. W. Stubbs. C. S. A. |
| Wm. C. Trueheart | Prince Edward | C. S. A. |
| A. A. Wash | Montpelier | Son of J. C. Wash. C. S. A. |
| John N. Williams | Norfolk | Son of John Williams. C. S. A. |

## CATALOGUE OF ALUMNI. 155

### 1865-66.

| NAMES. | RESIDENCES. | REMARKS. |
|---|---|---|
| †A. J. Adams | Williamsburg | Son of C. J. Adams. |
| Laban J. Belote | Eastville | Son of Laban Belote. |
| †Tucker Brooke | New Kent. | |
| 'O. S. Bunting | Williamsburg | Son of J. Bunting. |
| Frank Camm | " | Son of Dr. E. Camm. |
| Charles Camm | " | " " |
| †J. G. Camm | " | " " |
| †E. P. Cole | " | Son of R. F. Cole. |
| †Jesse Cole | " | " " |
| †J. S. Charles | " | Son of John S. Charles. |
| †R. R. Cole | " | Son of R. F. Cole. |
| †C. W. Cosnahan | " | Son of J. B. Cosnahan. |
| †H. M. Cosnahan | " | " " |
| †R. W. Cosnahan | Richmond | " " |
| †A. S. Cowles | James City | Son of D. S. Cowles. |
| †H. B. Cowles | " | " " |
| †J. R. Darden | Williamsburg | Son of W. W. Darden. |
| †Z. G. Durfey | " | Son of R. G. Durfey. |
| †Wm. E. Durfey | " | Son of W. C. Durfey. |
| John G. Dix | " | Son of John S. Dix. |
| John B. Douglas | " | Son of William R. C. Douglas. |
| Samuel Dunton | Northampton | Geo. B. Taylor, Guardian. |
| †Alex. C. Garrett | Williamsburg. | |
| H. W. Garrett | " | Son of Dr. R. M. Garrett. C. S. A. |
| V. F. Garrett | " | Son of Dr. R. M. Garrett. |
| †T. J. Harrell | " | Son of M. R. Harrell. |
| T. G. Hallyburton | Richmond | Son of Judge Jas. D. Hallyburton. |
| †C. F. Hurt | Williamsburg. | |
| †D. S. Jones | " | Son of H. T. Jones. |
| R. T. Jones | Charles City. | |
| Wm. L. Jones | Williamsburg | Son of H. T. Jones. |
| †J. C. Lucas, Jr | " | Son of J. C. Lucas. |
| †J. T. Lucas | " | " " |
| †Frank Mallory | Hampton | Son of Charles K. Mallory. |
| †L. Martin | James City | Son of Dr. William Martin. |
| †W. Martin | " | " " |
| †J. L. Mercer | Williamsburg | Son of Dr. J. C. Mercer. |
| C. W. Mercer | " | " " |

† Those marked thus † are in the Preparatory Department.

All students who are known to have been in the Confederate army have the letters C. S. A., with known rank, attached to their names. Some, many in fact, are omitted, and as it is the desire of the Faculty to get a perfect war record of all students, additional information is solicited from all concerned.—EDITOR.

## CATALOGUE OF ALUMNI.

| NAMES. | RESIDENCES. | REMARKS. |
|---|---|---|
| †R. P. Mercer | Williamsburg | Son of Dr. J. C. Mercer. |
| †Nathan Metzger | " | Son of Joel Metzger. |
| †W. E. Mullen | " | |
| J. Munford | " | Son of Col. John D. Munford. |
| Robert P. Saunders | " | Son of Robert Saunders. |
| Wm. Sherwell | " | |
| †W. J. Small | " | Son of W. J. Small. |
| †A. E. Smith | " | Son of S. Smith. |
| †H. Smith | " | " " |
| †George T. Smith | " | Son of Isaac Smith. |
| †H. M. Sweeney | " | Son of M. T. Sweeney. |
| B. M. B. Tucker | " | Son of Judge Beverly Tucker. |
| T. S. B. Tucker | " | " " |
| H. R. Vaughan | " | John A. Henley, Guardian. |
| †H. S. Vaughan | " | " " |
| George S. Vest | " | Son of W. W. Vest. C. S. A. |
| †J. B. Waller | " | Son of C. C. P. Waller. |
| †James M. Wineberger | James City. | |
| †Jno. McCabe Wineberger. | " | |
| Charles P. Williamson | Caroline | R. W. McGruder, Guardian. |
| John A. G. Williamson | " | " " |

## 1866-67.

| | | |
|---|---|---|
| M. Dulany Ball, L. B. | Fairfax | Son of S. M. Ball. |
| Samuel J. Hough, L. B. | Baltimore | Son of Samuel Hough. |
| Wm. Reynolds, Jr., L. B. | " | Son of William Reynolds. |
| Thomas G. Jones, B. P. | Middlesex. | |
| †T. S. Brown | Williamsburg | Son of Dixon Brown. |
| John Camm | " | Son of Dr. E. Camm. |
| W. D. Clarke | " | S. S. Moore, Guardian. |
| Woody C. Constable | " | Mrs. Susan Curtis, Guardian. |
| H. D. Cole | " | Son of R. F. Cole. |
| C. R. Cowles | James City | Son of D. S. Cowles. |
| J. W. Daugherty | Williamsburg | Son of L. J. Daugherty. |
| S. J. Dixon | " | Mrs. Mary Williamson, Guard'n. |
| R. B. Douglas | " | Son of W. R. C. Douglas. |
| George E. Floyd | Locustville | Son of Thos. F. Floyd. |
| S. R. Hankins | Surry | Son of John H. Hankins. |
| W. A. Hankins | " | " " |
| J. S. Morris | Williamsburg | Son of Dr. Wm. S. Morris. |
| R. P. W. Morris | " | " " |
| T. Ellis Morrison | " | Son of R. J. Morrison. |
| B. D. Peachy | " | Son of William S. Peachy. |
| T. G. Peachy | " | " " |
| Charles D. Smith | " | Son of Isaac Smith. |
| John B. Spencer | James City | Son of William L. Spencer. |
| W. L. Spencer, Jr | " | " " |

## 1867-68.

| NAMES. | RESIDENCES. | REMARKS. |
|---|---|---|
| John T. Rothrock, A. B. | Tennessee. | |
| F. S. Taylor, A. B. | Norfolk | Son of Tazewell Taylor. |
| T. A. T. Joynes, B. P. | Accomac | Son of T. A. T. Joynes. |
| William D. Peachy, B. P. | Williamsburg | Son of Wm. S. Peachy. |
| Chris. Tompkins, B. P. | Richmond | Son of Col. C. Q. Tompkins. |
| †H. T. Armistead | Williamsburg | Son of R. H. Armistead. |
| †Thos. P. Barham | " | |
| †John H. Bowers | " | |
| †Archer Brooks, Jr | " | Son of A. Brooks. |
| †W. J. Barlow | " | Son of Ro. J. Barlow. |
| Frank Camm | " | Son of Dr. Ed. Camm. |
| J. G. Camm | " | " " |
| E. P. Cole | " | Son of R. F. Cole. |
| R. R. Cole | " | " " |
| W. C. Constable | " | Mrs. J. S. Curtis, Guardian. |
| †A. G. Cowles | James City | Son of D. S. Cowles. |
| J. S. Charles, Jr | Williamsburg | Son of J. S. Charles. |
| J. R. Darden | " | Son of W. W. Darden. |
| †W. T. Darden' | " | " " |
| †L. H. Davis | " | Son of J. A. Davis. |
| Z. G. Durfey | " | Son of R. G. Durfey. |
| †W. H. T. Hancock | " | Son of W. Hancock. |
| Thos. Harrell | " | Son of M. R. Harrell. |
| A. W. Johnson | Sussex | Son of T. L. Johnson. |
| †A. Carter Jones | Williamsburg' | Son of H. T. Jones. |
| †Frank P. Lipscomb | James City | Son of S. Lipscomb. |
| R. P. Mercer | Williamsburg | Son of Dr. J. C. Mercer. |
| †B. B. Morecock | " | W. H. E. Morecock, Guardian. |
| Chas. Morris | " | Son of Dr. W. S. Morris. |
| †A. A. Moss | " | Son of T. A. Moss. |
| †W. T. Moss | " | " " |
| †B. B. Munford | " | Son of Col. J. D. Munford. |
| John Munford | " | " " " |
| †W. E. Mullen | " | |
| †E. D. Murdaugh | Anne Arundel, Md. | Son of Rev. E. C. Murdaugh. |
| †P. E. Powell | Williamsburg | Son of Peter T. Powell. |
| A. E. Smith | " | Son of S. Smith. |
| Geo. T. Smith | " | Son of Isaac Smith. |
| †J. C. Slater | " | Son of Parke Slater. |
| H. M. Sweeney | Petersburg | Son of M. T. Sweeney. |
| †Ro. P. Taylor | Williamsburg | Son of R. P. Taylor. |
| W. F. Tompkins | Richmond | Son of Col. C. Q. Tompkins. |
| †Thomas M. Ware | Williamsburg | Jas. M. Mahone, Guardian. |
| John B. Waller | " | Son of Charles C. P. Waller. |
| †Thomas Walthall | " | Son of Jos. M. Walthall. |

## CATALOGUE OF ALUMNI.

### 1869-70.

| NAMES. | RESIDENCES. | REMARKS. |
|---|---|---|
| †James T. Blair............ | York............ | Son of Edward F. Blair. |
| †John H. Bowers............ | Williamsburg. | |
| P. M. Boyden............ | Cobham............ | Son of E. Boyden. |
| †Thos. S. Brown............ | Williamsburg. | Son of Dixion Brown. |
| Frank Camm............ | " | Son of Dr. Ed. Camm. |
| J. G. Camm............ | " | " " |
| †John Camm............ | " | " " |
| †Benj. P. Catlett............ | Cloucester............ | Son of J. W. C. Catlett. |
| John S. Charles, Jr............ | Williamsburg. | Son of J. S. Charles. |
| †Henry C. Coke............ | Norfolk............ | Son of W. W. Coke. |
| E. P. Cole ............ | Williamsburg. | Son of R. F. Cole. |
| H. M. Cosnahan............ | " | H. M. Waller, Guardian. |
| †Thos. F. Curtis............ | " | |
| †L. H. Davis............ | " | Son of Joshua Davis. |
| †Logan D. Davis............ | Gloucester............ | Son of William K. Davis. |
| James M. Douglas............ | Williamsburg. | Son of Wm. R. C. Douglas. |
| †Robt. B. Douglas............ | " | " " |
| Z. G. Durfey............ | " | Son of R. G. Durfey. |
| R. S. Engle............ | New York............ | Son of Samuel Engle. |
| Leroy A. Farinholt............ | Gloucester C. H. | |
| †Lewis Garrison............ | Williamsburg. | |
| Samuel C. Goggin............ | Bedford............ | Son of Wm. L. Goggin. |
| Robt. Wash. Goode............ | St. Louis, Mo............ | Son of G. W. Goode. |
| R. S. Hall............ | Scotl'd Neck, N.C. | Son of A. S. Hall. |
| †Wm. H. T. Hancock, Jr... | Williamsburg. | Son of Wm. H. T. Hancock. |
| Geo. A. Hankins............ | James City............ | Son of George Hankins. |
| Reynolds Hankins............ | " | " " |
| †G. W. Harrison............ | Goochland............ | Son of Col. R. Harrison. |
| †Randolph Harrison............ | " | " " |
| Wm. E. Harwood............ | Petersburg. | |
| Z. Hofheimer............ | Norfolk............ | Son of I. Hofheimer. |
| †Carter Jones............ | Williamsburg. | Son of H. T. Jones. |
| Robt. S. Jones............ | Warrenton, N. C. | Son of A. S. Jones. |
| McLeod Kasey............ | Liberty............ | Son of Col. John G. Kasey. |
| †Wm. B. Lamb............ | Williamsburg. | Son of J. Lamb. |
| R. P. Mercer............ | " | Son of Dr. John C. Mercer. |
| John S. Morris............ | " | Son of Dr. Wm. S. Morris. |
| †Wm. T. Moss............ | " | Son of Thomas A. Moss. |
| †Robt. S. Morecock............ | " | Wm. H. E. Morecock, Guardian. |
| †Beverley B. Munford............ | " | Son of Col. J. D. Munford. |
| Edmund Murdaugh............ | Anne Arundel, Md. | Son of Rev. E. C. Murdaugh. |
| †B. D. Peachy............ | Williamsburg. | Son of Wm. S. Peachy. |
| †Thos. G. Peachy............ | " | " " |
| †P. E. Powell ............ | " | Son of P. T. Powell. |
| †John Ross............ | " | Alex. Maclean, Guardian. |

CATALOGUE OF ALUMNI. 159

| NAMES. | RESIDENCES. | REMARKS. |
|---|---|---|

R. B. Scott..................Princess Anne......Son of Wm. C. Scott.
†Thos. W. Sharp..............Williamsburg........Son of C. A. Sharp.
A. L. Smith..................Scotl'd Neck, N.C.Son of Wm. R. Smith.
Geo. T. Smith................Williamsburg.......Son of Isaac Smith.
†Henry Smith.................        "         ......Son of Sydney Smith.
†Henry D. Spear..............James City.........Son of John Spear.
†John B. Spencer.............James City.........Son of W. L. Spencer.
†Robt. P. Taylor.............Williamsburg.......Son of R. P. Taylor.
J. W. Turner.................Goochland..........Son of George W. Turner.
John B. Waller...............Williamsburg.......Son of C. C. P. Waller.
C. W. Wharton................Liberty............Son of J. A. Wharton.
John T. Wilkins..............Northampton........Son of Dr. J. T. Wilkins.
†C. B. Wilmer................Williamsburg.......Son of Rev. G. T. Wilmer, D. D.
†G. T. Wilmer................        "         ......     "         "
E. C. Wynne..................James City.........H. L. Taylor, Guardian.
†Robt. J. Wynne..............        "

## 1870–71.

E. L. Adair..................Accomac............Son of John W. Adair.
†C. P. Armistead.............Williamsburg.......Son of Col. R. H. Armistead.
†H. T. Armistead.............        "         ......     "         "
†John H. Bowers..............        "         ......Son of James M. Bowers.
†J. J. Bowie.................Baltimore.
P. M. Boyden.................Albemarle..........Son of Rev. E. Boyden.
†A. Brooks, Jr...............Williamsburg.......Son of A. Brooks.
†T. S. Brown.................        "         ......Son of Dixon Brown.
†John Camm...................        "         ......Son of Dr. E. Camm.
J. G. Camm...................        "         ......     "         "
John S. Charles, Jr..........        "         ......Son of John S. Charles.
†E. H. Clowes................        "         ......Son of John Clowes.
E. P. Cole...................        "         ......Son of R. F. Cole.
†H. D. Cole..................        "         ......     "         "
W. C. Constable..............        "
H. M. Cosnahan...............        "         ......Dr. R. P. Waller, Guardian.
A. S. Cowles.................James City.........Son of D. S. Cowles.
H. B. Cowles.................        "         ......     "         "
†T. F. Curtis................Williamsburg.
†L. H. Davis.................        "         ......Son of J. A. Davis.
†R. B. Douglas...............        "         ......Son of W. R. C. Douglas.
†L. E. Garrison..............        "
R. W. Goode..................Missouri...........Son of G. W. Goode.
T. H. Hammond................Sussex.
†W. H. T. Hancock............Williamsburg.......Son of W. H. T. Hancock.
George A. Hankins............James City.........Son of George Hankins.
†W. Hankins..................        "         ......     "         "
John Hare....................North Carolina.....Son of John B. Hare.

160    CATALOGUE OF ALUMNI.

| NAMES. | RESIDENCES. | REMARKS. |
|---|---|---|
| †G. W. Harrison | Williamsburg | Son of Col. R. Harrison. |
| †R. Harrison | " | " " |
| W. E. Harwood | Petersburg. | |
| J. de Bree Higgins | Norfolk. | |
| Z. Hofheimer | " | Son of Isaac Hofheimer. |
| R. M. Hughes | Abingdon | Son of Col. R. W. Hughes. |
| †A. C. Jones | Williamsburg | Son of H. T. Jones. |
| R. S. Jones | North Carolina | Son of A. S. Jones. |
| McL. Kasey | Liberty, Va | Son of Col. John G. Kasey. |
| †F. M. Lamb | Williamsburg | Son of J. Lamb. |
| †W. B. Lamb | " | " " |
| J. P. Little | " | Son of Dr. J. P. Little. |
| Isaac N. Martin | James City | Son of John T. Martin. |
| W. Martin | " | Son of Dr. W. Martin. |
| R. P. Mercer | Williamsburg | Son of Dr. J. C. Mercer. |
| †R. S. Morecock | " | W. H. E. Morecock, Guardian. |
| J. S. Morris | " | Son of Dr. Wm. S. Morris. |
| †W. T. Moss | " | Son of T. A. Moss. |
| †B. B. Munford | " | Son of Col. John D. Munford. |
| †A. C. Peachy | " | Son of William S. Peachy. |
| †B. D. Peachy | " | " " |
| †T. G. Peachy | " | " " |
| †T. F. Piggott | James City | Son of B. F. Piggott. |
| P. E. Powell | Williamsburg | Son of P. T. Powell. |
| †John Ross | " | Son of John Ross. |
| †T. W. Sharp | Prince George | Son of Clem. A. Sharp. |
| G. T. Smith | Williamsburg | Son of Isaac Smith. |
| †Henry Smith | " | Son of Sydney Smith. |
| †H. D. Spear | James City | Son of J. J. Spear. |
| W. Stoddert | Charles Co., Md. | |
| †R. P. Taylor | Williamsburg. | |
| †W. S. Tilford | " | Son of J. C. Tilford. |
| B. T. Turner | Goochland | Son of George W. Turner. |
| G. C. Turner | " | " " |
| M. T. Turner | " | " " |
| E. D. Tuttle | Williamsburg | Son of Friend Tuttle. |
| Robert F. Wall | Williamsburg | Son of M. Wall. |
| Thomas H. Wall | " | " " |
| †C. C. P. Waller | " | Son of C. C. P. Waller. |
| John B. Waller | " | " " |
| †Thomas Ware | " | James Mahone, Guardian. |
| C. W. Wharton | Liberty | Son of Rev. J. A. Wharton. |
| John T. Wilkins | Northampton | Son of Dr. J. T. Wilkins. |
| †C. B. Wilmer | Williamsburg | Son of Rev. G. T. Wilmer, D. D. |
| †G. T. Wilmer | " | " " " |
| W. S. Wilson | Norfolk | Son of George R. Wilson. |

## 1871-72.

| NAMES. | RESIDENCES. | REMARKS. |
|---|---|---|
| J. W. Turner, A. M. | Goochland | Son of G. W. Turner. |
| R. W. Goode, A. B. | Missouri | Son of G. W. Goode. |
| P. M. Boyden, B. P. | Albemarle | Son of Rev. E. Boyden. |
| R. S. Jones, B. P. | North Carolina | Son of A. S. Jones. |
| C. W. Wharton, B. P. | Liberty. | Son of Rev. J. A. Wharton. |
| James M. Ambler | Fauquier | Son of John Ambler. |
| †C. P. Armistead | Williamsburg | Son of Col. R. H. Armistead. |
| W. H. T. Barron | Richmond county. | Son of Com. Samuel Barron. |
| H. W. Booker | Hampton | Son of George Booker. |
| †A. Brooks. | Williamsburg. | Son of A. Brooks. |
| W. N. Brown | Westmoreland. | |
| F. Camm | Williamsburg | Son of Dr. E. Camm. |
| †John Camm | " | " " |
| J. G. Camm | " | " " |
| H. D. Cole. | " | Son of R. F. Cole. |
| †J. R. Coupland | " | Son of J. R. Coupland. |
| H. B. Cowles. | James City. | Son of D. S. Cowles. |
| †L. Davis. | Williamsburg. | Son of J. A. Davis. |
| J. L. Duncan. | Butler, Md. | |
| W. B. Finney | Accomac. | Son of A. G. Finney. |
| †J. H. Flippen | Pittsylvania | Son of C. W. Flippen. |
| T. S. Foster | Norfolk | Son of W. C. Foster. |
| †J. P. Gilmer. | Pittsylvania | Son of John Gilmer. |
| John C. Gresham | Lancaster C. H. | Son of Samuel Gresham. |
| †W. H. T. Hancock. | Williamsburg | Son of W. H. T. Hancock. |
| W. N. Hankins, | James City. | Son of George Hankins. |
| John Hare. | North Carolina. | Son of J. B. Hare. |
| †G. W. Harrison | Williamsburg | Son of Col. R. Harrison. |
| †R. Harrison | " | " " |
| †F. Hughes. | Abingdon | Son of Col. R. W. Hughes. |
| R. M. Hughes | " | " " |
| †A. C. Jones. | Williamsburg | Son of H. T. Jones. |
| †G. S. King | Hampton | Son of Dr. J. R. King. |
| †F. M. Lamb | Williamsburg. | Son of J. Lamb. |
| W. B. Lamb | " | " " |
| J. P. Little. | " | Son of Dr. J. P. Little. |
| †C. L. Mahone | " | Son of J. H. Mahone. |
| S. B. Mallory | Hampton | Son of Col. C. K. Mallory. |
| Isaac N. Martin | James City. | Son of John T. Martin. |
| James M. Matthews | Tappahannock | Son of James M. Matthews. |
| R. P. Mercer. | Williamsburg | Son of Dr. John C. Mercer. |
| W. F. Mitchell. | Towsontown, Md. | |
| J. D. Montague | Middlesex | Son of Hon. R. L. Montague. |
| †R. S. Morecock | Williamsburg | W. H. E. Morecock, Guardian. |
| B. B. Munford | " | Son of Col. John D. Munford. |

14

## CATALOGUE OF ALUMNI.

| NAMES. | RESIDENCES. | REMARKS. |
|---|---|---|
| R. W. Nicolson | Middlesex | Son of G. L. Nicolson. |
| W. H. N. P. Parker | Northampton | Son of Wm. H. Parker. |
| †A. C. Peachy | Williamsburg | Son of Wm. S. Peachy. |
| †B. D. Peachy | " | " " |
| T. G. Peachy | " | " " |
| †John H. Pigg | Pittsylvania | Son of H. Pigg. |
| John William Rice | Northumberland | Son of John Rice. |
| †John Ross | York county | Son of John Ross. |
| H. L. Schmelz | Hampton | Son of F. A. Schmelz. |
| A. E. Smith | Williamsburg | Son of S. Smith. |
| George T. Smith | " | Son of Isaac Smith. |
| Henry Smith | " | Son of S. Smith. |
| †R. F. Smith | York | Son of B. F. Smith. |
| †Albert Southall | Williamsburg | Son of Tyler Southall. |
| †E. D. Spencer | James City | Son of W. L. Spencer. |
| S. L. Straughan, Jr. | Northumberland | Son of S. L. Straughan. |
| †R. P. Taylor | Williamsburg | Son of R. P. Taylor. |
| B. T. Turner | Goochland | Son of G. W. Turner. |
| M. T. Turner | " | " " |
| E. D. Tuttle | Williamsburg | Son of F. Tuttle. |
| R. F. Wall | " | Son of M. Wall. |
| T. H. Wall | " | " " |
| †C. C. P. Waller | " | Son of C. C. P. Waller. |
| †T. M. Ware | " | J. M. Mahone, Guardian. |
| T. N. Williams | Pittsylvania. | |
| C. B. Wilmer | Williamsburg | Son of Rev. G. T. Wilmer, D. D. |
| †G. T. Wilmer | " | " " " |
| W. S. Wilson | Norfolk | Son of George R. Wilson. |
| †C. D. Witherspoon | Petersburg. | |
| E. C. Wynne | James City. | |
| †John A. Young | Warwick | Son of W. G. Young. |

### 1872–73.

| | | |
|---|---|---|
| R. M. Hughes, A. B | Abingdon | Son of Col. R. W. Hughes. |
| C. P. Armistead | Williamsburg | Son of Col. R. H. Armistead. |
| †N. Carey Brand | Alabama | Son of James W. Brand. |
| A. Brooks, Jr | Williamsburg | Son of A. Brooks, Sr. |
| C. J. Brown | Orange county. | |
| F. Camm | Williamsburg | Son of Dr. Ed. Camm. |
| †John Camm | " | " " |
| †E. H. Clowes | " | Son of John Clowes. |
| H. D. Cole | " | Son of R. F. Cole. |
| W. C. Constable | " | |
| †J. R. Coupland, Jr | " | Son of John R. Coupland. |
| †R. B. Daugherty | " | |
| †L. Davis | " | Son of J. A. Davis. |
| †Bascum Dey | " | Son of Rev. J. B. Dey. |

## CATALOGUE OF ALUMNI. 163

| NAMES. | RESIDENCES. | REMARKS. |
|---|---|---|
| †George Dilworth | James City. | |
| J. L. Duncan | Maryland | Son of William Duncan. |
| Thomas J. Edwards | Prince George. | |
| John W. Embrey | Falmouth | Son of Wesley Embrey. |
| †J. H. Flippen | Pittsylvania | Son of C. W. Flippen. |
| J. Waller Ford | Stafford | Son of N. W. Ford. |
| R. D. Gilliam | Pr. George C. H. | Son of Robert Gilliam. |
| †W. H. T. Hancock | Williamsburg | Son of W. H. T. Hancock. |
| G. W. Harrison | " | Son of Col. R. Harrison. |
| R. Harrrison | " | " " |
| †John H. Johnson | " | |
| A. C. Jones | " | Son of H. T. Jones. |
| †G. S. King | Hampton | Son of Dr. John R. King. |
| W. B. Lamb | Williamsburg | Son of J. Lamb. |
| J. P. Little | " | Son of Dr. J. P. Little. |
| R. C. Maclean | Alabama. | |
| †C. H. Mahone | Williamsburg. | |
| Joseph Martin | Henry | Son of William Martin. |
| W. F. Mitchell | Towsontown, Md. | Son of J. B. Mitchell. |
| †Robert S. Morecock | Williamsburg. | |
| B. B. Munford | " | Son of Col. J. D. Munford. |
| W. H. N. P. Parker | Northampton | Son of William H. Parker. |
| †A. C. Peachy | Williamsburg | Son of William S. Peachy. |
| B. D. Peachy | " | " " |
| T. G. Peachy | " | " " |
| †John Piggott | James City. | |
| †Thomas F. Piggott | " | |
| †F. U. Powell | Williamsburg | Son of P. T. Powell. |
| †W. O. Roper | " | Son of R. R. Roper. |
| †W. Schenck | York. | |
| G. T. Smith | Williamsburg | Son of Isaac Smith. |
| H. Smith | " | Son of Sydney Smith. |
| †R. F. Smith | " | |
| †Albert M. Southall | " | Son of Tyler Southall. |
| H. D. Spear | James City | Son of John Spear. |
| E. D. Spencer | " | Son of W. L. Spencer. |
| B. Jones H. Spruill | North Carolina | Son of Col. S. B. Spruill. |
| James E. Stewart | New Kent | Son of Richard A. Stewart. |
| James L. Taliaferro | Gloucester | Son of Gen. Wm. B. Taliaferro. |
| †R. P. Taylor | Williamsburg | Son of Robert P. Taylor. |
| B. T. Turner | Goochland | Son of G. W. Turner. |
| Thomas H. Wall | Williamsburg | Son of M. Wall. |
| †Thomas Ware | " | |
| †Thomas Williams | James City | Son of George Williams. |
| †W. C. Williams | " | Son of W. Williams. |
| C. B. Wilmer | Williamsburg | Son of Rev. G. T. Wilmer, D. D |
| George T. Wilmer, Jr. | " | " " " |
| John A. Young | Warwick | Son of W. G. Young. |

## 1873-74.

| NAMES. | RESIDENCES. | REMARKS. |
|---|---|---|
| J. P. Little, A. B. | Williamsburg | Son of Dr. J. P. Little. |
| J. L. Taliaferro, A.B. | Gloucester | Son of Gen'l W. B. Taliaferro. |
| W. H. N. P. Parker, B. P. | Northampton | Son of William H. Parker. |
| C. P. Armistead | Williamsburg | Son of Col. R. H. Armistead. |
| †N. Carey Brand | Alabama | Son of James W. Brand. |
| A. Brooks, Jr. | Williamsburg | Son of A. Brooks. |
| James Brooks | Woodbury, Md. | Son of William Brooks. |
| John Camm | Williamsburg | Son of Dr. E. Camm. |
| J. G. Camm | " | " " |
| H. D. Cole |  | Son of R. F. Cole. |
| W. C. Constable | " |  |
| †H. L. Darlington | York. |  |
| †Bascum Dey | Williamsburg | Son of Rev. J. B. Dey. |
| †R. B. Daugherty | " |  |
| T. J. Edwards | Prince George. |  |
| A. W. Ensor | Baltimore Co., Md. | Son of William O. Ensor. |
| R. D. Gilliam | Pr. George C. H. | Son of Robert Gilliam, Sr. |
| †W. H. T. Hancock | Richmond | Son of W. H. T. Hancock. |
| G. W. Harrison | Williamsburg | Son of Col. R. Harrison. |
| R. Harrison | " | " " |
| A. C. Jones | Williamsburg | Son of H. T. Jones. |
| †G. S. King | Hampton | Son of Dr. John R. King. |
| Charles Lamb | Norfolk | Son of W. W. Lamb. |
| †F. M. Lamb | Williamsburg | Son of J. Lamb. |
| W. B. Lamb | " | " " |
| R. C. Maclean | Mobile, Ala. | Son of Andrew Maclean. |
| J. Martin | Henry county | Son of William Martin. |
| †G. W. Mercer | Williamsburg | Son of Dr. J. C. Mercer. |
| †R. S. Morecock | " |  |
| †J. C. Motley | " | Son of John Motley. |
| B. B. Munford | Botetourt Co. | Son of Col. John D. Munford. |
| †W. R. Munford | " | " " " |
| J. A. Nicol | Prince William | Son of A. Nicol. |
| †A. C. Peachy | Williamsburg | Son of William S. Peachy. |
| B. D. Peachy | " | " " |
| T. G. Peachy | " | " " |
| †F. Upshur Powell | Williamsburg | Son of P. T. Powell. |
| Eston Randolph | Clarke county | Son of Bev. Randolph. |
| †W. O. Roper | Williamsburg | Son of R. R. Roper. |
| C. S. Scott | Powhatan | Son of E. Scott. |
| P. W. Smith, Jr | Gloucester C. H. | Son of P. W. Smith. |
| †Sydney Smith, Jr | Williamsburg | Son of Sydney Smith, Sr. |
| A. M. Southall | " | Son of Tyler Southall. |
| E. D. Spencer | James City | Son of W. L. Spencer. |
| G. D. Taylor | Accomac | Son of T. H. Taylor. |

| NAMES. | RESIDENCES. | REMARKS. |
|---|---|---|
| †R. P. Taylor | Williamsburg | Son of R. P. Taylor. |
| J. B. T. Thornton | Prince William | Son of W. W. Thornton. |
| Thomas H. Wall | Williamsburg | Son of M. Wall. |
| J. A. Watts | Roanoke | Son of Col. William Watts. |
| †W. C. Williams | James City | Son of W. Williams. |
| C. B. Wilmer | Williamsburg | Son of Rev. G. T. Wilmer, D. D. |
| G. T. Wilmer | " | " " " |
| †W. L. Wilson | Petersburg | Son of Dr. Samuel Wilson. |
| E. C. Wynne | James City | Son of Thomas Wynne. |

## DEGREES

### "In Course," given since 1858.

| NAMES. | RESIDENCES. | DEGREE. | DATE. |
|---|---|---|---|
| Robert J. Graves | U. T. Seminary | A. M | 1859 |
| Reginald M. Murphy | Maryland | A. M | " |
| James H. Barnes | James City county | A. M | " |
| William C. Parham | Arkansas | A. M | 1866 |
| A. S. Furcron | Chesterfield | A. M | 1868 |
| Edmund R. Bagwell | Accomac | A. M | " |
| Thomas J. Stubbs | Gloucester | A. M | 1869 |
| Samuel W. Murphy | Maryland | A. M | " |
| Frank H. Alfriend | Richmond | A. M | " |
| William I. Clopton | " | A. M | 1870 |
| J. F. Hubbard | Yorktown | A. M | 1872 |

## NAMES

Of those on whom Honorary Degrees have been Conferred.

| NAMES. | RESIDENCES. | DEGREE. | DATE. |
|---|---|---|---|
| Benjamin Franklin | | A. M | 1755 |
| Chevalier de Chastellux | General in French army | LL. D | 1782 |
| John F. Coste | First Physician " | M. D | " |
| Thomas Jefferson | | LL. D | " |
| Rt. Rev. James Madison | Williamsburg | D. D | 1790 |
| George Wythe, Judge of the Court of Chancery | | LL. D | " |
| St. George Tucker | State Judge | LL. D | " |
| Robert Andrews | Williamsburg | A. M | " |
| Charles Bellini | " | A. M | " |
| Granville Sharp | London | LL. D | 1791 |
| Humphrey Harwood | Williamsburg | A. B | " |
| Rev. John Bracken | " | D. D | 1793 |
| Rev. John Cameron | Bristol Parish | D. D | " |
| Rev. Jas. Maury Fontaine | Gloucester | D. D | " |

## CATALOGUE OF ALUMNI.

| NAMES. | RESIDENCES. | DEGREE. | DATE. |
|---|---|---|---|
| Rev. Sam'l S. McCrosky | Gloucester | D. D | 1793 |
| Rev. Thomas Andrews | Williamsburg | D. D | " |
| Rev. James Craig | Lunenburg | D. D | 1794 |
| Rev. John Buchanan | Henrico | D. D | " |
| Marquis de La Fayette | | LL. D | 1824 |
| Rev. William Meade | Frederick | D. D | 1827 |
| Rev. Robert B. Semple | Fredericksburg | D. D | " |
| Henry St. George Tucker | Winchester | LL. D | 1837 |
| Benjamin Watkins Leigh | Richmond | LL. D | " |
| Wm. H. Prescott, historian | Boston | LL. D | 1841 |
| Right Rev. John Payne | Missionary Bishop to Africa | D. D | 1851 |
| Rev. M. Wing | Gambier Collège, Ohio | D. D | " |
| Alexander Shiras | Rappahannock Academy | A. M | " |
| Hubert P. Lefevre | Williamsburg Female Acad. | A. M | " |
| George P. Scarburgh | State Judge | LL. D | 1852 |
| William H. Gilham | Virginia Military Institute | A. M | " |
| Charles S. Venable | Prof. at Hampden Syd. Col. | A. M | " |
| Richard Ford | Williamsburg Male Acad | A. M | " |
| John Blair Dabney | Campbell county | LL. D | 1853 |
| Dr. G. L. Upshur | Norfolk | A. M | " |
| Rev. Charles Minnegerode | " | D. D | 1854 |
| Rev. Geo. D. Armstrong | " | D. D. | |
| Hon. Litt. W. Tazewell | " | LL. D | " |
| Hon. Jno. Tyler, ex-Pres. U. S | | LL. D | " |
| John Tyler, Jr | | A. M. | |
| C. White | Rumford Academy | A. M | " |
| John B. Strange | Norfolk Academy | A. M | " |
| John B. Cary | Hampton Academy | A. M | " |
| Robert Gatewood | Norfolk | A. M | 1855 |
| Hugh B. Grigsby | " | LL. D | " |
| Right Rev. John Johns | Bishop of Virginia | LL. D | " |
| C. J. D. Pryor | Williamsburg | A. M | 1856 |
| William Green | Richmond | LL. D | " |
| Rev. E. A. Dalrymple | Pres. University of Maryl'd | S. T. D. | 1857 |
| Rev. George Woodbridge | Richmond | D. D | " |
| Rev. N. A. Okeson | Norfolk | D. D | 1858 |
| D. Lee Powell | Richmond | A. M | " |
| Robert J. Morrison | " | A. M | " |
| Rev. Cornelius Walker | Winchester | D. D | July 4th, 1859 |
| Rev. J. J. McElhenny | Kenyon College | D. D | " " |
| Rev. John A. Broaddus | Charlottesville | D. D | " " |
| Rev. J. C. McCabe | Richmond | D. D | " " |
| Rev. Richard H. Wilmer | Bishop of Alabama | D. D | " " |
| Rev. Silas Totten, D. D | Pres't of Iowa University | LL. D | " 1860 |
| Rev. George T. Wilmer | Williamsburg | D. D | " " |
| Rev. William Hodges | North Carolina | D. D | " " |
| H. B. Browne | Prince Edward | A. M | " " |
| Caleb Hallowell | Alexandria | A. M | " " |

## CATALOGUE OF ALUMNI. 167

| NAMES. | RESIDENCES. | DEGREE. | DATE. |
|---|---|---|---|
| Rev. Chan'g M. Williams | Bishop of China and Japan. | D. D...... | "   1866 |
| James Barron Hope | Norfolk | A. M...... | "   " |
| Rev. Edmund C. Murdaugh. | Anne Arundel co., Md | D. D..... | "   1868 |
| Rev. George H. Norton | Alexandria | D. D...... | "   " |
| Gen. Joseph E. Johnston | Virginia | LL. D..... | "   " |
| William G. McCabe | Petersburg | A. M...... | "   " |
| Rev. Francis Vinton, S. T. D. | New York city | C. L. D... | 22d Feb., 1869 |
| Rev. Christopher B. Wyatt. | San Francisco, Cal | D. D...... | "   " |
| Rev. M. Mahan, D. D. | Baltimore | LL. D.... | 22d Feb., 1869 |
| Rev. A. Paul Repiton | North Carolina | D. D...... | "   " |
| Rev. J. M. Banister | Alabama | D. D...... | 4th July, " |
| Rev. J. H. D. Wingfield | Petersburg | D. D..... | "   " |
| Rev. O. S. Barten | Norfolk | D. D...... | "   " |
| Prof. Basil L. Gildersleeve. | University of Virginia | LL. D.... | "   " |
| Prof. Wm. Dwight Whitney. | Yale College | LL. D.... | "   " |
| Rev. Henry N. Pierce, D.D. | Bishop of Arkansas | LL. D.... | "   " |
| Prof. Frank Preston | Lexington | A. M...... | "   " |
| Dr. Richard A. Wise | Richmond | A. M...... | " . " |
| Rev. Churchill J. Gibson | Petersburg | D. D...... | 22d Feb., 1870 |
| Rev. R. D. Nevius | Mobile, Ala | D. D...... | "   " |
| Rev. J. H. Wingfield | Portsmouth | D. D..... | "   " |
| Rev. Henry Wall | Richmond | D. D...... | "   " |
| Rev. Samuel Benedict | Savannah, Ga | D. D...... | 22d Feb., 1870 |
| Rev. John F. Hoff | Baltimore, Md | D. D...... | "   " |
| Rev. C. H. Shield | Washington, D. C | D. D...... | "   " |
| Hon. James Lyons | Richmond | LL. D.... | "   " |
| General R. E. Colston | Cape Fear Mil. Acad., N. C. | A. M...... | "   " |
| Rev. W. C. Williams | Rome, Ga | D. D...... | "   " |
| Hon. W. H. Macfarland | Richmond | LL. D...... | "   " |
| Henry A. Strode | Petersburg | A. M...... | "   " |
| Rev. Horace Stringfellow | Montgomery, Ala | D. D...... | '  " 1871 |
| Rev. W. C. Meredith | Winchester | D. D...... | "   " |
| Rev. Wm. Treble Saunders. | Key West, Fla | D. D...... | 4th July, 1871 |
| Rev. Q. Q. Scott | Pensacola, Fla | D. D...... | "   " |
| Rev. John A. Harrison | Tennessee | D. D...... | 22d Feb., 1872 |
| Rev. Robert J. Graves | Sharon, Pa | D. D...... | "   " |
| Rev. C. B. Coffin | New York | A. M...... | "   " |
| Dr. Henry Shield | Yorktown | A. M...... | 4th July, 1872 |
| Prof. John R. Tucker | Washington and Lee Uni. | LL. D.... | "   " |
| C. B. Duffield | Norfolk | LL. D... | "   " |
| Prof. John W. Mallett | University of Virginia | LL. D... | "   " |
| Rev. William Fulton | Salisbury, Md | D. D...... | "   " |
| Rev. J. R. Hubard | Washington, D. C | D. D...... | "   " |
| Dr. John Clopton | Ass't Sup't E. L. Asylum. | A. M....... . | "   " |
| Hon. Legrand W. Perce | Mississippi | LL. D.... | 22d Feb., 1873 |
| Hon. George F. Hoar | Massachusetts | LL. D.... | "   " |
| Robert Potts | Trinity College, England | LL. D.... | "   " |

## CATALOGUE OF ALUMNI.

| NAMES. | RESIDENCES. | DEGREE. | DATE. |
|---|---|---|---|
| Rev. Wm. G. Farrington | New Jersey | D. D | 4th July, 1873 |
| General F. H. Smith | Virginia Military Institute | LL. D | " " |
| Prof. C. S. Venable | University of Virginia | LL. D | " " |
| Rt. Rev. Wm. Pinkney | Maryland | LL. D | " " |
| Rt. Rev. Henry C. Lay | Maryland | S. T. D | " " |
| Rev. Robert Nelson | Missionary to China | D. D | " " |
| Rt. Rev. F. McN. Whittle | Virginia | LL. D | " " |
| Rev. R. C. Stocking | Chicago | D. D | " " |
| Rev. James H. Ticknor | Opelika, Ala | D. D | " " |
| Rev. John Muehleisen Arnold, P. D. | London, England | D. D | 22d Feb., 1874 |
| Rev. J. M. T. Otts | Wilmington, Del | D. D | " " |

# ORGANIZATION

## OF THE

# COLLEGE OF WILLIAM AND MARY,

*July 4th, 1874.*

---

### VISITORS AND GOVERNORS.

HON. HUGH BLAIR GRIGSBY, LL. D., CHANCELLOR.
HON. JAMES LYONS, LL. D., RECTOR.

| | |
|---|---|
| REV. GEORGE WOODBRIDGE, D. D. | REV. CHARLES MINNEGERODE, D. D. |
| TAZEWELL TAYLOR. | HON. ROBT. L. MONTAGUE. |
| GEN'L H. A. WISE. | GEN'L WM. B. TALIAFERRO. |
| JUDGE W. W. CRUMP. | JUDGE WARNER T. JONES. |
| MAJ. C. S. STRINGFELLOW. | REV. J. H. D. WINGFIELD, D. D. |
| WM. S. PEACHY. | DR. A. N. WELLFORD. |
| P. M. THOMPSON. | COL. WM. LAMB. |

HON. JOHN GOODE, JR.

---

*Clerk:*
WM. H. E. MORECOCK.

*Bursar:*
TAZEWELL TAYLOR.

---

### FACULTY.*

BENJ. S. EWELL, LL. D., PRESIDENT.

REV. GEORGE T. WILMER, D. D., Professor of Moral and Intellectual Philosophy and Belles Lettres.

REV. L. B. WHARTON, A. M., Professor of Latin, French, and Roman and French History.

REV. L. B. WHARTON, A. M., Professor of Greek, German, and Grecian and German History.

BENJ. S. EWELL, LL. D., Professor of Natural and Experimental Philosophy and Mathematics.

DR. RICHARD A. WISE, A. M., Professor of Chemistry, Geology and Physiology.

CHAS. S. DOD, A. M., Master of the Grammar and "Matty" School.

---

*The faculty each year select competent students from the senior classes to assist in teaching in the junior departments. During the late session the following students have acted as assistants: C. B. Wilmer, J. P. Little, J. L. Taliaferro.

# COURSE OF INSTRUCTION.

The Subjects taught in the College are Latin, Greek, Mathematics, French, German, Natural Philosophy, Mixed Mathematics, Chemistry, Geology, Mineralogy, Physiology, Moral and Intellectual Philosophy, and Belles Lettres.

## Department of Latin.

### PROFESSORS WHARTON AND WILMER.

*Junior Class.*—Cæsar, Sallust, Cicero's Orations; Gildersleeve's Latin Grammar; Arnold's Prose Composition; Andrew's Lexicon.

*Intermediate Class.*—Virgil, Livy, Horace; Gildersleeve's Latin Grammar; Arnold's Latin Prose Composition; Latin Prosody; Liddell's History of Rome.

*Senior Class.*—Juvenal, Terence, Tacitus; Harrison's, Zumpt's and Madvig's Latin Grammars; Latin Prosody; Roman Literature; Liddell's Rome.

## Department of Greek.

### PROF. WHARTON.

*Junior Class.*—Xenophon's Anabasis and Memorabilia; Hadley's Grammar; Oral and Written Exercises; Smith's History of Greece; Liddell and Scott's Lexicon.

*Intermediate Class.*—Homer, Herodotus, Demosthenes; Exercises; Greek Prosody, (Hadley;) Smith's History of Greece.

*Senior Class.*—Thucydides, Plato, Sophocles, Euripides; Exercises; Theory of Forms, (Hadley;) Lectures on Literature; Lectures on the Principles of Indo-European Comparative Grammar.

## Department of Mathematics.

### PROF. EWELL.

*Junior Class.*—Davies' Arithmetic, Algebra, Geometry and Plane Trigonometry.

*Intermediate Class.*—Algebra, Geometry, and Trigonometry completed; Davies' Surveying; Church's Analytical Geometry.

*Senior Class.*—Differential and Integral Calculus, (Courtenay); Des. Geometry.

## Department of French.

PROF. WHARTON.

*Junior Class.*—Fasquelle's French Course; Exercises; Lectures on Grammar; Collot's Dramatic Reader; Spiers and Surenne's Lexicon.

*Senior Class.*—Noel and Chapsal's Grammar; Exercises in Writing and Speaking French; Moliere, Racine, Lamartine; French History and Literature.

## Department of German.

PROF. WHARTON.

*Junior Class.*—Otto's Grammar and Exercises; Adler's Reader; Adler's Lexicon.

*Senior Class.*—Schiller, Goethe; Exercises in Writing and Speaking German; Lectures on German Literature.

## Department of Natural Philosophy and Mixed Mathematics.

PROF. EWELL.

*Junior Class.*—Popular and Practical Course of Mechanics, Acoustics, Electricity, Optics, Astronomy.

*Senior Class.*—Bartlett's Analytical Mechanics, Acoustics and Optics.

## Department of Chemistry, Geology, Mineralogy and Physiology.

DR. WISE, PROFESSOR.

*Junior and Senior Class.*—Usual course of Heat, Light and Electricity; Organic and Inorganic Chemistry, theoretical and practical, with their application to the principles of Agriculture and the Arts.

*Authors Used.*—Attfield's and Miller's Chemistry; Dalton's Physiology.

## Department of Moral and Intellectual Science and Belles Lettres.

REV. GEORGE T. WILMER, D. D., PROFESSOR.

*Junior Class—Middle Class—Senior Class.*

*Authors Used.*—Hamilton, Cousin, Jouffroy; Kame's Elements; Blair's Rhetoric.

# EXPENSES AND COLLEGE FEES.

Tuition, - - - - - $30 00
Matriculation Fee, - - - - 5 00
Servant's Hire and Contingent Expenses, - 5 00
Board at College Hotel, - - - 160 00
Use of Room and Furniture, - - 5 00
Fuel, Lights and Washing, - From $25 to 35 00

☞ Board may be obtained of families at advanced rates.
☞ There is no extra fee for Modern Languages.

Thus a Student's expenses at this College need not be more than $230.00, or if he enters on a scholarship, $200.00.

There is connected with the College a Preparatory Department, called the Grammar and "Matty" School, founded by Mrs. Mary Whaley, of Bruton Parish, Virginia, in 1742.

This School, which opens the 1st of October, and closes the 20th of July, is under the supervision of the Faculty. The Scholars are taught the usual English branches, with Latin, Greek and Mathematics, and are prepared for College. They are subjected to proper restraint and discipline. Boys under twelve not admitted.

All College charges are payable, half-yearly, in advance.

Those joining the department of Natural Philosophy and Chemistry, shall pay an additional fee of five dollars for the use of the apparatus.

Students may reduce the charges for Board to at least *one-half by renting rooms, providing their own furniture, and forming messes*, obtaining supplies from their homes if practicable. This plan has been found, *on trial, to be a success*, and to prove a *great saving*.

To give meritorious young men in limited circumstances the means of obtaining an education, FIFTEEN SCHOLARSHIPS, exempting those admitted on them from the payment of tuition fees, have been founded in the College.

Applications for these scholarships must be made before the beginning of the session.

☞ In addition to the above number of scholarships, each Professor has the power to confer a scholarship on two students, selected annually from their classes, as a reward of merit, and for good standing in their classes.

# DEGREES.

There are three regular Degrees, viz: BACHELOR OF PHILOSOPHY, BACHELOR OF ARTS, and MASTER OF ARTS.

*Required for B. P.*—The three years' Course. Latin and Greek omitted; or its equivalent, *i. e.*, proficiency in two Departments, and in the Junior Classes of three of the remaining Departments.

*Required for A. B.*—The three years' Course; or its equivalent, *i. e.*, proficiency in four Departments and in the Junior Classes of the remaining Departments.

*Required for A. M.*—The Degree of Bachelor of Arts, and in addition proficiency in any two Modern Languages, in the advanced Metaphysical Course, in English Literature, in Analytical Geometry, in Differential and Integral Calculus, and in Mixed Mathematics.

Certificates of Proficiency may be awarded, upon examination in any class or department, to those whose preparation before coming to College warrants it.

Every candidate for a degree shall, at least thirty days before Commencement, hand to the President an essay prepared to be spoken in public; from which the Faculty shall select a certain number to be spoken on the day of Commencement. No speech not so selected shall be delivered on that day; nor shall a diploma be granted to any student who shall fail to hand in such an essay, and deliver it publicly, if required to do so.

Any student, not a candidate for a Degree, shall be entitled to a certificate of his progress with the College Seal annexed.

The fee for graduation shall be five dollars, and for a certificate with the College Seal annexed, two dollars.

The Faculty have power to confer Honorary Degrees at their discretion.

# EXTRACTS FROM THE LAWS
## OF THE
# COLLEGE OF WILLIAM AND MARY.

CHAPTER I.—*Opening of Session.*

The session shall open on the second Wednesday of October, and close on commencement day, the 4th of July. From commencement to the beginning of the next session shall be the vacation. The Faculty may suspend recitation for a few days at Christmas, on the 22d of February and on Good Friday.

CHAPTER II.—*Terms of Admission.*

1. Candidates for admission to William and Mary College shall, within two days after arriving at Williamsburg, make themselves known to the President and pay their fees. The President shall give each one a copy of the laws, and within one week submit to him the following interrogatory: Have you read and understood the laws of this College, and do you acknowledge your obligation to obey them? Upon his replying in the affirmative he shall be considered as having fully matriculated.

2. No one shall be admitted under the age of fifteen, or of bad moral character; nor shall a student from another college be allowed to matriculate, unless he can show he is not, at the time of his application, under censure.

3. The fees for the session must be paid half in advance, unless the Faculty grant indulgence. No student will be permitted to attend any lecture until he has complied with this condition.

4. Those who enter before the 22d of February shall pay the full fees; those entering at or after this time shall pay half fees. No candidate shall be admitted for a less time than until the end of a session.

5. Each student shall be permitted to attend such classes as he may select, provided, in the opinion of the Faculty, he be competent to pursue the studies of such class with profit; and further, provided he attend at least three departments, unless the Faculty shall allow him to attend a less number.

6. After a student has selected his studies he shall not change during the session, without the permission of the Faculty.

7. Candidates for the ministry, or indigent young men, of good moral character and respectable abilities, may be admitted without the payment of fees.

8. Resident graduates, of the degree of Bachelor of Arts, may attend the classes in any department without paying a tuition fee; or may pursue their studies under the instruction of any of the Professors, on such terms as may be agreed.

## Chapter III.—*Faculty.*

1. The Corporation, consisting of "the President and Masters or Professors," known as "the Faculty," have possession, under the Charter, of all College property, and, subject to the inspection, direction and statutes of the Visitors and Governors, the control and management of it, together with the care, government, and instruction of the students.

2. It shall be the duty of the Faculty faithfully to instruct the several classes in the prescribed studies; to have a care and oversight of the morals of the students; strictly and impartially to administer the laws; and to propose to the Visitors such changes or additions as they may deem advisable.

3. There shall be meetings of the Faculty once a week, and oftener, if required by the President or two Professors. A record shall be kept of their proceedings by the Secretary, which shall be subject to the inspection of the Visitors. Nothing done by the Faculty shall be valid unless so recorded.

4. No member of the Faculty shall have the right to reveal their proceedings, or to make known, directly or indirectly, the votes or opinions of any one belonging to the body, unless permitted by a unanimous vote.

5. The Faculty have the right to employ assistant instructors in any of the departments, selecting such assistants from the students if they deem fit.

6. The Faculty shall have power to license teachers of studies not pursued in College, or of such accomplishments as may be proper to be taught; but no student shall attend such teacher until he is so licensed; nor shall any student engage in teaching, during a session, without permission.

7. No Professor shall engage in any occupation that interferes with his Professorship.

8. Before entering on the duties of his office, each Professor shall, in the presence of at least two Visitors, take the following oath: I, —— ——, do hereby swear that I will, well and truly, execute the duties of my office of —— —— according to the best of my abilities. So help me God.

9. The Faculty shall have power to regulate or suppress any society formed by students. None but students shall, without permission, be present at the meetings of any society in College.

10. The President and Professors shall, at the close of each session, report to the Visitors the state of discipline; the number of students in their respective classes; their general standing and progress in study; and also the state of the library, apparatus, and all other property of the College.

11. The Faculty shall have power to determine the times and number of recitations, and the study hours, and to select text books, subject to the control of the Visitors.

12. The President shall exercise all the powers conferred on him by the charter; shall have a general supervision of the College; see that the laws are faithfully executed, making such suggestions for this purpose as he may deem expedient. He shall preside at all the meetings of the Faculty, and on public academic days; shall have the right to vote on all questions before the Faculty, and in case of a tie to give a casting vote. He shall carry on the official correspondence of the College that does not devolve on the Secretary or Librarian; and shall give private and public admonition and counsel to the students when needed.

13. In the absence of the President the Faculty shall designate one of their body to exercise his authority.

14. It shall be the duty of each member of the Faculty to aid the President in the preservation of discipline, and in the enforcement of the College laws; to suppress all disorders or disturbances created by students, and, if necessary, to require them to retire to their rooms.

15. The Secretary of the Faculty shall keep a "Matriculation Book," in which the students shall enter their names and ages, and, unless over twenty-one, the name and postoffices of their parents or guardians.

CHAPTER IV.—*Government of Students.*

1. The principal object of these laws is to promote the comfort, respectability and welfare of the students, restraining them from vice, and inciting them to industry, by appeals to their reason and

sense of right and wrong, and by such censures as will not dissolve their connection with the College. But where the laws are wilfully broken, the peace of the better disposed students disturbed, and a pernicious example set them, it will be necessary to send the offender away.

2. A candid confession of a fault and a promise of amendment may, in most cases, mitigate the punishment or entirely prevent it.

3. The punishments shall be private admonition; public admonition; probation; suspension; dismission, and expulsion.

4. A student may be privately admonished by any member of the Faculty, at his discretion, without its being recorded.

5. A suspended or dismissed student shall, under pain of expulsion, within twenty-four hours after his sentence is made known, leave the College premises, and within two days he shall leave Williamsburg, unless permitted by the Faculty to remain.

6. It shall be lawful for the Faculty to question any student as to his participation in any offence against the College laws.

7. Where several students are engaged in breaking the College laws, in combination or otherwise, the Faculty may confine their censures and punishments to those who appear to be the ringleaders, or to those whose deportment is most reprehensible.

8. If the Faculty think that a student is habitually negligent in his studies, or that he is addicted to any vice or immorality, or that his example is pernicious to his fellow-students, they may, although without positive evidence, advise his parent or guardian to withdraw him without delay. Should this be declined, they may dismiss him quietly without disgrace, restoring to him a proper proportion of the fees he has advanced.

9. A student sending or accepting a challenge to fight a duel, or in any manner engaged therein as principal, shall be expelled.

10. A student conveying a challenge to fight a duel, or being second therein, or in the duel that may be the consequence, shall be expelled.

11. No student shall keep in his possession deadly weapons, nor resort to them in a fray.

12. No student shall, without permission, keep in his room firearms, nor shoot them, nor make loud noises of any kind within the College enclosures, or in the streets of Williamsburg.

13. No student shall, by words or blows, insult a fellow-student, nor a citizen.

14. No student shall game, become intoxicated, keep or have intoxicating drinks in his room, or possession; injure the property

of the College, or of citizens; nor be guilty of any conduct rendering him an unfit associate for young gentlemen of correct habits. Those who commit any of these offences shall be punished at the discretion of the Faculty.

15. If students treat with disrespect Visitors, or members of the Faculty, or combine to interfere with their authority, they shall be dismissed, or otherwise punished.

16. No student shall, without permission, visit any tavern or tippling house, nor be guilty of profanity.

17. Students shall not, without the consent of the Faculty, form, or join in, any public procession; nor take part in any public exhibition; nor deliver any speech in public until it has been revised and approved by the President.

18. Students shall not give parties, unless by the consent of the Faculty.

19. Students shall not unnecessarily absent themselves from their rooms during study hours, nor after bed-time; nor shall they play at such times on musical instruments, or make any noises whereby the attention of their fellow-students may be distracted or their repose disturbed.

20. Students shall not, without good excuse, absent themselves from prayers; nor from recitations, unless excused by the instructor of the class; nor leave the room; nor while at recitation read any book or paper, without permission; nor lie down on the benches; but shall demean themselves with propriety, and pay proper attention. If negligent, disorderly, or disrespectful, they may be required to leave the room.

21. If a student write for publication, or be instrumental in causing to be published, statements or pieces reflecting on the Visitors, Faculty, or any of his fellow-students, he shall be dismissed, or otherwise punished.

22. No student shall, without permission, go more than five miles from Williamsburg.

23. The Faculty shall have power to forbid and punish any offences against good order or propriety not herein enumerated.

CHAPTER V.—*Prayers and Church.*

1. There shall be daily prayers in the Chapel.

2. All students are expected to attend church on Sunday morning. They may indulge their religious preferences by choosing between the churches of the different religious denominations in Williamsburg; which preference shall be made known at the time of matric-

ulation. Nothing disorderly or irreverent shall be tolerated during chapel exercises or church.

3. On Sundays students shall abstain from ordinary diversions, and shall conduct themselves in a manner becoming the day.

4. A course of Biblical study, and on the evidences of Natural and Revealed Religion, may be conducted by the President or one of the Professors.

CHAPTER VI.—*Merit Rolls and Examinations.*

1. The Professors shall keep rolls of their classes, and regularly designate, by one common system of marks, the value of the recitation of each student. These marks, together with those given at the examinations, shall determine the scholarship of the students.

2. A weekly report shall be made to the Faculty by the Professors of all absences, irregularities and violations of the College laws of which they have any knowledge.

3. Reports shall be made to the parents or guardians of students, every month, of their scholarship and of all delinquencies and absences, whether excused or not.

4. No Professor shall, without the knowledge and consent of the Faculty, give to any student a certificate or recommendation.

5. There shall be two public examinations of all the classes, beginning, the first on or about the 23d of February, and the second immediately before commencement.

6. Each class shall be examined, in the following manner, by a committee of the Faculty, consisting of two Professors, to one of whom the class recites. A list of questions shall be prepared by the instructor of the class, to each of which he shall attach a numerical value—such that the sum of all the values shall equal the number denoting the highest grade of scholarship. After the examination, which may be either oral or written, he shall assign values to the answers. The sum of the values of the answers given by any student shall be the number obtained by him at the examination.

7. In the determination of the scholarship the examination shall be considered equivalent to one-third the value of the whole number of recitations.

8. No student shall be entitled to a certificate of proficiency in a class, unless the number denoting his scholarship be at least seventy, and the number obtained at the examination be at least seventy.

9. In no case shall a student be entitled to a certificate of proficiency until he has presented himself for examination.

## Chapter VII.—*College Buildings.*

1. The Faculty may, when necessary, appoint one of their number to direct, in conjunction with the President, the repairs of the College buildings and enclosures, and to take care of all the College property that is not in the possession of some one properly authorized.

2. Damages to any College property done by students shall be charged to them generally, if the authors are not known. Damages to a room in the College Hotel shall be repaired at the expense of the occupants. Intentional damages shall be charged twice the cost of repairing them.

## Chapter VIII.—*Library.*

1. The Faculty shall annually appoint a Librarian, with a reasonable salary, payable out of the Library Fund.

2. The Library shall be kept open once a week for two hours at such time as the Librarian may prefer.

3. None but Visitors of the College shall be allowed to enter the Library without the presence of the Librarian or a member of the Faculty.

4. The right to borrow books from the Library shall be confined to Visitors, members of the Faculty and students. The privilege of borrowing books may be extended to others.

5. Books borrowed shall be recorded by the Librarian, together with the names of the borrowers, in a book kept for that purpose. The Librarian shall, in his annual report, state what injuries have been done to books belonging to the Library, the amount of fines imposed and collected, and what books have been lost or destroyed. He shall also present a list of any that have been added to the Library since his last report, by gift or purchase.

6. Students shall not be permitted to borrow from the Library more than two volumes at a time. Books of reference, and others, designated by the Faculty, shall not be taken from the room.

7. No books shall be kept out of the Library by a student for a longer time than two weeks, under a penalty of twenty-five cents for each additional week. If books are defaced or injured out of the Library, the borrower shall pay a fine, or buy a new set, at the option of the Librarian; in which case the injured set shall be the property of the borrower. The Librarian shall be the judge of the amount of all fines.

8. Students shall not go beyond the counter of the Librarian

without his permission; nor shall any one, without such permission, except members of the Board of Visitors or Faculty, take a book from the shelf. Books may be handed from the shelf, and returned to it by the Librarian.

9. Borrowers of books from the Library shall not loan them to others.

10. Books shall not be kept out of the Library for more than four weeks by any but Visitors or members of the Faculty. All books shall be returned at least twelve days before commencement. Those who violate either of these provisions shall be fined.

11. Persons in the Library shall abstain from all loud talking, noise, and from smoking.

12. Books shall not be taken from the Library by any who owe fines. If students refuse to pay these fines they may be dismissed or otherwise punished.

13. No one shall be allowed, under any pretence, to carry a book away from Williamsburg.

14. The matriculation fees and fines collected by the Librarian shall constitute the Library Fund.

CHAPTER IX.—*Boarding and Steward.*

1. Students who do not live at the College Hotel may board or take their meals, by permission of the Faculty, with private families in Williamsburg, or form messes.

2. Students shall not be allowed to board at a tavern.

3. The Faculty may annually elect a Steward. He may reside in the College Hotel, unless some other building be designated by the Faculty, and have the use of it, the yard and garden, free of rent. His charges for board, washing, and hire of room furniture, shall be such as the Faculty may, from time to time, prescribe. He may be required to purchase fuel for the students, and have it delivered to them, for which he shall be allowed a reasonable per centage. He shall preserve order and decorum among his boarders. The Faculty shall have power, for reasons satisfactory to them, to discharge the Steward.

4. The Steward shall furnish such students as live in the College Hotel with plain and comfortable fare. He shall have their rooms cleaned up; their fires made; and fresh water carried to them once a day. They have no right to call on the Steward's servants for any other service.

5. The Steward shall be paid in advance for board, one-half at the beginning of the session, and one-half on the 22d of February.

6. If a student leave College from any cause, during the session, he shall be charged for board up to the time of his leaving only; and any excess which he may have advanced shall be refunded to him.

7. The Steward shall not supply students with any spirituous or intoxicating drink; nor shall he in any manner encourage them in the violation of the College laws. He shall keep no other boarders, without permission, during the session, than academic students or members of the Faculty; nor shall he furnish a suspended or dismissed student with meals for more than twenty-four hours after the publication of his sentence.

CHAPTER X.—*College Funds and Bursar.*

1. The Faculty shall, on the day preceding commencement, present to the Visitors an accurate account of all moneys received for profits on stock and interest of money, rents, or from any other source, keeping the income separate from the principal; and also a detailed statement of all payments made by the College. They shall, at the same time, present a separate statement of the productive and reproductive funds, or of any sum loaned on which interest has not been paid regularly, half-yearly; and also any change in the investment of money, and the reasons therefor; which accounts and statements, if approved by the Visitors, shall be recorded in a book kept for that purpose.

2. The salaries of the Professors shall be paid out of the income of the year in which they fall due, or out of the arrears of income of preceding years, after deducting the cost of necessary repairs and expenses of the College, and not out of the income of succeeding years.

3. The Faculty is enjoined to use none of the capital stock.

4. The Faculty appoint the Bursar, or financial agent of the College, determine his compensation, and require sufficient security.

CHAPTER XI.—*Servants.*

1. The Faculty shall hire as many servants as may be necessary.

2. No servants, but those authorized by the Faculty, shall be allowed to enter the College yard or building.

CHAPTER XII.—*Miscellaneous.*

1. The Faculty shall have power to require payment from the students, at any time during the session, for wilful damages to the College buildings or grounds.

2. If a student be dismissed before the 22d of February, or leave of his own accord, one-half the fees he has advanced shall be refunded to him. If after the 22d of February, none.

3. It is earnestly recommended to the parents or guardians of the younger students especially, to put the money intended to defray their expenses at College in the hands of a member of the Faculty, or of some citizen of Williamsburg.

4. All laws made by the Faculty, not in conflict with these, shall have their force and authority. The Faculty shall have power to delay enforcing any law herein contained until they have consulted the Visitors in relation to its amendment or repeal.

# PIEDMONT AND ARLINGTON

### Life Insurance Com'y,

*Home Office, Richmond, Va.*

This successful VIRGINIA COMPANY has established Agencies in every section of the country, North, South and West, and is the only SOUTHERN LIFE COMPANY that has complied with the Insurance Laws of New York, Pennsylvania, Ohio, &c., and secured business in those States.

## ANNUAL INCOME OVER ONE AND A QUARTER MILLION DOLLARS.

## 20,738 Policies Issued to September 24th, 1873.

## OVER $1,250,000 PAID IN DEATH LOSSES.

All Desirable Forms of Life and
      Endowment Policies Issued.
Policies Liberal and Non-Forfeitable.
      All Claims Promptly Paid.
Surplus (Dividends) Returned to Policy-Holders
      On the Contribution Plan.

No Company in America has been more successful, and no Company can present superior advantages to those who desire A LIFE POLICY.

   W. C. CARRINGTON, President.
   Rev. J. E. EDWARDS, D. D. Vice-Pres't.
   D. J. HARTSOOK, Secretary.
   J. J. HOPKINS, Assistant Secretary.

# ERRATA.

Page 84, line 10 from top, after name of Benj. Harrison, instead of "Son of Benj. Harrison, Signer, &c.," read son of Benj. Harrison. Signer of declaration of Independence, member of U. S. Constitutional Convention, and member of Congress.

Page 125, in list of 1835–6, and on page 127, in list of 1836–7, instead of W. H. I. Anson, read W. H. I'Anson.

Page 136, bottom line, instead of Lunanic, read Lunatic.

Page 145, for W. H. Shield, read W. H. Sheild.

Page 148, list of 1855–56, after name of James H. Barnes, for C. S. A. read Episcopal clergyman.

Page 149, after name of T. P. McCandlish, A. M., add A. B. Prof. Latin, College of William and Mary.

Page 168, bottom line, for Rev. J. M. T. Otts, read Rev. J. M. P. Otts.

Page 170, Dep't of Latin, for Arnold's Prose Composition, read Gildersleeve's Exercises.

Page 171, Dep't of French, for Fasquelle's French Course, read Otto's French Grammar and Reader.

# ADDENDA.

Add to the Honorary Degree list, on page 168, the names of the following persons—on whom degrees were conferred after this work went to press—viz:

Rev. Philip Slaughter.......Virginia.....................D. D......July 4th, 1874
Rev. J. W. Claxton..........Pennsylvania..............D. D......    "       "
Rev. D. F. Sprigg...........Virginia........................D. D......    "       "
Prof. Alex. Hogg............Agricultural & Mechanical College of Ala...A. M......    "       "
E. Morrissett...............Virginia........................A. M......    "       "
W. Frank Mitchell..........Maryland......................L. B......    "       "

☞ The note on page 117 shows that from 1786 to 1823 the average number of students at the College was about 45. Since that time the average has increased a great deal; but the lists for the different sessions, as contained in this catalogue, would make it appear to be less—as the plan has been adopted, to save space, of only inserting the name of each student *once*, and not repeating for each session he attended.

Hence the lists for the most part only show the number of *new* matriculates for each year. The name of each student (with few exceptions) is inserted the year he entered College—or, in case he took a degree, in the list of the year he graduated.

☞ The attention of the Alumni, and all interested in the College, is called to the note at the head of the catalogue, on page 74; also to the note at the foot of page 155. The Faculty, assisted by many of the Alumni, have labored very hard to make this catalouge as near perfect as possible. Should errors, and there are yet we fear very many, be detected and a correction of them sent to the secretary of the Faculty, they will be properly preserved and the corrections made in the next edition, whenever published.

Parties will please make no changes that they do not personally know to be correct.

www.ingramcontent.com/pod-product-compliance
Lightning Source LLC
Chambersburg PA
CBHW031441160426
43195CB00010BB/805